BTRIPP BOOKS

BOOK REVIEWS FROM

2012

BY
BRENDAN TRIPP

These reviews originally appeared on the "BTRIPP'S BOOKS" book review blog: http://btripp-books.livejournal.com/

Copyright © 2016 by Brendan Tripp

ISBN 978-1-57353-412-3

An Eschaton Book

http://www.EschatonBooks.com

Front cover photo courtesy Kenn W. Kiser via morguefile.com.
Back cover photo courtesy Sebastian Santana via morguefile.com.

PREFACE

From 1993 through 2004, I ran the *first* manifestation of Eschaton Books (now in its third revival). Initially started as a vehicle to publish my poetry, it soon became evident that the market for poetry is vanishingly small, and in 1994 we "pivoted" into being a metaphysical press.

During this time, I was largely a one-man shop, doing everything from editorial to shipping, which was a huge time commitment, and I typically worked 14 hour days, 7 days a week to keep things moving. I bring up all this here because, despite having been a life-long avid reader, during this period I had precious little time for reading, and what reading I *did* get done was largely reviewing book submissions. However, I never stopped *buying* books, which began to stack up in prodigious "to be read" piles.

When Eschaton went out of business (in a not unusual *denouement* for a small press – we had a distributor who ended up never paying us, while selling through all our stock) in 2004, I found myself with a lot of reading to catch up on, and a need to keep my writing chops sharp. So, I began to pen little reviews of what I was reading through, and post those on the web.

As the years went by, this became "a thing" that I was doing, and, for a while, I was targeting a fairly aggressive goal of getting at least 72 non-fiction books read per year. By 2015, this had resulted in my having read and reviewed 700 books over that 12-year span.

In recent years (since the upswing in print-on-demand publishing), I have had *numerous* acquaintances suggest that I put out my reviews as books. I was, at first, rather hesitant on the concept (as, after all, the material was free to read on the web), but I eventually figured that if various people thought it was a good idea, I might as well give it a shot.

While I could have started at the beginning, with the reviews from 2004, I decided that those were less representative of the whole, so opted to begin with the most recent ones.

This is the fourth of these collections, and the first from the seven-year span where I was reading more that 72 books per year. There are 75 reviews in this volume, a considerable increase from any of the previous (later) books. I was a bit confused when working on it, because the page count was ending up significantly less than the 2015 book, which had ten fewer reviews. I eventually realized that over the four years between the books, my average review length had been growing … when I started writing, I had been targeting the average length of a particular type of column in the Chicago Tribune, which were running 400-600 words. However, recently, if I've not knocked out 1,000 words on a review I feel like I've "let my readers down", and some have recently topped 2,000 words.

So, while this covers more books than the 2015 collection, it's got fewer pages per review. I'm anticipating that, going back through the years, this is going to continue, as the average word count heads towards that earlier, less expansive level.

A note on my review "style": I do not write classic reviews, but more a telling of my personal interaction with a particular book. This means that I talk about where and how I got the book, how it relates to other things I've read, what sort of reactions it triggered in me (and why), and how one can get a copy if it sounds appealing. Needless to say, if the reader is devoted to standard book reviewing styles, this might be an irritation … however, it does make these reviews somewhat idiosyncratic to *me*, resulting in a collection that is something of a "my encounters with books" sort of deal, which will, hopefully, be of interest to many readers.

- Brendan Tripp

CONTENTS

v - **Preface**

vii - **Contents**

1 - Tuesday, January 3, 2012
  Towards a secular ethics ...
  Beyond Religion: Ethics for a Whole World
  By H.H. The Dalai Lama

4 - Wednesday, January 4, 2012
  Some core teachings ...
  The Dhammapada: The Path of Perfection
  By Juan Mascaro

7 - Sunday, January 8, 2012
  And so it goes ...
  And So It Goes: Kurt Vonnegut: A Life
  By Charles J. Shields

10 - Sunday, January 15, 2012
  Long ago and far away ...
  Tourist's Guide - Agra & Fateh Pur Sikri
  By Lal Chand & Sons

12 - Monday, January 16, 2012
  Or not so funny ...
  101 Funny Things About Global Warming
  By Sidney Harris & Colleagues

13 - Tuesday, January 17, 2012
  Greeks bearing rules ...
  The Ten Golden Rules: Ancient Wisdom from the Greek Philosophers on Living the Good Life
  By M. A. Soupios & Panos Mourdoukoutas

15 - Wednesday, January 18, 2012
  A food journal ...
  America the Edible: A Hungry History, from Sea to Dining Sea
  By Adam Richman

17 - Tuesday, January 24, 2012

Not as in nervous cats with rocking chairs
**The Long Tail:
Why the Future of Business is Selling Less of More**
By Chris Anderson

20 - Thursday, January 26, 2012

A narrow focus ...
**The Google Resume: How to Prepare for a Career
and Land a Job at Apple, Microsoft, Google,
or any Top Tech Company**
By Gayle Laakmann McDowell

22 - Friday, January 27, 2012

Getting to the "Plus"
**Google+ for Business:
How Google's Social Network Changes Everything**
By Chris Brogan

24 - Saturday, January 28, 2012

A very modern voice ...
Civil Disobedience and Other Essays
By Henry David Thoreau

26 - Saturday, February 4, 2012

Eh ...
**Manage Your Depression Through Exercise:
The Motivation You Need
To Start and Maintain an Exercise Program**
By Jane Baxter, PhD

28 - Sunday, February 5, 2012

You want potatoes with that?
A Modest Proposal and Other Satirical Works
By Jonathan Swift

30 - Monday, February 6, 2012

Plausible deniability ...
**Enter the Past Tense:
My Secret Life as a CIA Assassin**
By Roland W. Haas

32 - Monday, February 13, 2012

Pushing my buttons ...
The Dip: A Little Book That Teaches You When to Quit
By Seth Godin

35 - Tuesday, February 14, 2012

Only moderately of approval ...
Digital Leader: 5 Simple Keys to Success and Influence
By Erik Qualman

37 - Saturday, February 18, 2012

A different evolution ...
**Darwin Among The Machines:
The Evolution Of Global Intelligence**
By George B. Dyson

39 - Sunday, February 19, 2012

A brighter light ...
Gurdjieff: Making a New World
By J.G. Bennett

43 - Tuesday, February 21, 2012

When the moon is in the seventh house?
**Aquarius Now: Radical Common Sense
And Reclaiming Our Personal Sovereignty**
By Marilyn Ferguson

45 - Thursday, March 8, 2012

Ill which the gods have sent thou canst not shun ...
The Seven Against Thebes
By Aeschylus

47 - Friday, March 9, 2012

Is not our fortune famous, brave, and great?
**Essence of the Bhagavad Gita:
A Contemporary Guide to Yoga, Meditation,
and Indian Philosophy**
By Eknath Easwaran

50 - Tuesday, March 20, 2012

Bird Talk ...
Winging It: A Memoir of Caring for a Vengeful Parrot Who's Determined to Kill Me
By Jenny Gardiner

52 - Monday, April 2, 2012

Fresh fruit for ...
Rubies in the Orchard: How to Uncover the Hidden Gems in Your Business
By Lynda Resnick

55 - Saturday, April 7, 2012

No clothes and a collar ...
The Pluto Files: The Rise and Fall of America's Favorite Planet
By Neil deGrasse Tyson

57 - Sunday, April 8, 2012

Sometimes "no plan" is the best plan ...
Six Tires, No Plan: The Impossible Journey of the Most Inspirational Leader That (Almost) Nobody Knows
By Michael Rosenbaum

59 - Friday, April 13, 2012

An encouraging look towards the future ...
Abundance: The Future Is Better Than You Think
By Peter Diamandis

62 - Saturday, April 14, 2012

Society fought the law, and the law won ...
The Laws of Disruption: Harnessing the New Forces that Govern Life and Business in the Digital Age
By Larry Downes

65 - Monday, April 16, 2012

Perhaps in some other universe ...
Résumé 101: A Student and Recent-Grad Guide to Crafting Resumes and Cover Letters that Land Jobs
By Quentin J. Schultze

68 - Wednesday, April 18, 2012

Some splainin' about human origins ...
Lucy's Legacy: The Quest for Human Origins
By Donald Johanson & Kate Wong

70 - Saturday, April 21, 2012

"Put the glasses on! Put 'em on!"
Blink: The Power of Thinking Without Thinking
By Malcolm Gladwell

74 - Sunday, April 22, 2012

"Who controls the present ..."
Socialnomics: How Social Media Transforms the Way We Live and Do Business
By Erik Qualman

77 - Monday, April 23, 2012

Holey moley!
A Black Hole Is Not a Hole
By Carolyn Cinami DeCristofano

80 - Wednesday, April 25, 2012

Paraphrasing from the Persian ...
The Rubáyát of Omar Khayyám: First and Fifth Editions
By Edward FitzGerald

82 - Friday, April 27, 2012

We all need control.
R.U.R. (Rossum's Universal Robots)
By Karel Capek

84 - Saturday, April 28, 2012

the sky tumbling down
Groundswell: Winning in a World Transformed by Social Technologies
By Charlene Li & Josh Bernoff

87 - Sunday, April 29, 2012

Her name is written on the Clouds
Bliss Now!: My Journey with Sri Sri Anandamayi Ma
By Swami Ramananda

89 - Friday, May 18, 2012

Anachronistic advice?
Networking: 150 Ways to Promote Yourself
By Bette Daoust

91 - Saturday, May 19, 2012

A book from a book ...
A Continual Feast: Words of Comfort and Celebration, Collected by Father Tim
By Jan Karon

93 - Sunday, May 20, 2012

"Does a dog have Buddha-nature?"
The Big Moo: Stop Trying to Be Perfect and Start Being Remarkable
By Seth Godin & "The Group of 33"

95 - Monday, May 21, 2012

More as branding than as a quality statement...
The Damn Good Resume Guide, Fifth Edition: A Crash Course in Resume Writing
By Yana Parker & Beth Brown

98 - Tuesday, June 12, 2012

So tempting to quote Hamlet ...
I Know I Am, But What Are You?
By Samantha Bee

100 - Wednesday, June 13, 2012

Do-it-yourself Psychology!
The Next Ten Minutes: 51 Absurdly Simple Ways to Seize the Moment
By Andrew Peterson, EdD

103 - Sunday, June 17, 2012

What a long strange trip it's been ...
Masters of the Planet: The Search for Our Human Origins
By Ian Tattersall

106 - Wednesday, June 27, 2012

Vive le Roi!
**Return On Influence:
The Revolutionary Power of Klout, Social Scoring, and Influence Marketing**
By Mark W. Schaefer

109 - Wednesday, July 11, 2012

The Transmedia Process ...
**A Creator's Guide to Transmedia Storytelling:
How to Captivate and Engage Audiences across Multiple Platforms**
By Andrea Phillips

112 - Thursday, August 23, 2012

Rewiring the brain ...
**The Little Book of Talent:
52 Tips for Improving Your Skills**
By Daniel Coyle

114 - Saturday, August 25, 2012

Two Sides to the Social Media Coin ...
**The Book of Business Awesome:
How Engaging Your Customers and Employees Can Make Your Business Thrive /
The Book of Business UnAwesome:
The Cost of Not Listening, Engaging, or Being Great at What You Do**
By Scott Stratten

117 - Sunday, August 26, 2012

Not the book I would have liked it to be ...
The Reality of Being: The Fourth Way of Gurdjieff
By Jeanne de Salzmann

119 - Thursday, August 30, 2012

An interesting half a book ...
**Mob Rule Learning:
Camps, Unconferences, and Trashing the Talking Head**
By Michelle Boule

122 - Friday, August 31, 2012

Exploring the darkness behind 9/11
**Masterminds of Terror:
The Truth Behind the Most Devastating Terrorist Attack the World Has Ever Seen**
By Yosri Fouda & Nick Fielding

125 - Saturday, September 1, 2012

The commercial conversation ...
**Word of Mouth Marketing:
How Smart Companies Get People Talking**
By Andy Sernovitz

128 - Tuesday, September 4, 2012

Once upon a time ...
America A.D. 1000: The Land and the Legends
By Robert Fisher

130 - Thursday, September 6, 2012

I dropped the good brain, Master ...
The Guinea Pig Diaries: My Life as an Experiment
By A.J. Jacobs

133 - Friday, September 7, 2012

Beauty and suffering ...
The Birth of Tragedy
By Friedrich Nietzsche

136 - Wednesday, September 12, 2012

How do you know who to trust?
**Liars and Outliers:
Enabling the Trust that Society Needs to Thrive**
By Bruce Schneier

139 - Tuesday, September 18, 2012

Auschwitz and unemployment?
Man's Search for Meaning
By Viktor E. Frankl

142 - Saturday, September 29, 2012

Brutal ...
**Death Metal Music:
The Passion and Politics of a Subculture**
By Natalie J. Purcell

145 - Sunday, September 30, 2012

Ancient Chinese wisdom ...
Mencius
By Mencius

147 - Tuesday, October 2, 2012

The math of making an impact ...
**The Impact Equation:
Are You Making Things Happen or Just Making Noise?**
By Chris Brogan & Julien Smith

150 - Saturday, October 6, 2012

"Anticipate the difficult by managing the easy."
**The Tao of Twitter: Changing Your Life and Business
140 Characters at a Time**
By Mark W. Schaefer

153 - Sunday, October 7, 2012

A vision of the visual ...
**Pinterest for Business: How to Pin Your Company
to the Top of the Hottest Social Media Network**
By Jess Loren & Edward Swiderski

156 - Tuesday, October 9, 2012

Brothels for the Mouth?
Kitchen Con: Writing on the Restaurant Racket
By Trevor White

159 - Wednesday, October 10, 2012

Hard advice ...
**No Time for Tact: 365 Days of
the Wit, Words, and Wisdom of Larry Winget**
By Larry Winget

162 - Thursday, October 11, 2012

Uncertainty, Chaos, and Luck
**Great by Choice: Uncertainty, Chaos, and Luck-
-Why Some Thrive Despite Them All**
By Jim Collins & Morten T. Hansen

165 - Friday, October 12, 2012

Don't shoot ...
**The Millionaire Messenger:
Make a Difference and a Fortune Sharing Your Advice**
By Brendon Burchard

169 - Saturday, October 13, 2012

Reframing reality?
**Reinventing the Sacred:
A New View of Science, Reason, and Religion**
By Stuart A. Kauffman

173 - Saturday, October 20, 2012

Gold, Natives & Wild West Shows ...
**Ho! For the Black Hills: Captain Jack Crawford Reports
the Black Hills Gold Rush and Great Sioux War**
By Paul L Hedren

176 - Wednesday, October 24, 2012

Being Indispensable ...
Linchpin: Are You Indispensable?
By Seth Godin

180 - Sunday, November 25, 2012

To thrive in chaos ...
Risky is the New Safe: The Rules Have Changed
By Randy Gage

184 - Monday, November 26, 2012

Pretty mechanical ...
**Robot Haiku: Poems for Humans to Read
Until Their Robots Decide It's Kill Time**
By Ray Salemi

186 - Wednesday, December 5, 2012

COIN for Brands
Brand Resilience: Managing Risk and Recovery in a High-Speed World
By Johnathan R. Copulsky

189 - Wednesday, December 19, 2012

With or without a cause ...
The Rebel's Guide to Email Marketing: Grow Your List, Break the Rules, and Win
By DJ Waldow & Jason Falls

192 - Thursday, December 20, 2012

In changing worlds ...
The Classmates: Privilege, Chaos, and the End of an Era
By Geoffrey Douglas

194 - Sunday, December 30, 2012

Legendary ...
Origins of Arthurian Romances: Early Sources for the Legends of Tristan, the Grail and the Abduction of the Queen
By Flint F. Johnson

197 - Monday, December 31, 2012

Old #10 ...
Ron Santo: A Perfect 10
By Pat Hughes & Rich Wolfe

199 - **QR Code Links**

219 - **Contents - Alphabetical By Author**

225 - **Contents - Alphabetical By Title**

Tuesday, January 3, 2012[1]

Towards a secular ethics ...

This is another book that came into my hands via the "Early Reviewer" program over on LibraryThing.com ... sometimes I'm confused as to why I get selected (by "the almighty algorithm") to get a book, but in this case, I would have been rather surprised if I hadn't been. Back in the 80's/90's I took the Kalachakra initiation three times (Madison, L.A., and NYC) and the Avalokitesvara initiation twice (Madison and NYC) from H.H. The Dalai Lama, and read quite a lot of Vajrayana tradition material, which is in my collection[2] over on LT (which is the primary consideration for the A.A. to pick who gets what), so I would have been quite pouty had I not gotten this book! Needless to say, I was very happy when Beyond Religion: Ethics for a Whole World[3] by the Dalai Lama arrived.

On the surface, this seems to be a somewhat counter-intuitive book. One of the biggest names in religion (and the head of one of the last Theocratic states, if in exile) looking at moving *beyond* religion ... but that's essentially what His Holiness is talking about here ... moving towards a global secular ethic which is a *human* system and not based on any one religion. While I'm sure that the Dalai Lama would not see it in these exact terms, I'm reminded of a line from the late Christopher Hitchens: *"Since it is obviously inconceivable that all religions can be right, the most reasonable conclusion is that they are all wrong."* ... and it seems to me that this particular reality check is the obstacle that this book is attempting to get past.

A decade ago the Dalai Lama wrote *Ethics for a New Millennium*, and this is somewhat of a follow-up to that, as indicated by the sub-title "Ethics for a Whole World". The book is in two parts, A New System of Secular Ethics, and Educating the Heart through Training the Mind, with the former setting up the argument for an ethical secularism, and the latter providing some guidance, from a Vajrayana perspective, for how to make this ethical stance part of one's inner life. In the introduction, he writes:

> ... as the peoples of the world become ever more closely interconnected in an age of globalization and in multicultural societies, ethics based in any one religion would only appeal to some of us; it would not be meaningful for all. ... Today, however, any religion-based answer to the problem of our neglect of inner values can never be universal, and so will be inadequate. What we need today is an approach to ethics which make no recourse to religion and can be equally acceptable to those with faith and hose without: a secular ethics.

It is interesting in the first part watching his examination of the secular from his situation of having been a life-long monk, and he certainly operates with the filter of basic Buddhist concepts of consciousness, empathy, suffering, compassion and justice. Having lived in a secular environment, some of the angles he takes here seem a bit odd, but he is obviously attempting to extract an ethical core from his reality which will stand on its own merits when shifted to the secular mode.

The second half of Beyond Religion[4] sort of turns the equation around and seeks to provide exercises or perceptions to make the secular world more ethical ... here's a bit about developing "contentment":

> *Cultivating contentment is especially important, I feel, in today's materialistic world of global consumerism. Materialistic society puts people under constant pressure to want more and to spend more long after their basic needs are satisfied. ... The materialism of modern society therefore makes the practice of moderation and contentment a daily necessity if we are to resist succumbing to a sense of personal dissatisfaction born of unrealistic craving.*

I was somewhere between amused and impressed at how well His Holiness managed to "repackage" essential meditations and reflection practices into formats which would be accessible to the average MBA (to pull a "non-spiritual" type out of the air). Here's how he makes this clear:

> *Yet, for all the associations of meditation or mental cultivation with religion, there is no reason why it should not be undertaken in an entirely secular context. After all, mental discipline itself requires no faith commitment. All it requires is a recognition that developing a calmer, clearer mind is a worthwhile endeavor and an understanding that doing so will benefit both oneself and others.*

I was very surprised to read another part of this. Over the years, I had never developed even a marginal mediation practice, launching into one discipline or another, trying to make progress, and then falling away from it soon after. I wish I'd read this thirty years ago:

> *It is also important to bear in mind that we should never force ourselves to practice. As noted earlier, beginners will inevitably experience many distractions. It takes time to accustom the mind to the discipline of formal meditation practice. It is therefore essential to remain patient and not to become discouraged. If we find ourselves having to struggle, this can be a sign that it is time to break off the session. Trying to continue under such circumstances*

> *will not be effective. The more we struggle, the more exhausted the mind becomes. If we carry on under these circumstances, we will soon begin to dislike practicing. Eventually, even the sight of the place where we conduct our practice may cause feelings of revulsion. So it is important not to reach this point.*

I have to wonder, however, how well this would play to other religious traditions. Buddhism is essentially atheistic (despite the multitudes of deities involved in the various sects), and is, generally speaking, not an "expansion-ist" religion. How Dominionist Xtians or Islamist Muslims would take a call for secular ethics is probably way on the other side of the scale! There are millions of people out there who can't believe you can be a "good person" without reference to their particular imaginary friend or specific "sacred" fairy tale collection, and I doubt they would be willing to make the effort to detach themselves from their delusions.

In any case, I found Beyond Religion[5] a delightful, enlightening, and even entertaining read, and would recommend it to all and sundry (well, perhaps with the exclusion of the folks discussed at the end of the previous paragraph), although the individuals that I was thinking of personally suggesting picking this up were all on the atheist end of the spectrum! This came out just in the past month, so should be available at your local book store, and the on-line guys have it at about a third off of cover price. If you have any interest of developing your inner life, or getting past the religious modality, this will be a great book for you to read.

Notes:

1. http://btripp-books.livejournal.com/121971.html

2. http://btripp-books.com/

3-5. http://amzn.to/1Jb7ZE5

Wednesday, January 4, 2012[1]

Some core teachings ...

I'm *almost* done with the books I scored at the last Newberry Library Book Fair, and this is one of those. As I've noted in previous reviews, this is frequently a source of "dead people's books", and the current book had both a smattering of pencil marks *and* a sheet of notes in it, which had the original price sticker, from ASUCLA, which operates the UCLA bookstores ... so this managed to migrate from southern California to Chicago at some point between 1973 and 2011.

This is the Penguin Classics edition of the Dhammapada, translated by Juan Mascaro, and entitled The Dhammapada: The Path of Perfection[2]. The Dhammapada is one of the core scriptures of Theravadan Buddhism, written in Pali. I have read other editions of this before, and I was quite impressed with how accessible Mascaro's translation is ... which is enough to recommend this version. However, one of the most useful things here is his Introduction. About 1/3rd of this rather slim volume is taken up by Mascaro's essay, which provides a wealth of information on this work. Not only does he discuss the history and language issues, but he makes an effort to place this within the context of both other religious scriptures, from the Bhagavad Gita and the Upanishads to the Bible, the Christian mystics, and Sufi writings, and the expressions of poets from Rumi to Shakespeare, Shelley, Keats and Wordsworth. Here's how he closes the essay:

> The message of Buddha is a message of joy. He found a treasure and he wants us to follow the path that leads to the treasure he found. He tells man that he is in deep darkness, but he also tells him that there is a path that leads to light. He wants us to arise from a life of dreams into a higher life where man loves and does not hate, where a man helps and does not hurt. His appeal is universal, because he appeals to reason and to the universal in us all ... He achieves a supreme harmony of vision and wisdom by placing spiritual truth on the crucial test of experience; and only experience can satisfy the mind of modern man. He wants us to watch and be awake and he wants us to seek and to find.

The Dhammapada is purportedly a record of the actual words of the historical Buddha, prince Siddhattha Gotama (to use the Pali spelling), although these were only preserved in oral transmission until a century or two past his death. Which brings me to the difficult question of "what do I say about a 2,500-year-old collection of teaching materials?", especially when my sense of how these were in the original is only 2nd or 3rd hand. There are parts of this which are, to the modern ear, *very* repetitive ... but that makes sense in the context of something originally intended for oral transmission. The document here is divided into 26 chapters which contain a total of 423 verses ... here's one section, Chapter 3 – The Mind:

> *33 – The mind is wavering and restless, difficult to guard and restrain: let the wise man straighten his mind as a maker of arrows makes his arrows straight.*
>
> *34 – Like a fish which is thrown on dry land, taken from his home in the waters, the mind strives and struggles to get free from the power of Death.*
>
> *35 – The mind is fickle and flighty, it flies after fancies wherever it likes: it is difficult indeed to restrain. But it is a great good to control the mind; a mind self-controlled is a source of great joy.*
>
> *36 – Invisible and subtle is the mind, and it flies after fancies wherever it likes; but let the wise man guard well his mind, for a mind well guarded is a source of great joy.*
>
> *37 – Hidden in the mystery of consciousness, the mind, incorporeal, flies alone far away. Those who set their mind in harmony become free from the bonds of death.*
>
> *38 – He whose mind is unsteady, who knows not the path of Truth, whose faith and peace are ever wavering, he shall never reach fullness of wisdom.*
>
> *39 – But he whose mind in calm self-control is free from the lust of desires, who has risen above good and evil, he is awake and has no fear.*
>
> *40 – Considering that this body is frail like a jar, make your mind strong like a fortress and fight the great fight against MARA, all evil temptations. After victory guard well your conquests, and ever for ever watch.*
>
> *41 – For before long, how sad, this body will lifeless lie on the earth, cast aside like a useless log.*
>
> *42 – An enemy can hurt an enemy, and a man who hates can harm another man: but a man's own mind, if wrongly directed, can do him a far greater harm.*
>
> *43 – A father or a mother, or a relative, can indeed do good to a man; but his own right-directed mind can do him a far greater good.*

I have to assume that this has become a standard college text, as it is still in print and it has a fairly high cover price (for being under 100 pages). You can certainly find the *text* (in a different translation) out there for free on the web, but if you can get a hold of a used copy of The Dhammapada: The Path of Perfection[3] the introductory material (and Mascaro's translation) is well worth it. This is available via the on-line guys, and I'm guessing it could obtained from the brick-and-mortars as well. If you want to dip into the basics of Buddhism, this would be a good place to start.

Notes:

1. http://btripp-books.livejournal.com/122307.html

2-3. http://amzn.to/1Jb7pWQ

Sunday, January 8, 2012[1]

And so it goes ...

This is only the second time that I've been in danger of running up on the "deadline" for getting books reviewed in the LibraryThing.com "Early Reviewer" program. This was "won" in the September 2011 batch, and arrived on October 15th ... theoretically we have 3 months before not having a review in will start inhibiting our ability (via "the almighty Algorithm") to win subsequent books, and so I'm right on the edge of that now.

Unlike a previous E.R. Program book, it's not that I wasn't enjoying reading Charles J. Shields' And So It Goes: Kurt Vonnegut: A Life[2], but it was somewhat longer than a lot of the books I've been reading of late, and got "moved to the back burner", as it were, while I was trying to push through some shorter reads to make my 72 book target for last year. I will admit, however, that there were parts of this which echoed situations in my life at the moment that made it very uncomfortable reading at times, which also led me to opt for other books.

I understand that this "official" biography of Kurt Vonnegut is not without controversy. Amazingly (if I'm reading the introductory material here correctly), the author only met with his subject *twice* before his death, and was faced with assembling all the details on Vonnegut's life without the benefit of on-going communications with him. He also, I gather, was stonewalled by certain parts of the family, from those who did not wish to participate at all, to those who would not allow for full access and use of assorted background and accessory information.

Shields had approached Vonnegut a couple of times with the suggestion that they work on a biography, and Vonnegut had "taken a pass" on the concept. However, eventually he relented, having been long irritated that he seemed to have a less "secure" place in history (and in various books, directories, and catalogs) than many other writers. Given the above challenges (Vonnegut suffered the fall from which he never recovered very soon after his second meeting with the author), it is rather remarkable what Shields was able to assemble for this book (there are *55 pages* of notes, nearly all dealing with the source of particular bits of information).

Over all, Vonnegut did not have a very happy life. In his youth he was regularly "failing" at things his family expected of him (his lack of a college degree haunted him for decades until he was able to "bargain" for one prior to a teaching assignment), especially compared to his elder brother (who was a noted atmospheric scientist). Family tragedies (his mother's suicide, his sister's early death) also seemed to produce a theme of fatalism in his life. Of course, his most famous life experience (courtesy being the central event of *Slaughterhouse-Five*) was being a prisoner of war in WW2, and living through the Allied bombing of Dresden ... which produced a series of impressions that played a part in both his personality and his writing for the rest of his life.

Success did not come early or easily to Vonnegut, he was considered something of a hack writer producing material for the lower end of the publishing world for many years. Slowly his luck changed and he moved up the scale into better-known national magazines, and eventually into writing books. His family was "complex", having both his natural kids and nephews whose parents had died (hours apart from one another) living in his household, which for most of the time was just barely functioning on a financial basis.

Vonnegut was fortunate, however, to have had a writing voice which was right for the zeitgeist of the 60's and 70's, and as the years rolled on, his works began to sell and he became very popular as a speaker on very lucrative college tours. Towards the end of his life, his "back catalog" was selling in excess of a hundred thousand copies per year in the US, a remarkable number when you consider that only the top 2% of new books sell as many as 5,000 copies!

Much of the book is given over to detailing family stress, affairs, divorces, and re-marriages, with his last wife being painted in particularly unpleasant tones (perhaps due to her refusal to have anything to do with the biography). As a former publisher, I would have like to have had the bits about his interaction with agents and presses more fleshed out (they are a secondary element here, but the material is more about the *relationships* he had with various characters in the book business than the inner workings of the business itself), but this would probably not be of much interest to the general reader.

One theme that keeps surfacing is how great a divergence there was between the "public image" of Vonnegut and the man himself. He was perceived as the counter-cultural icon (and *philosophically* he was that, but more in a liberal "freethought" way), but was given to wearing suits and mixing with "establishment" types. It's suggested here that even his "look" was somehow a pretense ... that, having been stylistically compared to Mark Twain, he took to sporting mustache and hair styles reminiscent of Samuel Clemens' alter ego.

In the end, one has mixed feelings about And So It Goes[3], while the commercial and cultural success of Vonnegut is undeniable, his life was sufficiently stressful and alienated (feelings which creep into the reading), that the take-away is rather uncomfortable. I had a personal connection with one data point here, one of my college professors, Mark Dintenfass, is name-checked in the book in the section dealing with Vonnegut's time teaching at the University of Iowa, when he was a student in the graduate writing program.

This is, of course, very new (Vonnegut only died in 2007), so should be available in your local bookstores, but the on-line guys have it at 35% off of cover. Over the years I'd been somewhat of a fan of Vonnegut, so I'm coming to this with a reasonably solid familiarity with his major works (although I was surprised at the extent that he'd written in vehicles other than the books). I'm guessing that one would at least have to have an active *interest* in him as a public figure to slog through the 400+ pages of this, as it was fairly uncomfortable read to one for whom the books had "meant something" at one point. If you've been a fan of the books, or of the man (or his public persona), this will certainly give you a new perspective, but I'm suspecting it's "not for everybody".

Notes:

1. http://btripp-books.livejournal.com/122380.html
2-3. http://amzn.to/1Jb6CVV

Sunday, January 15, 2012[1]

Long ago and far away ...

Aside from three 2ft stacks of recent "to be read" acquisitions, I also have a half a dozen file storage boxes filled with books I've picked up in the past, but never got around to reading. Every now and again, I take a look through those to see if there's something that I'm in the mood to read. Last month, *Tourist's Guide - Agra & Fateh Pur Sikri* seemed to want to be read, so I fished it out of one of the more-buried boxes.

Back in the early 80's (I couldn't figure out exactly which year, need to dig out my photo binders!) I spent a couple of weeks in north India and Nepal. A buddy of mine from college had gotten a Fulbright and was over in Benares doing research for his doctoral thesis. His brothers and I coordinated our vacation schedules and flew in for a visit, with the four of us running around to New Delhi, Agra, Katmandu, and Benares.

I picked up this guide while there, very likely (given the "look & feel" of the volume) from a souvenir stand somewhere in Agra, home of the Taj Mahal (although, 30 years later, I don't recall the specifics!). Now, I usually make an effort to let folks know how they can get a copy of a book I'm reviewing, however, I was unable to dig up any information on this beyond what's in it, which has no photo, map, or writing credits, just the publisher info (Lal Chand & Sons, New Delhi).

This is one of those charming, older, foreign books that looks like it was hand-set in metal type (there are a couple of "o"s that appear set upside down, for instance), with text that suggests that those composing it, while *familiar* with English (as one would expect in India), were not "native speakers". It features, within its just-over-100 pages, sixteen full-page photos, all but one in quite passable color, plus two maps. The publishers obviously paid a lot of attention to what the tourist would like to know, and the book starts with a couple of sections on history, first that of Mughal empire and then of Shah Jahan and the wife for whom he'd built the Taj Mahal as a mausoleum. It then moves through descriptions and backgrounds about 60 various structures in Agra and the surrounding area, and finishes with a section on things a traveler might have interest in, from seasonal temperatures, to hair dressers and golf courses.

As I recall it, we only spent a day (perhaps two) in Agra, so hit the major sites, and the descriptions here (as well as the photos) helped bring the visit back to me, even decades later, so kudos to the prose in this aspect. In all of the sections the history is brought to bear, so everything has a context within the extensive time-line of the Mughal Empire. Obviously, with sixty sites and four "background" info sections in about 110 pages, nothing is covered in *depth* here, but one does not feel like one is being "cheated" on any particular place.

To help remind myself of the area, I pulled it up on Google Maps' satellite view[2], and was able to check out where things were in relation to each other (although there is no "street view" per se, there are *hundreds* of snapshots linked out from the blue dots).

Anyway, reading *Tourist's Guide - Agra & Fateh Pur Sikri* was quite a trip down memory lane for me. I wish I could point you to a copy, but I couldn't even find anything solid about *the publishers*, let alone this book, so I guess you're out of luck unless you stumble across a copy in a used book store!

Notes:

1. http://btripp-books.livejournal.com/122746.html
2. https://goo.gl/maps/zFyV5BrNYK82

Monday, January 16, 2012[1]

Or not so funny …

So, I was worried at the end of the year that I wasn't going to be able to make my "72 non-fiction books" reading target, as I'd fallen behind and was enmired in a couple of thicker, denser books that I was pretty sure weren't going to be done by 12/31. I must admit to looking for some "quick reads" to slip in the last couple of weeks of 2011, and found 101 Funny Things About Global Warming[2] by Sidney Harris (& Colleagues) at the dollar store. This is a collection of environmentally-themed cartoons from back in 2008 … 101 of them … not exactly a "major" reading project!

This is not to say it was an "easy" read, as most of the material here is snide, nasty, and deeply spun to the Left … with most, if not all, the 21 contributors being of the "chorus" of liberals who were hell-bent on painting George W. Bush as some sort of demon monkey, surrounded by monsters doing his diabolical (yet incompetent?) will. At its best, the material here is archly ironic, at its worst, it's plain partisan broadsides against the Bush administration. The *worst* of this is the work of Sidney Harris, the nominal "author", so one has to assume that he had an idea of being "clever" (in that smarmy "all my friends will think I'm SO smart" way) with a book attacking Bush, and got the other cartoonists (all the way up to the brilliant Gahan Wilson) to submit their own pieces on global warming, environmentalism, etc.

While there are some honestly funny bits in here, the feeling at this point is that of going back to that insane period when the voices of the mainstream media (press and entertainment) were constantly trying to one-up each other with barbs at Bush and his administration. This is, as that was, juvenile, snarky, and mean-spirited … but I suppose there are people out there who would find that appealing. If this was a regular book, I'd bring you some quotes, but I assume that scanning and reproducing any of the cartoons here would be "frowned upon" … you can see a few of these, though, via the Amazon Look Inside![3] view.

Anyway, I really disliked 101 Funny Things About Global Warming[4], but it helped me to get to 72 books for the year and only cost me a buck. If you're on the other side of the fence politically, however, this might be something you'd love … so you might want to check it out. It's still available from the on-line guys' used channels for a couple of bucks (plus shipping, of course) new, or, if you want to spend nearly ten bucks (!) you can get an e-book version. Personally, I'd say skip it, but there's no accounting for taste.

Notes:

1. http://btripp-books.livejournal.com/123104.html
2. http://amzn.to/1YKQOLy
3. http://www.amazon.com/gp/reader/B001P80L8C/ref=sib_dp_pt#reader-link
4. http://amzn.to/1YKQOLy

Tuesday, January 17, 2012

Greeks bearing rules ...

This was another "small book" (it's 116 pages) that I picked up towards the end of last year to help me get to my 72-book reading target for the year. I found this on the clearance table over at the Barnes & Nobel where I usually write these book reviews (although this weekend I'm writing from home while watching the NFL playoffs). The Ten Golden Rules: Ancient Wisdom from the Greek Philosophers on Living the Good Life by M. A. Soupios & Panos Mourdoukoutas is an interesting book, with an odd origin ... it started out being published in Greece as The Ten Rules of Spiritual and Professional Fulfillment, I guess being a "business strategy" sort of thing, although this is not particularly evident in the the English version. Both of the authors are long-time professors at Long Island University's C.W. Post Campus, Dr. Soupios being an expert in History and Politics, and Dr. Mourdoukoutas an expert in Economics and Business Strategy.

The authors put forth the reason of the book in the introduction:

> For centuries, most discussions of spirituality in Western culture have concentrated on the precepts and practices of the Judeo-Christian tradition. For more than two thousand years, any consideration of the spiritual life fell within the privileged domain of organized religion. But the rise of modern secularism in the eighteenth and nineteenth centuries severely compromised the credibility of the religious path, raising a serious dilemma for the modern West – the spiritual imperatives of life continue to demand our attention at a time when traditional mechanism for addressing these needs have become increasingly dysfunctional and ineffective.

The book is structured, as one might expect, in ten chapters, one for each of the "Ten Golden Rules". Each chapter is connected to a Greek Philosopher, with an appropriate quote, then a "story" about how the particular "Rule" worked in somebody's life, a statement summing up the rule, a discussion on the rule relating to the story, and, finally, a "Mediation Grid" featuring a handful of concepts for further consideration.

Here's how the chapters are set out:

> 1. - Plato - "Examine Life"
>
> 2. - Epictetus - "Worry Only About the Things You Can Control"
>
> 3. - Aristotle - "Treasure Friendship"

4. - Epicurus - "Experience True Pleasure"
5. - Epictetus - "Master Yourself"
6. - Solon - "Avoid Excess"
7. - Pythagoras - "Be a Responsible Human Being"
8. - Aeschylus - "Don't Be A Prosperous Fool"
9. - Hesiod - "Don't Do Evil to Others"
10. - Aesop - "Kindness Toward Others Tends to Be Rewarded"

{Yes, it bugs me too that Epictetus shows up twice in this!}

As is often the case, the "stories" in these are fairly lame, attempting as they do to force in a "moral teaching" in a page or so of text, but the discussion of the concepts are pretty solid, making good points in a relatively small space.

Again, I very much like the direction of The Ten Golden Rules[3], and the authors make a very good case for a reconsideration of Greek philosophy as a basis for a modern ethics, with these ten rules being the touchpoints for guiding one's actions. Here's a bit from the Epilogue:

> Spiritual living is not an exclusive preserve of religious teaching. There are alternative paths to spiritual contentment, one of which involves the examined life afforded by reason. Among reason's many blessings are a capacity to examine life; to understand what we can and what we cannot control in life; to discriminate between false and true pleasures; to identify true friendships; to attain a properly balanced existence – all of which can contribute to a meaningful spirituality, such as that outlined by the wisdom of the ancient Greek sages.

Obviously, I'd recommend this to anybody ... but, unfortunately, it looks like the specific edition that I have (which was a discount pressing, which I then got at clearance) isn't available, but the more expensive one is, with a few copies in the used channels. It's a bit steep at cover price (for such a slim volume), but it's a very worthwhile read!

Notes:

1. http://btripp-books.livejournal.com/123360.html
2-3. http://amzn.to/1OtFILd

Wednesday, January 18, 2012[1]

A food journal ...

Here is another awesome dollar store find ... as I have probably already mentioned here, I used to be quite confused at how books, such as this, which are still in print (and, in this case, being offered at *full cover price* on-line) can end up on the $1 shelves ... a while back, however, a manager up at Dollar Tree was at the check out and he told me that they get books that Walmart has had and discontinued, so that's how reasonably new, quality books end up retailing for a buck! Needless to say, these don't stay on the shelves long, so it's a impetus to visit the dollar stores with some regularity.

I'm guessing that anybody with cable/satellite TV knows the author of this one ... Adam Richman, who has hit it big as the host of Travel Channel's "Man vs. Food" and its various spin-offs. His America the Edible: A Hungry History, from Sea to Dining Sea[2] is evidently a collection of entries from his journal, spanning 10 locations and five years, from 2004 to 2009 (during which period he scored his show). Most of this is like a written version of the "non-challenge" parts of *Man vs. Food*, where he goes places, finds great food, and raves about it.

This isn't, however, a print companion to the show, and there are a number of surprising points here. First of all, on the show one takes it that he's a food industry guy who happened to land an on-camera gig ... not (really) so. He's an *actor* who, in the first chapter here, is striving to get his career off the ground in L.A. ... much of the "location" elements are due to him being some place for an acting gig (he did a lot of regional stage work). Frankly, aside from a few "context" paragraphs, there's not much here about him working in the restaurants ... he mentions being a waiter, a sushi chef, and a few other things, but these all seem to have been in the course of keeping his acting career funded.

The places featured here are Los Angeles, Honolulu, Brooklyn (where he's from), St. Louis, Cleveland, Austin, San Francisco, Portland (Maine), Savannah, and back, five years later with a hit show, to L.A. These, however, are *not* presented in a "travel/dining" mode, but more like being pulled out of a diary, with Richman describing what he was doing, what he was feeling, where he was staying, etc., with the food stuff just the central element in the narrative.

This "journal" aspect is both the strength of the book and a nagging weakness, as it also brings in what I felt to be a rather discordant note. In almost every one of these places he's either just broken up with somebody and looking for some "rebound action", or getting together with some gal that he knew from some other time, or chasing down some random woman that he encountered in that city. To me, this was simply "TMI" and his various presentations of the details, or smugly "not telling", was not *adding* anything, and the book would have been improved with not having that aspect.

Of course, maybe the author was needing to *express himself* as a whole human being, with the struggles of his career and his love life there to make this less of a "food book". At least America the Edible[3] is fairly consistent in tone, whether he's describing life-long haunts, finding places serendipitously, or even just driving around looking for the next place to stop and eat.

Over the years of keeping his journal it appears that he was also snapping some pictures, as there are a smattering of snapshots of food which generally relate to what he's talking about in the text. There are also black boxes with what I'm guessing to be white text to look like a menu blackboard which bring in historical facts, interesting food info, bits of trivia, local tips, and assorted lists (from places to get pizza outside New York to food-related songs), and a few recipes, all of which certainly make the book a more informative read.

Again, this is sort of "in between" genres, it's autobiographical more than you'd expect (want?) in a food journal, but it's not exactly a straight forward food book either. While the effect does come across as *charming*, you get the feeling that Richman is trying a bit *too hard* to BE "charming" with personal details that seem only to be in the book to get people to *feel* some connection with him. This is not to say that the book's not a delightful read, just that (and I realize that I'm a stick-in-the-mud about this) it could have used a firmer hand on the editorial side.

America the Edible[4] is out there, but (oddly enough) both of the big on-line guys have it for full cover price, so if you were looking for a new copy, you might be able to do as well at your local brick-and-mortar book vendor. As noted, I got this a couple of weeks ago at a Dollar Tree, so if you have one of those nearby, you might want to try there ... the next best deal would be the new/used guys on Amazon where you can score an "acceptable" copy of the hardcover for just 1¢ (plus the $3.99 shipping, of course). Given the above caveats, I enjoyed reading this, and got a lot of good, very interesting, information from it, so I'm glad I picked up a copy ... you probably would be too.

Notes:

1. http://btripp-books.livejournal.com/123493.html
2-4. http://amzn.to/1OtF0xv

Tuesday, January 24, 2012[1]

Not as in nervous cats with rocking chairs

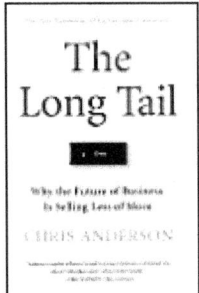

This was another of those amazing dollar store finds ... a classic book, in hardcover, for a buck. This is a Happy Thing in my life. The Long Tail: Why the Future of Business is Selling Less of More[2] came out of Chris Anderson's famed *Wired* magazine piece[3] (the most downloaded article in their long history) which introduced the concept.

"The Long Tail" is a way of visualizing sales, a chart will have a "big end" where the real popular stuff is, and then "a long tail" running off into the less requested stuff. This is pretty constant across all types of sales, but it tended to be more cut-and-dried in the days of "scarcity distribution" ... now, given the on-line possibilities, that "tail" can pretty much go on forever. This stuff is so counter-intuitive that I'll just let Anderson tell you:

> *[Trend-spotting] is what I was doing in January 2004, in the offices of ... a "digital jukebox" company. Digital jukeboxes ... have a broadband connection to the Internet and patrons can choose from thousands of tracks that are downloaded and stored on a local hard drive.*
>
> *During the course of our conversation [the CEO] asked me to guess what percentage of the 10,000 albums available on the jukeboxes sold at least one track per quarter.*
>
> *I knew, of course that [he] was asking me a trick question. The normal answer would be 20 percent because of the 80/20 Rule ... That is: 20 percent of products account for 80 percent of sales ...*
>
> *But [he] was in the digital content business which is different. So I thought I'd go way out on a limb and venture that a whopping 50 percent of those 10,000 albums sold at least one track a quarter.*
>
> *Now, on the face of it, that's absurdly high. Half of the top 10,000 books in a typical book superstore don't sell once a quarter. Half of the top 10,000 CDs at Wal-Mart don't sell once a quarter; indeed Wal-Mart doesn't even carry half that many CDs. It's hard to think of any market where such a high fraction of inventory sells. But my sense was that digital was different, so I took a chance on a big number.*

> I was, needless to say, way, way, off. The answer was 98 percent.
>
> It's amazing, isn't it?" [he] said. "Everybody gets that wrong." ...
>
> He called this the "98 Percent Rule." As he later put it to me, "In a world of almost zero packaging cost and instant access to almost all content in this format, consumers exhibit consistent behavior: They look at almost everything.

He then continues:

> Throughout the first half of 2004 I fleshed out this research ... by then I had some hard data ... [Rhapsody] had given me a month's worth of customer usage data, and when I graphed it out, I realized that the curve was unlike anything I'd seen before.
>
> It started like any other demand curve, ranked by popularity. A few hits were downloaded a huge number of times at the head of the curve, and then it fell off steeply with less popular tracks. But the interesting thing was that it never fell to zero. I'd go to the 100,000th track, zoom in, and the downloads per month were still in the thousands. And the curve just kept going: 200,000, 300,000, 400,000 tracks – no store could ever carry this much music. Yet, as far as I looked, there was still demand. Way out at the end of the curve, tracks were being downloaded just four or five times a month, but the curve still wasn't at zero.

These economies aren't just in music, either:

> Take books: The average Borders carries around 100,000 titles. Yet about a quarter of Amazon's book sales come from <u>outside</u> its top 100,000 titles. Consider the implication: If the Amazon statistics are any guide, the market for books that are not even sold in the average bookstore is already a third the size of the existing market – and what's more, it's growing quickly.

This, of course, comes through a filter of consumer action, and this is an interesting point on that:

> The other thing {aside from acting as guides for each other} that happens when consumers talk amongst themselves is that they discover that, collectively, their tastes are far more diverse than the

> marketing plans being fired at them suggest. Their interests splinter into narrower and narrower communities of affinity, going deeper and deeper into their chose subject matter, as is always the case when like minds gather.

All of this material comes from the first quarter of the book, with the remainder of it being case studies, additional mathematical analysis, and lots of amazing data. The author looks at numerous industries, media, and institutions, and how moving from the "scarcity" model is changing them. While bits and pieces of this do sound dated 6 years down the road (see the Borders mention above), it is rather forward looking, with a late chapter even projecting what the effects will be when 3D printers become commonplace.

Anderson shows where the business model is heading: *"The secret to creating a thriving Long Tail business can be summarized in two imperatives: 1. Make everything available. 2. Help me find it."*, but also notes that *"legal restrictions will continue to be the primary barrier to growing the Long Tail"*, which is certainly chilling in light of SOPA/PIPA and similar attempts for government meddling in the Internet!

I would certainly recommend The Long Tail[4] to all and sundry ... it's a fascinating piece of cultural reporting, with things to recommend it to anybody with interest in media, marketing, the arts, or pretty much anything which is distributed and sold. Again, I found my copy of this up at the dollar store, but it's still in print, so you are likely to be able to find it at your better-stocked brick-and-mortar book vendors. The on-line guys have it at their usual 32% discount from cover price, however, and the new/used channels have "like new" copies for as little as a penny (well, four bucks after shipping's added), so you have a choice of source on this one.

Notes:

1. http://btripp-books.livejournal.com/123898.html

2. http://amzn.to/1YKN9x6

3. http://www.wired.com/wired/archive/12.10/tail.html

4. http://amzn.to/1YKN9x6

Thursday, January 26, 2012[1]

A narrow focus ...

This was a book that I actually got queried about from the good folks at Wiley ... since it was evidently a "job search" book, I said "yes", figuring that it would be good for my The Job Stalker[2] blog over on the Tribune's "ChicagoNow" site. However, Gayle Laakmann McDowell's The Google Resume: How to Prepare for a Career and Land a Job at Apple, Microsoft, Google, or any Top Tech Company[3] has an *awfully* narrow focus, being primarily targeted at recent college (engineering and computer science) grads looking to get hired by the "big boys" of the tech community. I suppose I could have "gotten that" from the sub-title, but I was really expecting something more *general*. Of course, if you *are* a recent graduate hoping to *"land a Job at Apple, Microsoft, Google, or any Top Tech Company"*, this is the book for you!

The author is a third-generation female engineer who added a Wharton MBA to her Computer Science degrees while working at Microsoft, Apple (although these were internships), and Google. Considering that she's (triangulating from her resume) not quite 30, that's a lot of experience, and this is her second book. She's since left "the big boys" and forged off on her own ... interestingly not being a software engineer, but doing career consulting for college grads who want to get hired by those "Top Tech Companies".

One of the things that stood out to me in this book is the assumption (or even encouragement) that people won't stay in a job more than four years. This very brief time-line keeps cropping up, and it's mind-boggling to me (having had two positions I was in for over a decade, and another I'd have been happy to have run out that long). This is frustrating to me (being in a seemingly unending job search, myself) as I keep hearing that companies are hesitant to hire older "more experienced" workers to mid-level positions because they're afraid that we'll bolt to a better gig after a while ... if the "new model" is only staying in a job 2-3 years for the *kids*, what the heck are they worried about with us *geezers*?!

This passage stood out as an example of how "planned" careers seem to be these days:

> No matter how happy you are in your current job, with any luck, this role will end up as a stepping stone to a new position or to a new company. Suddenly, all your years of work get mashed into a tiny five-bullet box on your resume and you picture yourself with a T-shirt saying, "I slaved away for five years and all I got were these lousy bullets."
>
> Your five-bullet box should be planned while you're working, not after you leave. Seek out meas-

urable, tangible accomplishments. Build something, create something, lead something. If you've tackled a major issue for your company, can you qualify its impact in terms of dollars, hours, or reduced sales calls? Seek out this information when it happens to ensure that you can get the most precise, accurate data.

So, let me get this straight, one should be constantly angling for *quantifiable* projects, for the benefit of one's resume, rather than what your company *needs* to have done? No wonder I can't quantify anything on my resume ... there were never any debriefings that let me know if the client moved X more cases of product in Y market where we'd done a program ... we figured if they re-upped the contract they were happy, and I doubt that they would have shared the details with us anyway!

Given these caveats, The Google Resume[4] is pretty much a soup-to-nuts overview of what it (presently) takes to get a job at one of the big tech companies. McDowell talks about what colleges are the best bets, what activities *in* college will help most, and how to find those internships (and she certainly has experience in that aspect). She goes over resumes, cover letters, references, and a whole bunch of interview particulars (since tech interviews are a different beast than most). She goes into balancing offers from different companies, and talks about how to best manage the on-the-job aspects of one's career (for instance, showing one case where a gal was in a job she loved at Amazon, but "gained nothing" from staying there five years instead of jumping ship after two!).

One of the more interesting parts of the book is where she presents questions she's been asked by various job seekers, at the end of each chapter. Their situations, and her answers, put a somewhat more concrete focus on the subject matter ... although, generally speaking, it's in a "cold, calculating – me, me, me!" light most of the time.

Overall, I found The Google Resume[5] a bit of a slog to get through, but this is largely due to it being targeted to a *very* different person than myself, and my being somewhat aghast at the tone of the book. However, if one is in the intended audience for this (and I'm considering passing it along to my highschool-aged daughter who wants to be an engineer for the general guidance of what sort of notches to get in one's belt), this is probably a great resource. I'd definitely recommend it as a gift to the appropriate college students, but I get a sense that if you're over 25 and not a computer science grad, there's not that much you'll get from this.

Notes:

1. http://btripp-books.livejournal.com/124001.html
2. http://jobstalker.info/
3-5. http://amzn.to/1YKJWO2

Friday, January 27, 2012[1]

Getting to the "Plus"

Every once in a while I get wind of a book that I'd like to review, and that the publishers haven't seen fit to contact me about (not that I'm "all that" in the reviewing field, but there *are* a couple of publishers who do have me on their promo lists). Being as I've previously looked at Social Media Guru Chris Brogan's *Trust Agents* and *Social Media 101*, I was interested to see his new publication, Google+ for Business: How Google's Social Network Changes Everything[2]. This came out from QUE publishing (a tech publisher rather than a business press this time), and so I dug around, found a contact for their marketing folks, and requested a review copy. Needless to say, being able to point them to my previous reviews of Chris' books no doubt helped in this.

As I've pointed out in my reviews of a number of older tech-niche books, early impressions on things have a way of going "stale" pretty quickly, so Brogan was taking a bit of a chance here, jumping in with a book on Google+ so soon after its debut. In fact, the official publication date of Google+ for Business[3] came just six months and a day after the launch of G+. Of course, the author is pretty up-front about this, being clearly aware that things would be changing very quickly (amusingly, just this past week Chris had posted on his G+ about a feature he wished they'd implement, and the feature went live two days later!), but this is likely to be the Achilles heel of the book: while it's reasonably "fresh" now (less than five weeks past its publication date), every month that goes by is going to make this more anachronistic ... much like my old Netscape manuals.

However, this might not ultimately matter, as this book is targeted for a business audience who want to know *now* what this new platform is about. And, of course, G+ isn't *just* another new generating-a-lot-of-buzz social media vehicle, it's *Google's* playground, and it's pretty clear that what happens on G+ will be effecting rankings on the flagship search engine ... so it's *important* for the folks who stay up at night wondering how to tweak the SEO voodoo of their sites to improve their Google appeal!

Now, I know Chris from Twitter, and had the pleasure of meeting him at a couple of Social Media "industry events" (is this an *industry*?), and I was aware of him "jumping in with both feet" on G+ early on. Honestly, one of *my* "desired features" on G+ (which did eventually get implemented) was wanting to have post comments collapsed, as it used to be that Chris would put up something and one would have to scroll and scroll and scroll to get past the 80 or so comments that folks had made in response. While I liked the "look and feel" of G+ better than Facebook, it had certain issues for me (still does) which made it far less appealing than Twitter, so I only occasionally checked in, and never quite "got" how much he was using it last year.

Anyway, Brogan certainly put in the time to become as much of an "expert" as one can be on a six-month-old, ever-evolving platform, and he brings that, along with his general Social Media expertise, to bear here. Again, this is (as clear from the title) a book *for Business*, and that's the focus here ... walking corporate readers through the process of creating a positive, profitable, presence on G+.

One of the author's on-going crusades is to make corporate presences in the Social Media sphere *personal*, with the folks who he holds up as "doing it right" generally being *people* representing companies, rather than corporate icons speaking through anonymous PR functionaries. I believe his stance on this is the best way of utilizing these channels, but I also understand what a hard sell that can be at places with bigger legal departments than communications groups, and recent events can be a sobering counterpoint (such as the case where a company sued its "Twitter guy" for "taking" "their" contacts with him when he left, or less antagonistic cases when somebody who had *personally* been very closely identified with the Social Media customer service face of a company had "moved on") to this approach.

Brogan pretty much assumes that Google+ for Business'[4] readers come to G+ pretty clueless, and walks them through all the basics of getting set up, and figuring out what they want to do once they're there. He then deals with how to post various types of content, talks about "content strategy", how to develop a "warm sell", grow one's audience, and share information. The model that he presents is that of a "magazine", that needs a particular focus, but has a lot of material that is at least generally related to that subject ... and while it can have *ads*, these are not the central part of what's in there (or you're not likely to have much "readership" for very long). He then addresses setting up specific business pages and points the reader to a half-dozen ones already up. He gives tips and tricks (several, such as the keyboard codes that G+ uses for italics, etc., I'd never heard of before) for using the interface, and what he calls "power plays" for maximizing the effectiveness of various options available on the platform (I have yet to have been in a "Hangout" video conference, but he notes cases where these have been very effective for certain individuals/companies, although they can only host up to 10 users at a time).

This is a very useful book (it has inspired me to tweak a few things that I was doing with G+ and try to make an effort to interact there more frequently), and it certainly is excellent for what it's intended to accomplish. It's brief enough (at under 200 pages) to not be a major slog, but still covers all the bases (as they're currently laid out) of the Google Plus environment. As noted above, however, this is something that one should "pull the trigger on" *now* rather than waiting because the platform is evolving before our eyes.

Since Google+ for Business[5] has only been out a few weeks, I'm pretty sure that you'd be able to find it in any bookstore that carried tech/business titles, and, of course, the on-line big boys have it, with both currently offering it at 39% below cover price. If you have an interest in getting on Google+ and "hitting the ground running", you should certainly pick up a copy of this!

Notes:
1. http://btripp-books.livejournal.com/124374.html
2-5. http://amzn.to/1OtC9ov

Saturday, January 28, 2012[1]

A very modern voice ...

Ah, another delightful Dover Thrift Editions book! These gems that can both nudge a sub-$25 on-line order up into the promised land of free shipping, but can also be called upon to pad one's reading totals in months when one is falling short of one's goals (remember, I try very hard to read 72 non-fiction books a year, and went into this past December in dire need of some "quick reads"), plus, they're a great way to fill in gaps in that otherwise-excellent Liberal Arts education.

Henry David Thoreau is one of those authors whose presence was certainly noted in the assorted English Major texts and collections, and I'm certain that I'd read *some* of his stuff back then, perhaps even his most-famous work *Walden*, but despite having dipped a toe into his writing (I have another couple of brief pieces by him in my library), I really didn't have much of a sense of the man's material.

I am *very* glad that I picked up Civil Disobedience and Other Essays[2], as its title work is *amazing* and should be required reading for everybody with an interest in Libertarianism and similar political philosophies. *Civil Disobedience*, however, is only one of five essays here (along with *Slavery in Massachusetts*, *A Plea for Captain John Brown*, *Walking*, and *Life without Principle*), and, unfortunately, the rest are not as strong at that. However, this is well worth the (very minor) cost of the volume, and here's a illustrative sampling:

> Unjust laws exist: shall we be content to obey them, or shall we endeavor to amend them, and obey them until we have succeeded, or shall we transgress them at once? Men generally, under such a government as this, think that they ought to wait until they have persuaded the majority to alter them. They think that, if they should resist, the remedy would be worse than the evil. But it is the fault of the government itself that the remedy *is* worse than the evil. *It* makes it worse. Why is it not more apt to anticipate and provide for reform? Why does it not cherish its wise minority? Why does it cry and resist before it is hurt? Why does it not encourage its citizens to be on the alert to point out its faults, and *do* better than it would have them? Why does it always crucify Christ, and excommunicate Copernicus and Luther, and pronounce Washington and Franklin rebels?
>
> One would think, that a deliberate and practical denial of its authority was the only offence never

> contemplated by government; else, why has it not assigned its definite, its suitable and proportionate penalty? If a man who has no property refuses but once to earn nine shillings for the State, he is put in prison for a period unlimited by any law that I know, and determined only by the discretion of those who placed him there; but if he should steal ninety times nine shillings from the State, he is soon permitted to go at large again.
>
> If the injustice is part of the necessary friction of the machine of government, let it go, let it go; perchance it will wear smooth, - certainly the machine will wear out. If the injustice has a spring, or a pulley, or a rope, or a crank, exclusively for itself, then perhaps you may consider whether the remedy will not be worse than the evil; but if it is of such a nature that it requires you to be the agent of injustice to another, then, I say, break the law. Let your life be a counter friction to stop the machine. What I have to do is to see, at any rate, that I do not lend myself to the wrong which I condemn.

These words could be coming from a Ron Paul campaign speech today, but they date back to 1849! Thoreau's situation here was the prospect of going to jail for non-payment of a tax ... *"It is for no particular item in the tax-bill that I refuse to pay it. I simply wish to refuse allegiance to the State, to withdraw and stand aloof from it effectually,"* ... very modern sentiments, and ones that would be as sure to draw the none-too-gentle attentions of the authorities today.

The next two essays deal, obviously, more with issues of slavery, more specifically in *Slavery in Massachusetts* (or how it manifested in a "free" state), and regarding the more direct abolitionist efforts in *A Plea for Captain John Brown*, and both of these are quite inspiring, if less universal. The last two essays are interesting but not as focused as the first three, but I suppose "your mileage may vary", as these are more railing against the failings of culture/civilization in general rather than that of the Government, so perhaps just don't appeal to me as much!

Anyway, the *cover price* of Civil Disobedience and Other Essays[3] is a whopping $1.50 so the odds of a brick-and-mortar book vendor having it taking up shelf space is unlikely, but, as noted above, it's an ideal throw-in for an on-line order needing to get up to the free shipping zone. I highly recommend putting this on your list for just that situation.

Notes:

1. http://btripp-books.livejournal.com/124662.html
2-3. http://amzn.to/1OtBDXE

Saturday, February 4, 2012[1]

Eh ...

This book came to me via the LibraryThing.com "Early Reviewer" program. I've been fortunate in that I've "won" a book in each of the past 11 months, although it's always a bit of a surprise. The way that works is that a number of books are made available by publishers and that LT members put in "requests" for the titles they find interesting. As I almost exclusively read non-fiction, and the list is *heavy* with fiction, the pickings are frequently quite slim for me, and I'll frequently click the request button for things that are just "sort of" interesting. Unfortunately, this was the case with Manage Your Depression Through Exercise: The Motivation You Need to Start and Maintain an Exercise Program[2] by Jane Baxter, PhD ... of the four books I clicked, this was the least "on target" for me, but it seemed like it might be useful, being that (with my on-going jobless state) I have to deal with depression, and I certainly could do with more exercise.

I don't know what I was expecting here, but it is a very detailed "plan" for a five-week program ... which, needless to say, I didn't actually *do* (although I did move it up to the top of my to-be-read pile when it came in). The author, who is presented as a psychotherapist, isn't a MD, but has degrees in Social Work, and is a "certified physical trainer". She tries to set up the book much like she might approach dealing with a client, in a somewhat chatty style, which, frankly, seems more aimed at what one would expect for the clinically depressed in an in-patient setting. She refers to her own "system" called PsychFit, and has "cutesy" names for other things, like the main exercise routine (the MMSMR, or "Move More, Smile More Routine"). Needless to say, this all was an immediate turn-off to me.

On the plus side, this is very systematic ... she has daily programs for the five weeks, and everything builds in a reasonably logical progression. Again, I didn't get the sense that this was for the "casually depressed" person, but (as noted above) folks unable to function in their lives. Each week has a "theme", with material brought in on nutrition, brain biochemistry (which I did find fascinating), etc. The last section (past week 5) was on "Stress, Loneliness, and Anger" which (in my case, at least) should have been where this *started* (and yes, it made me angry reading it).

I know that I've bitched in other books about authors who fill up their pages with lots of QR codes or MS tags, leading off to web-based resources, but this was one that *seriously* needed to have a source of material, as every few pages there's a questionnaire or chart to fill out, and places to make notes about what you're thinking, etc., and, unless you're going to have the book stuck under your arm for the five weeks, this is not going to be particularly handy. Bizarrely, in an appendix, there are copies of three of the charts, but with a *warning* that you can only copy these for your "personal use" and telling you to contact her *publisher* for permission to reproduce them otherwise! In a context where having a web page with the *necessary materials* easily printable would make a ton of sense, this all reminded me of the classic Monty Python sketch[3] where Anne Elk (Cleese) explains "her" theory of the brontosaurus ... it's evident that Dr. Baxter (or her publisher) is worried that this material will be "stolen" and suddenly there will be dozens of knock-off "PsychFit" operations cropping up everywhere.

I hate to be as negative about this as it sounds here, as the book/program does look like it could be helpful to folks who fit its profile ... it's just that this was *constantly* irritating me with one thing or another, but that's probably "just me" and I don't think I'm the target audience for this (notably, there is not a single picture of a guy doing the exercise routines here). As I mentioned, there are several quite informative bits (which I was planning on quoting here, but they didn't fit in how this ended up coming out) that I really appreciated reading, but it was an on-going struggle for me to just *read* his (and, again, this is structured to be *done* and not just read).

Manage Your Depression Through Exercise[4] came out last fall, so is probably still around in the health/exercise sections of your local bookstores, but the on-line guys have it at a discount of about 25% off of its very reasonable cover price. Again, this is the sort of thing that "pushes my buttons" and is probably aimed at a whole different demographic, so it may be something that you'd find very appealing (between B&N and Amazon, this had almost all 5-star reviews) instead of highly aggravating!

Notes:

1. http://btripp-books.livejournal.com/124868.html
2. http://amzn.to/1OtB8fW
3. https://youtu.be/qgxqkP5TZiw
4. http://amzn.to/1OtB8fW

Sunday, February 5, 2012[1]

You want potatoes with that?

Yes, here's another of those Dover Thrift Edition books ... once again doing triple duty for me, being a fast read when I was trying to get to my 72-book reading target last year, being a throw-in to get an on-line order up over $25 for free shipping, and filling in another gap in my Liberal Arts education. Now, I'm pretty sure that the title piece of Jonathan Swift's A Modest Proposal and Other Satirical Works[2] was in one of our text books (the Norton Anthology?), but it was one of those things that in highschool and college I likely read with only enough attention to shoot for a C on the next quiz, so coming back to it at this point at least informs me on it at a more substantial level.

Another book that I was reading recently was addressing the concept that before radio/television/internet the written word was a major entertainment field, and writers like Swift had a social role perhaps like that of a Steven Colbert ... commenting (or more likely mocking) on the issues and figures of the day. This becomes a problem in coming to this material some 300 years later, not only is the *style* of the writing alien, but the *context* is hard to appreciate, even with extensive footnotes. The first piece in this, "The Battle of the Books", pits different sections of a library (the "moderns" vs. the "ancients") against each other, but with almost every book, every reference, every description, aimed at figures of the day. Presumably, the reader in 1697 would "get the joke" but it's hard to make any sense of it on that level today. Imagine somebody in 2300ce watching a late-70s Saturday Night Live skit and trying to make sense of the cultural references in it.

This is the longest of the five pieces collected here (along with "A Meditation upon a Broomstick", "A Discourse Concerning the Mechanical Operation of the Spirit", which has interesting foreshadowings of several of Gurdjieff's themes, and "An Argument Against Abolishing Christianity in England") but it is the last which is the most famous (if not to say *notorious*), the title work "A Modest Proposal". This, of course, is Swift's satirical suggestion *"for preventing the children of poor people in Ireland from being a burthen to their parents or country, and for making them beneficial to the public"* by way of having their offspring be made a food source. Yes, *eating babies*.

Most of this is structured much along the lines of a business prospectus, with all the various costs and returns set out with various benefits to society (not least of which, this being Ireland, *"it would greatly lessen the number of papists"*), including providing a way for the poor *"to pay their landlord's rent, their own corn and cattle being already seized"*. A lot of this is not for the squeamish, as he goes into a fair amount of detail on the role of butchers, taverns, banquets, exports, etc. in the trade of Irish babies. Obviously, this is presented (albeit straight-faced) so over-the-top that it is evident that the author is addressing the oppression of the people rather than making an actual "proposal", but it is still a shocking piece. Here the subject matter is sufficiently universal that it is as disturbing now as it no doubt was back then.

Again, this is a slim (60-page) volume, with a cover price of $2.00 so you're quite unlikely to find it in a brick-and-mortar book store ... however, if you're interested in checking out the 17th Century's version of The Daily Show, you might want to add a copy of A Modest Proposal[3] to your next on-line order.

Notes:

1. http://btripp-books.livejournal.com/125087.html

2-3. http://amzn.to/1YKGldn

Monday, February 6, 2012[1]

Plausible deniability ...

I picked up Enter the Past Tense: My Secret Life as a CIA Assassin[2] by Roland W. Haas at the dollar store the other day. Having been sort of "full up" on business books, I jumped into this and read it over just a couple of days. It purports to be an autobiographical look at the career of a kid who sort of fell into doing CIA "black ops", but there are "issues" here with the truthfulness of this. To start out, even in the introductory materials in the book, the author is being defensive about being able to prove anything, and the few photos that are in the book only serve to "pin" the general arc of the story, but not the particulars.

I really try to avoid reading others' reviews of books before I slog into mine, but in this case I took a peek over on Amazon. This has quite a lot of reviews, with about 1/3rd of them quite negative, and 2/3rds of them being raves, or *defenses* of the book. I also found it interesting that the author jumped in to comment on many of the negative reviews, at least the ones posted before his accidental death (which was also detailed there) in August 2010. Some of the reviewers/commenters suggested that some of the defensive reviews were likely written by Haas as well. Many of the negative reviews go into a lot of detail about what is factually untrue in the book ... I have no way of judging these, but the number of them is suggestive.

Of course, in this area, it's hard to say for sure. Everything in this might be perfectly true, but the level of compartmentalization and deniability for "the agency" could easily prove to make confirming *anything* here difficult. Certainly, there is no reason to suspect the *early* parts of the book being untrue ... the author was the child of German immigrants who came to the US following WW2, and he was badly treated by kids where he grew up. Now, the specifics here are heavy on how smart he was and how much abuse he could take, etc., which does sound a bit like embellishment, but on the whole, it comes across as plausible. He ends up in NROTC at Purdue and is not particularly enthusiastic about either, being more interested in booze and drugs. One day he's called into the office and introduced to a guy from D.C. who proceeds to recruit him for clandestine work ... this was the first point where I had plausibility issues, as it was my impression that being as messed up as Haas indicates he was would immediately disqualify one for those sorts of attentions ... but this was the late 60's and things might have been different then ... and there *was* the element that he might have been just the "psychological profile" they were looking for.

He goes through training, and some odd twists (his CIA handler has Haas get himself arrested and expelled from school) and is then sent off to Germany, from where he's sent to Iran, Afghanistan, India, etc. for some hits. While this part of the book reads well, there are points that do seem "iffy" in terms of how they actually worked. When reading this, I simply assumed that he'd gathered bits of many different operations and wove them together into one narrative that lacked a certain continuity due to this. He does various projects from his West German base (it seemed odd how he was easily able to get teaching positions, but that was usually his cover) as the Cold War wound down. Following the reunification of Germany, he returns to the US and develops a health club in California (one of the things in the photo section is a newspaper piece about this club), which eventually gets co-opted by the Hells Angels (with some more implausible bits), making it so that he has to move again.

At this point the book changes and gets a lot more sketchy in the details, he mentions that he did a number of hits, but says he can't say *anything* about them, and he moves to the southeast and ends up, through several highly unlikely events (which he attributes to his CIA handler's influence), getting set up in an Intelligence job with the military. The focus here, however changes from his "black ops" work to his health, both his heavy drinking, his drug use, and the onset of diabetes. Most of the rest of the book deals with his problems with these issues.

This was the main problem I had with the book … it was at least a good *story* for the first 3/4 or so, and then just *stopped* and became something completely different. I don't know if Haas intended this to be somehow *inspirational* (when he eventually gets clean and sober), or just ran out of interesting things to write about, but the book "falls off the table" and drags on to the end.

Again, a lot of people think that Enter the Past Tense[3] is almost wholly a fabrication, but it's at least interesting for most of the way. I found it a quick, entertaining read, up until the point where it wasn't. I don't read many spy books, or thrillers, so this was a bit of "fluff" for me, and I don't know if it's something that I could recommend to those who typically read this sort of thing. It's still in print (so somebody must be buying it at retail!), but you can get "good" copies for a penny, and "like new" copies for under 50¢ (plus shipping, of course) from the new/used guys, which is probably where you'd want to go (unless you can find a dollar store copy like I did) if this sounds like something you'd want to read.

Notes:

1. http://btripp-books.livejournal.com/125270.html
2-3. http://amzn.to/1YKFFtY

Monday, February 13, 2012[1]

Pushing my buttons ...

I've been a pretty big fan of Seth Godin's books (and his blog), but for some reason The Dip: A Little Book That Teaches You When to Quit[2] simply pissed me off. I'd found this at a reasonable used rate on Amazon the other day and put it up top on the "to be read" pile (looking for a quick read while in the midst of a couple of rather dense books).

In many ways, what Godin is arguing for in The Dip[3] is the opposite of what Chris Anderson was talking about in *The Long Tail*. Godin here focuses on that top slice of everything, about being "the best in the world". He starts this off with a look at ice cream flavors ... listing the top 10 flavors industry-wide. Vanilla comes in #1, with nearly 30% of the market, with Chocolate a distant second at about 8%. The remaining eight flavors are virtually indistinguishable, all hovering around 5% of sales. Obviously, the point here is that if you're not Vanilla, you're way behind. He notes:

> *"People don't have a lot of time and don't want to take a lot of risks. ...*
>
> *With limited time or opportunity to experiment, we intentionally narrow our choices to those at the top.*
>
> *You're not the only person who looks for the best choice. Everyone does. As a result, the rewards for being first are enormous. It's not a linear scale. It's not a matter of getting a little more after giving a little more. It's a curve, and a steep one."*

The saving grace in this is that "best" and "world" are very subjective, so one can aspire to be the "best in the world" for a very particular finely defined niche (the examples he gives include *"the best gluten-free bialys available by overnight shipping"* and *"the best Thai restaurant in Queens"*). If you're able to pick your niche, and work real hard to be the *best* in that niche, you can have a realistic expectation of achieving that "best in the world" status for that "world".

Did I mention that he pissed me off? Well, it *starts* here. Basically, he argues that people like me, the well-rounded, the "jack of all trades", those aspiring to being polymaths or a "Renaissance Man", are *screwed*. Nobody wants to hire you if you're not the particular polygonal piece that fits into the specific polygonal hole they're looking to fill. That's why so many job listings these days specify "rock stars" or "ninjas"... they want one-dimensional unthinking robots who, like Colonel Sanders back in the 80's "do one thing right". Godin argues that if you can't be the "best in the world" at a given job/business/sport, *quit* ... and go do something else. I did an assessment exercise a few years back and identified *fifteen* different job slots that I was "plausible" (i.e., I'd be competent doing and wouldn't hate it too much) for ... that's a pretty damn wide skill set, but Godin would have me dump *fourteen* of those and pick ONE to focus on. Sounds like Hell to me.

Anyway, back to the book. There are three "curves" he defines for any activity, which chart effort on the horizontal axis and results on the vertical. These are "The Dip", "The Cul-de-Sac", and "The Cliff". The latter two are bad and lead to failure, one being pretty much a straight line across the chart, with no increase in results for added effort, and the other having an initial upwards slope, followed by a sudden downward plunge (the example he gives is cigarette marketing, where the addictive nature of the product keep sales moving up until emphysema sets in). The "Dip" looks like the blue area on the cover of the book, where initial growth in results slide down, and eventually pick up strongly once you're through the down phase.

The second thing that pissed me off here was that, to my reading, there is *nowhere* in here where one can realistically KNOW which curve one is on, or if one is *in* "The Dip", how deep and long that's going to be. Godin spends a lot of time talking about pushing through the dip (and ways to fail in doing so), but never shows *how* one can tell if there is a *possibility* of getting through it. He defines "The Dip" enough in various contexts, going to law school and passing the bar are a "dip" creating a scarcity pool of people (or at least lawyers) who have, the organic chemistry class that separates the M.D.s from the psychologists, manufacturers who make it past all the production and distribution challenges to successfully get a product out there, entrepreneurs who manage to weave through the mine field of start-up funding, etc. ... plus this is dynamic and "playable" in particular niches: *"That's the goal of any competitor: to create a Dip so long and so deep that the nascent competition can't catch up."* Again, this is all about *scarcity*, the big fat front end of the "long tail" distribution curve ... and, according to Godin, if you're not on the way to being "the best in the world" (navigating through the Dip) you should *quit*, even though there's no clear way to tell if that's going to happen or not.

> "The people who set out to make it through the Dip – the people who invest the time and the energy and the effort to power through the Dip – those are the ones who become the best in the world. They are breaking the system because, instead of moving on to the next thing, instead of doing slightly above average and settling for what they've got, they embrace the challenge. For whatever reason, they refuse to abandon the quest and they push through the Dip all the way to the next level."

What pissed me off in this is that, while he says: *"... it's pretty easy to determine whether something is a Cul-de-Sac or a Dip ... the hard part is finding the guts to do something about it"*, there's nothing here to help one make that determination, which sort of invalidates everything else in the book!

As one might expect, given Godin's popularity, The Dip[4] is still in print, and at a bit more reasonable price point that most of his "small" books (this is well under 100 pages). As noted above, I got this from the new/used vendors, and there are "very good" copies available for under three bucks (before shipping). I don't know if I can enthusiastically recommend this one, however, there's just too much about it which just doesn't connect for me ... although your reading might be different.

Notes:

1. http://btripp-books.livejournal.com/125500.html

2-4. http://amzn.to/1NMUqrb

Tuesday, February 14, 2012[1]

Only moderately of approval ...

A month or so back I attended an event hosted by Brickfish (they're a "social media platform" company) down at the House of Blues. They'd brought in Erik Qualman (who's best known for his *Socialnomics* book from a couple of years ago) to speak (he's one of their consultants, I take it), and provided attendees with copies of his new book, Digital Leader: 5 Simple Keys to Success and Influence[2], which he was also signing. So, if the FTC is peeking in, yes, this was a *free* copy.

As regular readers of my reviews probably have a pretty good sense of, I'm not fond of "cutesy" in books, and if you're going to come up with some mnemonic acronym, it had better be a *useful* one (such as the "trouble", TRBL, mnemonic for in-line CSS style calls) or I'm going to find it irritating at best. If I'm constantly having to check back to the introductory chapters to remind myself what your cute word "means", it's a #FAIL. Unfortunately, Qualman's book is based on one of these: S.T.A.M.P. ... and, as is frequently the case, I feel that it's somewhat "forced", but it's the organizing matrix for the book, with the various sections corresponding to the concepts hooked onto those letters:

> S – Simple: "success is the result of simplification and focus"
>
> T – True: "be true to your passion"
>
> A – Act: "nothing happens without action – take the first step"
>
> M – Map: "goals and visions are needed to get where you want to be"
>
> P – People: "success doesn't happen alone"

It is telling that I could *not* remember any past "simple" when typing this, and had to refer back to the index for the other four! Another bad sign was that I ended up with *no* little slips of paper bookmarking particular pages that I wanted to either come back to (for resources, etc.), or thought would make a good quote in my review ... which also indicates that a lot of this was being convolutedly pushed towards "stamp" imagery to the detriment of the material.

This is not to say the book is *bad*, but that it could have been *better* with a more straight-forward presentation. It starts out reasonably well, defining its concept:

> "At one time, if you reached a certain level of celebrity or significance, you may have been immortalized on a postage stamp. ... Few people, however, attained this level of notoriety. The digital age has changed this concept: now every single one of us

> has a <u>digital</u> stamp. ...
>
> *Digital footprints and shadows constitute our permanent imprint on the world: a detailed summary of our life for our contemporaries and for people of the future to view and consider. Digital footprints are the information we post about ourselves online, while digital shadows are what others upload about us. Collectively, these two items have changed the world forever, and as current or aspiring leaders it is necessary to adapt to this new reality. While others will help or hinder along the way, <u>you</u> will ultimately determine how effective a leader you become and your overall stamp on life."*

Each of the "STAMP" sections has 3-4 chapters, addressing some topic more-or-less connected with the acronym elements. Within the chapters are some very useful bits, "Digital Deeds" which are sections featuring tips and suggestions for using various platforms and programs, "Life Stamps" which are little biographical sketches about people that illustrate the topic at hand, plus brief quotes from famous "leaders" every few pages (although the editing slipped up on this, with a Ray Kroc quote repeating on 205 and 206). What I found most engaging here were the many "case studies" that Qualman dips into in the various chapters, from the evolution of Apple's web page (how it was simplified), to Magic Johnson's post-basketball business success (in the "connections" part of the "People" section), which were interesting windows into what the author saw as stories exemplifying his points.

Again, there's a lot of good stuff in here, but I really feel it would have been a lot more effective without the artificial structure of the "STAMP" concept. I also got the sense that there were some "editing issues" here (aside from the one noted above), on both a "why wasn't that fixed?" level, and in the feeling that certain elements (what *the heck* was that poem about in the introductory chapter?) had been fought over and not "smoothly" settled as far as the over-all tone was concerned (I realize I'm being both picky and vague here).

<u>Digital Leader</u>[3] has only been out for a couple of months now, so you should no doubt be able to find it at your local brick-and-mortar book vendor, but, as usual, the on-line guys have it at about 1/3rd off of cover, making it cheaper that what's available used (once you add the shipping). This is a "different kind" of book in its genre, being wider based across business and cultural trends than just the hard-core digital/social zone, and has its appeal primarily in that reach. I liked it well enough, and you certainly might find it more engaging than I did ... not a ringing endorsement, but not a "pan" either.

Notes:

1. http://btripp-books.livejournal.com/125867.html

2-3. http://amzn.to/1Zqjtrm

Saturday, February 18, 2012[1]

A different evolution ...

This is one that I've had sitting around for quite a while, probably going back to either a Newberry Library book fair, or another box sale at OpenBooks. A friend had borrowed it recently and "warned" me that it was a bit on the dense side, but, while it was a struggle when in the "reading chair" (Zzzzz!), it was just fine for on the subway, or at various coffee vendors (see pic[2]).

Darwin Among The Machines: The Evolution Of Global Intelligence[3] by George B. Dyson (son of Freeman "Dyson Sphere" Dyson) is an interesting look at the movement towards what has since been popularly known as "The Singularity". It's notable that, although this book dates from 1997 ("ancient history" for most computer books), the presentation here does not feel particularly dated. This is likely due to most of the book being backwards-looking, examining predecessors of the machines that were starting to proliferate at the time.

The title of this book is from a section of a book by Samuel Butler, who was something of a philosophical sparring partner of Charles Darwin, but that piece was more about his *grandfather*, Erasmus Darwin, whose theories (in the 18th century) preceded and provided a basis for Charles' work. Erasmus was both more "mystical" than his grandson, and more fascinated by machines, and Charles made a very significant effort to make sure nothing of his work was credited to his predecessor.

> Computers may turn out to be less important as catalysts facilitating technological evolution and more important as catalysts facilitating evolutionary processes through the incubation and propagation of self-replicating filaments of code. As Erasmus Darwin and his Lunar Circle characterized the age that brought mechanical and electromagnetic metabolism to life, so John von Neumann and his circle of engineers and programmers characterized the origins, two centuries later, of self-replicating strings of bits. In 1948, von Neumann delivered his "General and Logical Theory of Automata", from which my father, in his Origins of Life, condensed the essential truths that "metabolism and replication, however intricately they may be linked in the biological world as it now exists, are logically separable. It is logically possible to postulate organisms that are composed of pure hardware and capable of metabolism but incapable of replication. It is also possible to postulate organisms that are composed

> of pure software and capable of replication but incapable of metabolism".

Two elements of the book can be derived from this, the subtle, but noticeable, thread of the Darwin and Dyson families (and of sons/grandsons wishing to stand outside of their predecessors' extensive shadows), and of the concepts of software and hardware standing apart. Much of the book looks are the evolution of *software*, which has direct cognitive lineages into the past, rather than the machines of which it runs (although this evolutionary track is certainly addressed). It is probably this that makes Darwin Among the Machines[4] less anachronistic than many books of its vintage would tend to be.

On one level, the book could be taken as a series of papers, as most of the chapters a fairly self-contained, and only link together peripherally. The first few chapters *sort of* form a story arc, but most of the rest address a particular concept and delve back in time as much as they need to (such as "On Distributed Communications" which starts with a signaling system used by the Greeks in the siege of Troy in 1184bce, and runs into the mid-60s with the RAND Corporation work that laid the groundwork for the Internet), covering topics and figures all across the board.

Again, much of this is more about history and philosophy ... who developed what, who argued what and with whom, how wars steered developments (from Troy to the calculations of M.A.D. in the Cold War), and what influences came to bear on making the machines and the code come together. From a place where I have a computer (smart phone) on my belt which would run circles around most of the machines discussed here ... it is remarkable to look into the growth of the machines, and it does become tempting to look at this as something *organic*, if in the spirit of the late, great, George Carlin suggesting that humans only evolved to create *plastics* for the Earth. Dyson, in one paragraph, links our relationship with silicon, from knocking off razor-sharp chips from a hunk of obsidian, to *"increasingly complex chips of silica, given form by the force of information"*, and elsewhere notes: *"We shall not see biochemistry replaced by electronics; we shall see a merger that incorporates them both."* (hopefully not making these[5] prophetic!).

I was a bit surprised to see that Darwin Among the Machines[6] is still in print, 14 years after its publication ... somewhat unusual for a "tech" book, but as noted above, this is more about the *concepts* of artificial intelligence, and not so much about the technologies involved at the time of writing. However, since it *has* been out so long, there are a lot of copies in the "used" channels, and a "good" copy of the hardcover can be had for as little as 1¢ (plus shipping, of course) out there. I was fascinated by this book (it's an area that I'm quite interested in), but it was not exactly a light, breezy read. However, if you're willing to slog through it, there's great stuff to be found here!

Notes:
1. http://btripp-books.livejournal.com/125970.html
2. https://goo.gl/TsZdPh
3-4. http://amzn.to/1NMTaV3
5. http://goo.gl/m4MWFN
6. http://amzn.to/1NMTaV3

Sunday, February 19, 2012

A brighter light ...

This is a really, really interesting book ... *if* you are into the "Fourth Way" material of Gurdjieff, Ouspensky, and their assorted followers and interpreters. As regular readers of this space are no doubt aware, I have read quite deeply into this genre, although the *explosion* of third- and fourth-generation students producing books has made it nearly impossible to have read everything on the subject.

The reason that J.G. Bennett's Gurdjieff: Making a New World[2] is so fascinating is that it's *written by Bennett*, who was a major light in the mystical field in the mid-20th century in his own right, and a linchpin and pivot-point between many threads of occultism of the time. Bennett had been in British military intelligence in Turkey during the time of "the great game" between the U.K. And Russia ... and might well have known of Gurdjieff "professionally", as there are many rumors that much of Gurdjieff's ability to travel as he did was due to having been an agent of the Tsar. While Bennett met Gurdjieff in the 1920's while studying with Ouspensky, he did not work intensively with him until the late 40's, arriving in Paris right before Gurdjieff's near-fatal car crash.

The first part of this book discusses the region of Asia that Gurdjieff hailed from, including its culture, history, environment, and mystical traditions.

> *Strangely enough, the tradition of the Masters is almost unknown in India. When Helena Blavatsky published her books,* The Secret Doctrine *and* Isis Unveiled*, one of her chief claims was to have encountered in person some of the Masters in or beyond Tibet. The belief in Masters then became an integral part of the theosophical doctrine, but it acquired an occult character that weakened its credibility. Much of the mystery of the theosophical 'masters' derived from their supposed location in Tibet, though Helena Blavatsky herself asserted that their headquarters was beyond the mountains in the legendary 'Shamballa'. It never occurred to me that this was more than a pure invention until, quite recently, Idries Shah suggested to me that it could be derived from Shams-i-Balkh, the Bactrian Sun Temple, the ruins of which can still be seen at Balkh near the northern frontier of Afghanistan. Rudolph Steiner associated Balkh with Hraniratta, the centre of the Mithraic Sun worship. The point to be made here is that the belief in an ancient and continuing tradition is particularly strong in the regions of Central Asia in which Gurdjieff concentrat-*

> ed much of his search. In this chapter no attempt is made to settle the question whether or not a supreme spiritual hierarchy really does exist. I shall, however, carefully examine the suggestion that the name "Masters of Wisdom" comes from the Khwajagān who played such an extraordinary role in the heart of Asia between the eleventh and fifteenth centuries of the Christian Era. The word Khwaja means wise man or master, and is best rendered Master of Wisdom. … I have little doubt that Gurdjieff had heard of these Masters in his youth, and that one of the principal objects of his travels in Turkestan, Afghanistan and Tibet was to discover traces of their activity in order to reconstruct their teaching.

If anybody would have "inside knowledge" about these mystical threads in the area, it would be Bennett, who had the nearly-unique combination of having been an intelligence officer in the British military *and* a seeker & adept himself. These initial chapters trace where Gurdjieff likely got most of his concepts, with Bennett presenting tidbits that would be difficult for any others to offer:

> Even if the Khwajagān and the Sarmān were not identical, it is possible that individual Khwajas were associated with the Sarmān Brotherhood. This is suggested by Gurdjieff, and by comparing dates and activities, we may identify his Brother Olmantaboor with Ubeydullah Ahrar. Ahrar's biographer, Mēvlanā Djami, the greatest literary figure of Central Asia, was evidently aware that Ahrar's influence went far beyond his immediate environment.

The level of obscure historical data that Bennett introduces in these chapters is truly amazing, and leads the reader into wanting to dig deeply into the hints and trails sketched out. However, once established, the book turns to tracking Gurdjieff's early history, largely based on the information in *Meetings With Remarkable Men* and other materials that the author had access to. Again, one gets the sense here that Bennett had data from his intelligence work that allowed him to make more focused "guesses" than would be the case for anybody without his background.

About half way through the book, Bennett switches to looking at the actual teachings, and takes apart the literature in a way which surprised me (I had been unaware of how much editing had been done by Gurdjieff to his books over time). Most of this is probably too esoteric for those *not* familiar with Gurdjieff's books, but it is *fascinating* for those who have studied them.

> [One] might legitimately retort that it is useless to know how a machine works if one does not know what the purpose it is intended to serve. … Modern

> science is in this very situation. It is in process of discovering how the universe works but does not even ask what it is for. If the universe is too large a machine for us to think of as a whole, we have the solar system or even the 'space-ship earth' to study. Who asks the question: "What is this remarkable piece of mechanism for?" Man himself is another marvelously constructed machine closer to us than any other machine. Do we ask ourselves, "What purpose does this ingenious apparatus serve?"

This is "Gurdjieff's question", and sits at the core of "The Work" …

> The answer Gurdjieff gives to the questions - "What is the sense and significance of life on the earth?" - is radically different from any current views. Gurdjieff asserts in Beelzebub's Tales that the doctrine of reciprocal maintenance is derived from 'an ancient Sumerian manuscript' discovered by the great Kurdish philosopher Atarnakh. The passage quoted runs: "In all probability, there exists in the world some law of the reciprocal maintenance of everything existing. Obviously our lives serve also for maintaining something great or small in the world."
>
> This passage occurs in the description of a Central Asian fraternity called "The Assembly of the Enlightened", which had existed from Sumerian times and flourished openly in the Bactrian kingdom when Zoroaster was teaching. After Zoroaster, it disappeared for a hundred generations, and only now has again begun to send out into the world its 'Unknown Teaching'. I have suggested that this is the Sarmān society.
>
> What is this doctrine? Reciprocal maintenance in its special sense connotes that the universe has a built-in structure or pattern whereby every class of existing things produces energies or substances that are required for maintaining the existence of other classes.

On a personal note, I was quite surprised to see this concept put this way, as it is very close to the concept of "Ayni"[3] among the Q'ero people of the high mountains of Peru, whose Shamanic traditions I've studied. Gurdjieff's version of this has a lot more complex cosmology connected with it, but the parallels are very strong.

Most of the rest of the book has Bennett walking the reader through the details of this concept, with their associated graphs. While I'd been familiar with the "enneagram", there are other charts here, specifically dealing with levels of reciprocity from "heat" to "endlessness" (with all the other levels of existence in between) that I'd never encountered, and the complexity of this is somewhat off-putting.

Gurdjieff: Making a New World[4] is, oddly, shown by both of the on-line "big boys" as being out of print, although both have used copies in their listings. It is, however, available in paperback from Bennett Books[5]. I've noticed previously that they will have copies of things which don't seem to be generally available, so that's probably your best bet for finding this. However, I got my hardcover in "good" (pretty beat up) condition from one of the new/used vendors, so I can't speak to the "buying experience" with Bennett Books. If you've read some Gurdjieff, I would *highly* recommend picking up this book, as it "looks under the hood" on his life and teachings to an extent that I've never seen elsewhere … but if you're not familiar with the "Fourth Way" material, I think this would be a very confusing place to start (I'd recommend Ouspensky's *In Search of the Miraculous* for a first exposure).

Notes:

1. http://btripp-books.livejournal.com/126240.html
2. http://amzn.to/1ZqiyqW
3. http://goo.gl/umzNhL
4. http://amzn.to/1ZqiyqW
5. http://www.bennettbooks.org/

Tuesday, February 21, 2012[1]

When the moon is in the seventh house?

I picked this up a few years back at the dollar store, and it sat in my ever-growing "to be read" pile for a very long time, largely because I assumed that it was going to be a "woo-woo" newage book, as I (perhaps unfairly) recalled the author's previous (and far better known) book *The Aquarian Conspiracy* to be. I was probably a bit "burned out" by social media stuff last month, and picked this up just for a change of pace. So, I was *quite* surprised at what a level-headed book Marilyn Ferguson's Aquarius Now: Radical Common Sense And Reclaiming Our Personal Sovereignty[2] was.

Frankly, the signs were there, even in the sub-title, "common sense" and "personal sovereignty" are right out of Libertarianism, and the book starts out by discussing Thomas Paine! It's not, however, a particularly *political* book, as it weaves science, philosophy, mysticism, and, yes, *some* politics, into a very interesting tapestry. It is, unfortunately, not an easy book to say "what it's about", as it swings though a wide array of topics, most of which set up as "symbolized" by particular types (The Firemaker, The Sacred Warrior, The Navigator, etc.), although that connection tends towards being somewhat tenuous. I wonder how long it took Ferguson to write this, as it is *so* "chock full" of quotes, references, stories, and discussions of research, etc., that it must have taken a substantial effort to assemble all of this together. The book's 200 or so pages are divided into 14 chapters, and these contain various sections, each running from a half a page to about 3 pages, and (more or less) containing one idea, which in turn is sequenced with the others around it, and generally relates to the chapter topic.

Again, this makes it challenging to snag a chunk of text to put in here that would be illustrative of the book ... as each section has its own focus, its own "characters", and doesn't necessarily create a "story arc" with surrounding materials. To give you a bit of an example, the chapter that's sort of about ESP ("Tuning into the Field – The Dowser"), starts out quoting Tom Paine, moves into the theories of E.H. Gutkind, Henry Miller's reactions to those, which then dovetails into a quote by Ezra Pound ... all in the first page and a half of the chapter. Many, if not most, of the sections have as much "happening in them", making a rich mix of influences and cognitive threads, but making it very hard to sum up. It's almost as if Ferguson took everything she'd ever read in putting out her *Brain/Mind Bulletin*, cut it into bite-size pieces, and organized it into this book.

While I find it frustrating in the context of writing a cogent review, please don't take this as a *criticism* of the book. While it *is* a bit of a "fire hose" with concepts flying off the page in quick succession, it is an *amazing* collection of ideas and the people associated with those ideas, encapsulated just enough (in the sections and "themed" chapters) to give it a structure. The writing is generally accessible, despite the "depth" of some of the particular bits, and almost never veers off into too much (within the context of the book) detail on any one subject. As noted, I sort of expected the collectivist sensibility of the New Agers to be operating here, but the focus is very much on individual growth, responsibility, and freedom, and these linked into key thinkers of the past. One of the recurring themes here is of education/intelligence, and how our culture is being badly served by the systems which are in place currently ...for those who've been following my reading via these reviews, the concept of "attention" (which I've been running into a lot in a number of books) also plays a significant role here ... all very interesting.

Aquarius Now[3] is still in print, so could be found at your local better-stocked brick-and-mortar book vendor. Oddly, only one of the on-line big boys have it (and with no discount at that), but there are copies in the used channels, with a "like new" version of the hardcover going for as little as 1¢ plus shipping (which would probably be your best bet at this point). Again, I enjoyed reading this *way* more than I had anticipated, and I'd heartily recommend it to anybody with an interest in all that Mind/Brain stuff!

Notes:

1. http://btripp-books.livejournal.com/126666.html

2-3. http://amzn.to/1ZqikA7

Thursday, March 8, 2012[1]

Ill which the gods have sent thou canst not shun ...

Yes, here's another of those Dover Thrift Edition books that serve three functions in my reading ... first, pushing an online order up into the "over $25 free shipping" promised land, second, filling a gap in my otherwise-excellent liberal arts education, and third, well, being a fast read when I've been falling behind on my six-books-a-month reading target (72 books a year). This one, The Seven Against Thebes[2] by Aeschylus is one of the few remaining plays by that ancient Greek dramatist. Aeschylus wrote in the 5th century BCE, and preceded the better known Sophocles and Euripides. According to the introductory note here, it was Aeschylus who introduced a second actor in a scene (where formerly, all plays just featured one main actor with a chorus), greatly expanding the dramatic possibilities.

The Seven Against Thebes[3] is the third play of a trilogy, of which the first two are lost, dealing with the famous Oedipus tragedy (best known from Sophocles' masterpiece). In this third play, Oedipus' cursed progeny, Eteocles, ruler of Cadmea (later known as Thebes), and Polynices, the exiled brother seeking to take the city-state with the aid of the army of Argos, prepare to do battle. It's convenient that the storyline is so familiar in Western culture, as it makes this play considerably more accessible than if one only had the "backstory" elements included within the text itself. The chorus is supposed to be the "Cadmean Maidens", lending a certain pathos to the proceedings, as they have a pronounced interest in the results, and are in no way "detached" in their interactions with the featured characters.

The first three-quarters of this are exchanges between Eteocles, a Spy which is reporting on the Argive forces outside the seven gates of Cadmea, and the Chorus. The Spy reports on what champions of Argos are assigned to attack which gate, and Eteocles responds with what Cadmean warriors will be meeting them there (along with what deities are affiliated with both forces), and the Chorus expressing their hopes and concerns. Eteocles himself goes to defend the seventh gate, at which his brother Polynices is attacking.

I hate to bring in a "spoiler" here, but:

> O dark and all prevailing ill
>   That broods o'er Oedipus and all his line,
> Numbing my heart with mortal chill!
>   Ah, me, this song of mine,
> Which, Thyad-like I woke, now falleth still,
>   Or only tells of doom,

> And echoes round a tomb!
> Dead are they, dead! in their own blood they lie -
> Ill-omened the concent that hails our victory!
> The curse a father on his children spake
> Hath faltered not, nor failed!
> Nought, Laius! they stubborn choice availed -
> First to beget, then, in the after day
> And for the city's sake,
> The child to slay!
> For nought can blunt nor mar
> The speech oracular!
> Children of teen! By disbelief ye erred -
> Yet in wild weeping came fulfillment of the word!

While all the other Cadmean warriors successfully defended their gates, Eteocles and Polynices slay each other at the seventh. At this point Etocles (obviously) and the Spy are replaced by Oedipus' daughters Antigone and Ismene (although the latter has no specific lines) and a Herald from the ruling council. The Herald bears instructions that Polynices should be denied a funeral and be thrown to the dogs outside the walls, which Antigone refuses, insisting that both of her brothers will be given proper rites, and the play ends. It's primarily in this last quarter of the play that the Chorus (of the Cadmean Maidens) fills in the background on the family's dark history.

As you can tell by the quote above, this has been rendered into English rhyme (by an E.D.A. Morshead in 1928), and one has to wonder what liberties have been taken with the original (in ancient Greek rhyme) to force it into not only another language, but a rhyming scheme in that. The doom/tomb and mar/oracular rhymes stand in the above as possibly painful extrapolations!

Anyway, The Seven Against Thebes[4] was a reasonably entertaining read, and it's one of those "culturally significant" works that one really should be familiar with. As is usually the case with the Dover Thrift books, you're not likely to find these at your local brick-and-mortar store because their cover prices are so low (in this case $1.50) that they're hard to justify expending shelf space on, but they're ideal to have at the ready when you have a couple of twelve dollar books and need to bump things up to get free shipping from the on-line guys!

Notes:

1. http://btripp-books.livejournal.com/126915.html

2-4. http://amzn.to/1QJbt3u

Friday, March 9, 2012[1]

Is not our fortune famous, brave, and great?

This is another book that came my way via the LibraryThing.com "Early Reviewers" program. I'm not sure what I was specifically expecting this to be (in the LTER program, there's a big list of books that are being offered by publishers, with a brief description of each, and a button to "request" a book, and then it's up to the "almighty algorithm" to match up the requests to what seems to be the best match of reviewer ... you can request as many as you like, but you'll only get one "win", and that's not a sure thing). Anyway, I've had a long familiarity with the Bhagavad Gita, going back to the mid-70's when the Hare Krishna movement was wide-spread, and I actually had a subscription to their *Back to Godhead* magazine. One of the features of this was an on-going translation of the Gita by ISKCON founder Prabhupada, where there was the Sanskrit text, a transliteration of that into the Western alphabet, a linear translation, and an interpretive translation of the meaning of the passage ... I found these *fascinating*, as it was a window into Sanskrit that I didn't have otherwise. So, it wasn't much of a surprise when I "won" Eknath Easwaran's [Essence of the Bhagavad Gita: A Contemporary Guide to Yoga, Meditation, and Indian Philosophy][2], but I was thinking that this would simply be another translation of the Indian classic. Actually, Easwaran (who is the late founder of the Blue Mountain Center of Meditation) *has* a translation of the Gita, and this book is intended as a "companion" to that, outlining the "essence" of that text.

So, instead of having just another translation to wade through, this is a rather remarkable "explanation" of the book, which depends more on the author's personal relationship with the material than with the details of the material.

> Because we are not separate from [the] supreme reality, it follows that each of us is incomplete so long as we consider ourselves separate: that is, until we make this discovery ourselves. Whatever else we may achieve in life ... there will be a vacuum in our hearts that can be filled only by direct, experiential knowledge of reality. This is the message of the Gita in a nutshell: life has only one purpose, and that is to know the divine ground of existence and become united with it here and now.

This certainly is a different tone than the chanting and dancing of the mid-70's Krishna kids ... although I'm sure they'd have agreed with this passage in principle.

If you are unfamiliar with the Bhagavad Gita, it's one section of the sprawling historical epic poem, the Mahabharata, which describes events in India in the 8-9th centuries BCE. The core elements of this deal with a war between various elements of a dynasty, with relatives, teachers, and close friends arrayed on both sides. One key figure is the prince Arjuna, who is preparing for battle, and at the start of the Gita, is reviewing the assembled lines, with his chariot driver, Krishna. Arjuna, a great warrior, is having qualms about this battle, foreseeing the deaths of so many people he cares about, and expresses this to Krishna … who then reveals himself as the Godhead and goes through a whole exposition about "life, the universe, and everything", including how Arjuna must follow his dharma as a warrior and participate in the battle. Easwaran points out that the actual war is *within*, and the battle is with the illusion of separateness, or Maya.

Again, I was surprised at how little Essence of the Bhagavad Gita[3] actually dwells on the story, or even wording of the Gita. Rather, the author takes the Gita as a starting point to discuss the underlying *concepts* involved, and the tone is very much discursive, as though one was sitting at tea with Easwaran and listening to him expound on this. Indeed, there is a good deal of autobiographical material in this, discussing how he came to his faith, and became a teacher, etc., using elements from his own life to illustrate the ideas he's presenting.

Of course, when it's to the point, he will dip into the text of the Gita, such as in this passage where Krisha is instructing Arjuna on the illusion of death:

> *Death is inevitable for the living; birth is inevitable for the dead. Since they are unavoidable, you should not sorrow. Every creature is unmanifested at first and then attains manifestation. When its end has come, it again becomes unmanifested. What is there to lament in this? (2:27-28)*

Frankly, if one looked through the chapter titles here, one would not suspect that this was a book about, or even based on the Bhagavad Gita … as the chapters deal with reality, personality, yoga, meditation, the unconscious, reincarnation, and other more "philosophical" subjects whose natures are brought to light for Easwaran in the pages of the Gita. This is probably the most appealing part of the book for me, as, rather than "beating one over the head" with the insistence of entering a Krsihna practice (like the Hare Krishnas back in the day), he is taking the *teachings* of Krishna from the Gita and presenting these as a template for an approach that is quite in line with modern western psyches.

I very much enjoyed Essence of the Bhagavad Gita[4], and would generally recommend it to "all and sundry", with the one concern that it might not have the impact that it did for me if one was not as familiar with the source material. Obviously, one could pick up Easwaran's *translation* of the Gita (which would likely provide a seamless transition into this), but it is also available free on-line, from the basic text translated into English (http://www.sacred-texts.com/hin/gita/[5]), to Prabhupada's idiosyncratic presentation (http://www.asitis.com/[6]), and other detailed looks at this classic book (such as at http://www.bhagavad-gita.org/[7]). That said, I do think this would be a useful read for anybody. Being that it's new, you have a pretty good shot of finding it at your local bookstore that stocks "eastern religion" titles, and the on-line guys have it from a quarter to a third off of (a very reasonable) cover price.

Notes:

1. http://btripp-books.livejournal.com/127140.html
2-4. http://amzn.to/1NMQG92
5. http://www.sacred-texts.com/hin/gita/
6. http://www.asitis.com/
7. http://www.bhagavad-gita.org/

Tuesday, March 20, 2012[1]

Bird Talk ...

This was one of those Dollar Store finds ... I'd been up at the "new" one (I discovered that there was one straight up the Red Line which didn't involve changing trains) picking up a few things when I found they'd gotten in a new batch of books, and I scored $112 worth (at cover price) for just $5 ... gotta love that!

This sort of jumped out at me, as I've been a *parakeet* owner much of my life (we currently have two: Shadow and Aqua - see pic at right), and the general thesis of Jenny Gardiner's Winging It: A Memoir of Caring for a Vengeful Parrot Who's Determined to Kill Me[2] both sounded like a "light read" and something that might give some perspective on Aqua, our always-hostile older bird. Of course, there's a significant difference between domestically-bred parakeets and a wild-captured bird like Gardiner's African Grey parrot, Graycie, but both seemed to share a mean streak (made less bloody at our house by the relative smallness of Aqua's beak muscles!).

Again, what I had *anticipated* jumping into Winging It[3] was a light bird-centered collection of whacky stories about the author's learning to deal with this ill-tempered parrot. What I didn't expect was this was more of a personal reminiscence of her whole life, in which Graycie, while certainly being an on-going *theme*, was only one element in a house-full of pets (pretty much all of which, not being as long-living as a parrot, *die* at one point or another), a work-from-home husband, and three kids who go from birth through college in the telling.

The parts of the book that I found very uncomfortable were the ones where her kids had various serious health issues, and she takes up whole chapters on the subject. Needless to say, were I have to gone into this expecting an *autobiography* these elements wouldn't have stuck out like they did, but having thought this to be a "bird book", they were unwelcome (to the author, too, I suppose) sidetracks from the stuff that got me to pick it up and leap over dozens of other books in the "to be read" pile.

I also had some serious *"verklempt"* moments reading this. As a father with kids fast approaching college age, much of the reflection that Gardiner does about how quickly this all flies by, leaving one only the memories (or, in her case, a bird still repeating phrases from the children's early years), hit me hard ... sort of counter-acting the "light reading" aspects I'd looked for in this.

I know it's unfair to judge a book on what I had thought or hoped it was going to be, rather than what the author meant it to be (although, in my defense, it would be hard to guess that the book was more a family memoir than a book about raising a parrot from the dust jacket!), but I do wish there was more like this passage in place of the various "parental challenges" parts of the book:

> *On a recent night she wasn't content with simply plinking. Instead she grew silent. And then I heard he say out loud, "Jenny!" ... The sound came from an unfamiliar quadrant of the room. We are all so used to her voice coming at us from the corner in which she resides that it's jarring to hear it from anywhere else. I got up to search and found her in her favorite spot, by the parrot cabinet. She was standing in front of the cabinet, trying to open it up. For fun, because I had the time to actually supervise her, I decided to open the cabinet and let her have at it. So for a good forty minutes she happily hung out, pulling down little wooden blocks and toys and an old sock stuffed with pieces of wood and all the while talking, talking, talking.*

I suppose I also would have liked some additional expository material about African Grey parrots in general. There are bits and pieces woven through the narrative (coming in as the author found out about them), but it would have been interesting to have had some block elements with data on how long-lived parrots can be, how they are remarkable mimics (and the things Graycie says are pretty amazing), and maybe even some pictures (the only one of the bird here is on the cover ... the other pic up there in this review is a snapshot of *my* parakeets!).

I want to say the book is *sad*, but I guess it's just a *sentimental* look back on the author's family over a quarter century, much of which is spent "battling" with a particularly cranky (and early on, accident-prone) bird. There's no big pay-off at the end ... no happy bird-human détente ... just a reaching of the present, and, like closing a photo album, a stop (and I just now took a look at the Amazon reviews, and I see a lot of other folks found this more sad that funny).

Winging It[4] is only a couple of years old, and the on-line guys still have it. You can, however, pick up a "like new" copy for a penny (plus shipping) from the used vendors, and if you scurry out to your local Dollar Tree you might be able to find a copy there (I just got this last Friday, and they had several copies on the shelf). This wasn't the book I was hoping to read, but if a family memoir's your thing, this might be of interest.

Notes:
1. http://btripp-books.livejournal.com/127259.html
2-4. http://amzn.to/1NMPLFM

Monday, April 2, 2012[1]

Fresh fruit for ...

This was another dollar store find. It's not necessarily the sort of thing that I'd go *looking for*, but it seemed interesting enough, and fit into the sort of book that I could feature over on *The Job Stalker*[2]. Frankly, Lynda Resnick's Rubies in the Orchard: How to Uncover the Hidden Gems in Your Business[3] isn't really about what's suggested by the sub-title (or by the cover splash saying it contains "Secrets to Marketing Just About Anything"), but is more like a "business autobiography", walking the reader through her career. Now, her career has been rather remarkable, but this is more her life story than a "marketing treatise", save for a couple of dozen adage-like statements set out in boxes through the book.

This starts off strangely ... sure, the author is well-connected, but what does it say about you when your book starts with *thirty-six* blurbs from famous people (from Michael Eisner to Gloria Steinem to Queen Noor of Jordan) over 7 pages before even getting to the title page? That is either a particularly crude expression of braggadocio, or an extreme manifestation of self-doubt needing to be salved by Big Names saying nice things about you.

The litany of companies that Ms. Resnick has led is quite impressive, including Teleflora, the Franklin Mint, Fiji Water, and POM pomegranate products (the book largely hangs on that business, with the fruit being the "rubies" in the title). In each of these (and her experiences in the advertising business before) she faced different challenges, and came away with assorted life/business lessons. I assume the intended take-away would be these lessons, although they pretty much need to be extracted by the reader from the author's narrative about her life.

There are also some "colorful" aspects to the history presented here ... including a brush with *political* notoriety when, while doing other work for the Vietnam anti-war movement, she allowed Daniel Ellsberg to use her agency's copier at odd hours ... which ended up his copying the classified documents that later appeared as *The Pentagon Papers*. One would think "once bitten twice shy", but she was later blindsided, in her role with POM, by the same types when PETA fixated on their business' use of animal testing (necessary for making the sorts of health claims for their pomegranate products they were).

> The PETA campaign was loaded with falsehoods, whether intentionally or simply as a result on the group's lackadaisical research. But what PETA's attack inspired was far worse. Animal rights extremists, some with their faces covered to avoid identification, began protesting outside out house.

> It was unnerving to drive each day past a group of screaming protesters, who called us murderers and worse.

The tone here is of somebody who is shocked that she, who has all these hard-left friends (many of whom show up in the front blurbs), would be subjected to this sort of treatment. It evidently left a mark, as they subsequently bent over backwards on almost every front to make Fiji water appear "earth friendly", from doing rainforest conservation in the Fiji islands, to various approaches to make it look like they were creating a smaller "carbon footprint" than their competitors.

There are, however, several bits of business wisdom in here beyond the "personal story" of Ms. Resnick. The tale of each of the companies she's run is interesting in its own right, and general statements can be pulled out of the telling. Here's one that stood out for me:

> Successful advertising makes us register the moment and take notice. If you can generate a reaction in consumers, you've already achieved a major goal; you've become part of their life in that small but very critical moment. If you use that moment to land a solid message somewhere on the brain – a message grounded in your brand identity and value – then you've truly achieved a great deal.

Again, these sorts of "teaching moments" don't stand outside the main flow of the memoir ... it would have been (in my opinion) more useful had she created a "take-aways" section at the end of each chapter (which generally go company-by-company through her career) for the "business lessons" learned. As noted previously, there are also a number of one-liners sprinkled through the book, which do present an encapsulated "point":

> You get a lot further in life by showing what you don't know and asking for help than you do pretending you know it all.
>
> What good are advertising, marketing, and design if the product is junk?
>
> If you want to make money on a product, you have to learn how to give it away.

That has a certain resonance for me, as I was involved in a friend's promotional project for Fiji water (I was a judge in a city-wide "scavenger hunt"), and I've been aware of many other events where they've been quite prominent in providing cases and cases of the water. Obviously, the things highlighted in the book are things that Resnick holds as true and applies in her business.

Rubies in the Orchard[4] is also strange in terms of illustration ... it has a few, but they are oddly selected ... one page is a mass of clippings from the author's involvement with Daniel Ellsberg, another is a "cheesecake" shot of her from a poster promoting her agency in 1970, thee are a couple of charts and diagrams, but, again these are few and far between, and seem to have been almost randomly added (from what one must assume to be a vast amount of possible illustrative material that they'd have on hand). In addition, there's a section of *color photos* which are pretty much all reproductions of ads, billboards, etc. from her various companies. One of these is to-the-point (illustrating the Jackie Kennedy necklace that they'd bought for $211,000.00 at auction, and ended up selling 26 million dollars worth of copies through the Franklin Mint), but even that could just as well have been handled by a B&W illustration in the book, and certainly nobody else would care if the pictures of the outdoor advertising was in glossy color!

This is an interesting book for what it is, but a bit of a disappointment in terms of what it seems to think it is. I guess the author hopes that the reader will be so wowed by the opinions of her blurb-writing friends that they'll not notice the weaknesses here. I suspect that Resnick had an idea about creating a popular business book, but ended up writing a memoir instead. There's certainly an *attempt* to keep the story line tied in with the pomegranate business, but that becomes tenuous when dealing with pretty much every other company in here. Again, it's generally an agreeable read, and it's a fascinating look at one person's life who has been extremely successful, but the focus shifts around and ends up as being not-quite-this and not-quite-that. A paperback edition appears to still be in print on this, but there are "like new" copies in the new/used channel going for as little as 1¢ (plus $3.99 shipping, of course). If this sounds like something you'd be interested in checking out (and I was looking for extra copies to give to a couple of friends), you might first want to check the Dollar Tree stores, as I got this there only a few weeks ago.

Notes:

1. http://btripp-books.livejournal.com/127583.html

2. http://jobstalker.info/

3-4. http://amzn.to/1XaWiDT

Saturday, April 7, 2012[1]

No clothes and a collar ...

Ever since they *explained* it to me at the dollar store, I'm less incredulous at finding really cool books *for a buck*, but it still feels pretty remarkable when I show up there after a re-stock (of the books that they buy in bulk from places like Walmart when the stock cycles out of *their* book sections) and find real gems. Needless to say, Neil deGrasse Tyson's The Pluto Files: The Rise and Fall of America's Favorite Planet[2] (a book still in print) was a pleasant surprise.

I'm sure that most folks are at least peripherally aware of the subject of this book ... the "demoting" of Pluto from planetary status to a "dwarf planet", one among many existing out beyond the orbit of Neptune (although, interestingly, Pluto, with an "off kilter" orbit, sometimes is *closer* to the Sun than Neptune, but the two have managed to sync their orbits so there's no chance of a collision). I suppose it's some sort of consolation that this class of "dwarf planets" have been re-named "Plutoids", so that Pluto, rather than being the least of the planets is now the first among an ever-growing list of minor bodies (some a bit larger than Pluto) out on the edges of the solar system.

Neil deGrasse Tyson has become the media face for planetary studies, Director of New York's Hayden Planetarium, and an astro-physicist with the American Museum of Natural History, he is constantly in demand as a guest on TV shows and as a lecturer at schools across the country. Much of The Pluto Files[3] feels like it's addressed to a younger audience (although the book is not specifically targeted to kids), with lots of cartoons, Disney connections, song lyrics, and even reprints of a bunch of grade school kid's letters, but it, ultimately, is a pretty straight-forward telling of the history of Pluto in the sciences and popular culture.

There certainly is a lesson to be learned here ... Pluto was only discovered in 1930, so had been a planet for just over 75 years when it was re-classified in 2006 ... yet the level of public outcry, especially in the USA, was pretty extreme. If only three or four generations were told that the solar system had nine planets (the last of which was Pluto), yet the "demoting" of it caused so much hostility, it becomes easy to understand how *religion* keeps it hooks in believers.

The book looks at how a planet out beyond Neptune had been forecast from the orbital patterns of the outer planets, and how it was discovered, named, and taught in the developing astronomical sciences. However, it was the onward march of science that brought better telescopes and tracking machines (computers replacing film exposures), and suddenly there were many "trans-Neptunian objects" running around in the Kuiper belt ... at least eight around Pluto's size.

One of the key "set pieces" for the book was a new display at the Hayden, where Pluto was nowhere to be found. The inner "rocky" planets, Mercury, Venus, Earth, and Mars, were there, and the outer "gas giants", Jupiter, Saturn, Uranus, and Neptune, were there, but Pluto and other Kuiper belt "ice balls" were not represented. Strangely, there were even members of the scientific community who were angrily fighting to keep Pluto in the planetary mix … but most of the opposition came from folks who just weren't comfortable "having their universe changed" on them. While I did not have a strong reaction to Pluto's reclassification, I can sort of understand where they were coming from, as I felt a certain level of "personal affront" when I discovered that the creature I grew up knowing as a Brontosaurus had somehow morphed into an Apatosaurus without anybody seeking out my opinion on the matter.

Anyway, The Pluto Files[4] is a light, yet very informative read. There were a good half dozen things that were *completely* new to me here, and I'm reasonably well-read on the solar system, as well as information on how the name happened, and some details of astronomical research which were quite illuminating. It had its lesser moments (the recurring bickering between Tyson and a "pro-planet" guy got tiresome fast, and *why* did they bother including three appendices for *song lyrics* and another two for stupid tongue-in-cheek legislation on the matter from New Mexico and California? … those could have just as usefully been URLs in footnotes instead of 6% of the book), but those are just minor gripes (and I suppose the book *had* to have a picture of the author posing with the Disney character Pluto).

Anybody interested in astronomy, planetary science, scientific "politics" and history, as well as sociological issues of how belief systems become ingrained in the masses, should find this book fascinating. As noted, it's still in print (although I'm guessing it's long since been sold through in the dollar store channel), so might even be available via brick & mortar book stores, but the on-line guys have it at a discount, and "good" copies of the hardcover can be had for under a buck (plus shipping, of course) from the new/used guys. I certainly enjoyed this, and am glad I stumbled over it like I did!

Notes:

1. http://btripp-books.livejournal.com/127802.html

2-4. http://amzn.to/1QF678I

Sunday, April 8, 2012[1]

Sometimes "no plan" is the best plan ...

Although I crank out a vast lot of reviews (just this weekend I hit my 500th review posted to LibraryThing.com!), I haven't been particularly active in *soliciting* books for review. As I've mentioned, from time-to-time I get queried or have titles sent to me from a couple of publishers, especially for books dealing with the job search, due to featuring my reviews on the subject over in The Job Stalker[2] blog on the Tribune's "Chicago Now" site ... but every once in a while I'll run into something that sounds interesting, but might not be the sort of book that I'd have picked up in my general reading, so I'll make a request for a review copy. This is one of those. I'd seen Harvey Mackay's enthusiastic piece[3] about this in his newsletter a while back and thought it might be the sort of thing that would be of interest to my *The Job Stalker* readers, so you're getting it kind of "in the middle"!

Coincidentally, "cutting out the middle man" is one of the themes in the business bio of Bruce Halle, Six Tires, No Plan: The Impossible Journey of the Most Inspirational Leader That (Almost) Nobody Knows[4] by Michael Rosenbaum, a look at the owner of the Discount Tire company.

Those familiar with my reading patterns[5] might find this an odd book to grab my interest, but the way Halle went from "rags to riches" was deeply engrained in the same "openness", "customer service", and "treating people right" lessons constantly pushed by Social Media gurus like Scott Stratten, Chris Brogan, and Gary Vaynerchuk ... *decades* before they (or "social media") came on the scene. It's a testament to how *basic values* can make business thrive if consistently applied, without undo interference from MBAs and accountants.

Bruce Halle was a child of the (1st) Great Depression, hailing from small-town New England. His family barely was able to eke out a living, and came to depend on friends and relatives for food and shelter. This, no doubt, etched into young Halle a feeling of responsibility for others close to him. A middling student, he looked like the type that would get out of highschool and move into a factory job, but was encouraged by one of his teachers to at least give college a shot. This he did, but didn't fare particularly well through his first two years, so the timing of the Korean War was quite fortuitous for him, giving him a break to "get his head right". While in the service Halle manage to get married and start a family, so when he returned to college, he had both school and work hanging over his head, and, again, with the help of particularly interested teachers, managed to graduate. He was very successful selling cars, and things looked promising, but he then shifted into insurance sales, which did not work so well, and eventually partnered in an automotive service business which ended up failing (due to licensing issues with suppliers), leaving him with the title's "six tires, no plan".

However, Halle's genius lay in interpersonal connections, and he set up his half-dozen tires in a storefront he personally rehabbed and began to offer great value, personal attention, and a pattern of free services. He found he could get "off-brand" tires for a great deal less than the "names" (although these were frequently identical), and came up with the name Discount Tire. Just as he'd had success in selling cars, his skills caused the business to thrive.

As the business grew, Halle did things differently than most other companies. Firstly, he'd find guys with a lot of enthusiasm, but few prospects, and give them a clear path to both a solid paycheck, and a decent shot at moving up to management positions. Secondly, to get into management in the company, you *had* to start out "in the bays" installing tires ... he wasn't hiring the business school grads in suits, unless they were willing to get their hands dirty for a few years. This created an atmosphere of camaraderie on all levels of the company, as (after a while) your boss, your boss' boss, and your boss' boss' boss had all been right were you were now, and *knew* what your daily concerns, challenges, and frustrations were. Halle (initially with partners) also personally owned *all* the stores, so there were no outside interests and agendas ... making it possible for him to pluck an assistant manager from one place and offer him a new location on the other side of the country if he felt that was the right man for the job, and using what he called "the reset button" if one of these shifts had to be reconsidered.

As in any corporate story, there were ups and downs, experiments that didn't work, and decisions that went awry, but generally speaking, Discount Tire exhibited impressive growth, spreading around the country. Halle, himself, had personal challenges, with his wife of nearly 40 years succumbing to cancer before her 60th birthday, and his near-fatal mountain bike accident four years later. He survived both of these, appointing a new CEO following his recovery from his accident, and soon afterward re-marrying, bringing in a "new partner" on several levels.

The specifics in here of how Halle dedicates so much to the employees of Discount Tire should be inspiring to anybody in business ... and the practices he brought to bear in building his business should be a lesson to anybody looking to improve their life. Six Tires, No Plan[6] is a delightful read, and brings a whole different perspective on some "business teachings" of more recent vintage. This is a brand-new release, so should be available via your local bookseller, but it's also at a 33% discount at the on-line big boys. Even if you're not interested in business, careers, or the like, this is an inspiring read about somebody who made a great success of himself by "doing it right" ... so you should check it out.

Notes:
1. http://btripp-books.livejournal.com/128060.html
2. http://jobstalker.info/
3. http://harveymackay.com/column/don%E2%80%99t-discount-the-bruce-halle-story/
4. http://amzn.to/1SgJdT1
5. http://www.librarything.com/catalog.php?view=btripp&sort=tagsREV
6. http://amzn.to/1SgJdT1

Friday, April 13, 2012[1]

An encouraging look towards the future ...

Well ... you've had to wait a while to read this review. I was halfway into writing it five weeks ago when my much-beloved netbook up and died ... in the middle of a sentence. It's taken this long for me to a) get hooked up with a replacement and b) get back out to do some reviews ... and, of course, the material (which was fresh in my mind back then) has faded slightly in my recall.

However, I really, really liked Peter Diamandis' Abundance: The Future Is Better Than You Think[2], which I anticipated I would when I requested a review copy from Free Press. As you can guess from the subtitle, this is *not* your typical "the sky is falling" futurist book ... instead, it's a look ahead at all the stuff that is trending positively, and what might bring a very bright future. It will be interesting to see how this plays out in the "if it bleeds, it leads" mainstream media, which *thrives* on sensationalizing bad news, as Abundance[3] is very much the antithesis of that.

Diamandis works with a "pyramid" symbolism here, somewhat related to Maslow's, with "simple physiological needs" at the base: water, food, and shelter; the next level featuring energy, education, information and communications, and finally, at the top, health and freedom. All the elements in the book relate to one or another of these concepts, and how they can be brought to the whole of humanity. This is a challenging book to summarize, because there is *so much* in it, hundreds of case studies and reports of research and programs moving things forward toward the "abundance" of the title. As with most books that I have been enthusiastic for while reading, this has dozens of little slips of paper sticking out of the top, with pages that I noted as having particularly important passages, or things that I wanted to take a further look at later. Here are a few of the points made in the introductory sections:

> Our current educational system ... is built around fact-based learning, but the Internet makes almost every fact desirable instantly available. This means we're training our children in skills they rarely need, while ignoring those they absolutely do. Teaching kids how to nourish their creativity and curiosity, while still providing a sound foundation in critical thinking, literacy and math, is the best way to prepare them for a future of increasingly rapid technological change.
>
> ...
>
> Many of today's dangers are probabilistic – the economy might nose-dive, there could be a terrorist

> attack – and the amygdala can't tell the difference. Worse, the system is also designed not to shut off until the potential danger has vanished completely, but probabilistic dangers never vanish completely. Add in an impossible-to-avoid media continuously scaring us in an attempt to capture market share, and you have a brain convinced it's living in a state of siege ...
>
> ...
>
> In contemporary society ... very few of us actually maintain 150 relationships. But we still have this primitive pattern imprinted on our brain, so we fill those open slots with whomever we have the most daily "contact" - even if that contact comes only from watching that person on television. ... The reason we care so much about what happens to the likes of Lady Gaga is ... because our brain doesn't realize there's a difference between rock stars we know about and relatives we know.

This initial section is fascinating as it shows how we're not set up to see the good stuff that's happening, on both an organic and societal basis. It then presents a litany of "dire forecasts" of the (mainly recent) past that were just plain *wrong* ... and then moves into a wide array of exciting new things, which rarely make it onto the media's radar, and so don't get into the general population's minds.

These are all over the board ... with new subjects every few pages. There is Dean Kamen's water purification project, that started out as a way to help dialysis patients, but was scaled up to the point where *"The current version can purify 1,000 liters of water a day using the same amount of energy it takes to run a hair dryer."*. There are the "highrise farm" projects (this one has recently been in the news), with promises that *"One hundred fifty vertical farms could feed everyone in New York City."*. There are the "generation IV" nuclear reactors, being developed by the likes of Nathan Myhrvold and others, which are "backyard nukes" that have *"no moving parts, can't melt down, and can run safely for fifty-plus years, literally without human intervention ... We could power the world for the next one thousand years just burning and disposing of the depleted uranium and spent fuel rods in today's stockpiles."*, and are projected to be priced "to undercut coal".

Abundance[4] then moves into health care, and the remarkable advances in systems to diagnose, treat, and prevent illness ... and the evolving capabilities to address health at the genetic level. Advances in robotics are also promising to replace (or at least augment) surgeons, and nurses. Technology developed for (and made very inexpensive by) the Xbox Kinect is at the forefront for sensors that will allow for nearly-automated assisted living at a fraction of the current costs.

There is so much in this book that I've not even touched on. The scope here is really breathtaking, and the vision world-changing. There is a web resource for on-going research at AbundanceHub.com[5], which promises to keep updating material in line with what's in the book (although, at the moment - only a couple of months past its publication - it's mainly *about* the book). The last 20% of Abundance[6] is a remarkable collection of references with data related to elements covered in the book (one of my favorites is the side-by-side comparison of a Cray2 supercomputer from 1985 and the iPad2 from 2011, where the latter had almost everything the former did, at a bit over a pound vs. nearly three tons, and at less than 1/50,000th the cost!), which in many cases brings home the really remarkable advancements discussed in the main text.

Abundance[7] is one of those books that I wish EVERYBODY would read ... it's really *that* important. If people took the information in this to heart, it could radically change the future of the planet and the race dramatically for the better. Heck, there were a dozen projects described here I wish I could *work with*, given my current job search! As it's brand new, your odds of finding it at your local brick-and-mortar book store are very good, and the online big boys are currently both featuring it at a deep discount. Do get a copy ... it's a game-changer ... highly, highly recommended!

Notes:

1. http://btripp-books.livejournal.com/128282.html

2-4. http://amzn.to/1Xnn1aX

5. http://abundancehub.com/

6-7. http://amzn.to/1Xnn1aX

Saturday, April 14, 2012[1]

Society fought the law, and the law won ...

This is a somewhat odd book ... it's both a technology and a societal book ... it both looks at current trends and tries to forecast from them ... and yet, when it's over, it's become something of a look at actual *law* rather than a philosophical projection of "laws", which comes as something of a surprise. There's a quote by a federal judge towards the end of the book, which sums up a lot of the thrust here: *"Beliefs lawyers hold about computers, and predictions they make about new technology, are highly likely to be false. This should make us hesitate to prescribe legal adaptations for cyberspace. The blind are not good trailblazers."* Essentially, The Laws of Disruption: Harnessing the New Forces that Govern Life and Business in the Digital Age[2] by Larry Downes is about how the on-rush of technological change is changing everything, and the way that society is dealing with this is both complicated and not ideal. As any "digital native" will tell you, one of the biggest challenges out there is that most elected officials are technologically illiterate at best, with many being nearly Luddites in their resistance to the digital reality ... and the down-side of this appears again and again in totally disastrous legislation and regulation.

Frankly, I "had issues" with some of the places Downes was going here, with my background in publishing (and hence in intellectual property, copyright, etc.); he argues against a lot of things which have long been elements of our creative culture and proposes solutions which are not particularly palatable. An illustrative quote regarding this "new approach" is presented from the comic book icon Stan Lee, who says: *"In the digital age authors should be prepared to give away everything of value and make their money on the crap."* ... although how much imprinted swag the average author is likely to sell (and back in the day I had Cafe Press stores full of un-ordered merchandise sitting there for each of our books), is a good question. Downes says: *"The Law of Disruption always challenges the existing rules and profit allocations of industries, but in the end it creates more value than it destroys."*, but it certainly leaves destruction in its wake ... one hates to think that one's particular niche in the world is simply the next "sealing wax" or sheet music, soon to be inconsequential.

The book is arranged in four areas: "Digital Life", "Private Life", "Public Life" and "Information Life", the latter three of which each contain three of what Downes describes as the nine laws of disruption ... Law One: Convergence, Law Two: Personal Information, Law Three: Human Rights; Law Four: Infrastructure, Law Five: Business, Law Six: Crime; Law Seven: Copyright, Law Eight: Patent, and Law Nine: Software.

Historical antecedents are sketched out here, going back to the Middle Ages and how the "killer app" of the time, the *stirrup* (which allowed Charlemagne to develop mounted troops, evolving into Knighthood, and the Feudal system), and similarly through each law. Other "laws" underlie much of the book, the familiar "Moore's Law" (every 12-18 months the processing power of computers doubles while the price holds constant), and slightly less familiar "Metcalfe's Law" (the usefulness of a network is the square of the number of users connected to it), which lead to the (coined for this book, I take it) "Law of Disruption" - *technology changes exponentially, but social, economic, and legal systems change incrementally*. Obviously, this expresses itself in the nine "laws" across three spheres as noted above.

One thing that stands out is the idea of "non-rivalrous goods", unlike a physical object, information can be used simultaneously by many people, so have significantly different economics associated with their creation and use. Downes introduces the concept here of "The Five Principles of Information Economics" ... 1 – Renewability: *"Information cannot be used up."*, 2 – Universality: *"Everyone can use the same information at the same time."*, 3 – Magnetism: *"Use makes the brand more, not less, valuable."*, 4 – Lack of Friction: *"The more easily information flows, the more quickly its value increases."*, and 5 – Vulnerability: *"Value can be destroyed through misuse."*. Within the Information Economy there are also, as in the regular economy, what Ronald Coase described as "transaction costs", these being to costs of Search, Information, Bargaining, Decision, Policing, and Enforcement ... each of which will vary by situation and the nature of the transaction, with as much as 45% of total economic activity being taken up by these.

The Laws of Disruption[3] has a somewhat uneven arc ... starting out almost "philosophical" but, by the time the author gets to Copyright and Patent, it's nearly "polemical" in favor of massive change in these areas, and somewhat enmired in the legalistic details of these subjects. Of course, along the way, there are many fascinating expositions of what one might not have suspected in the digital field (for instance the *vast* differences between the thrust of "privacy" regulations between the USA and Europe, and even, in specifics, between the various European countries ... what would be a "who cares?" issue in one is frequently the "third rail" in another, and vice-versa), but I suspect that most folks reading it will find it far more engaging in some parts than others.

If you have an interest in the digital world (and, of course, more and more, the "digital world" is defining the "real world"), you might find this a source of unique context for consideration of some of the thornier issues of that environment. It certainly provides lessons to legislators (not that legislators are likely to be paying any attention) of how *not* writing laws is far more helpful in most situations than grinding out some short-sighted piece of regulation ... and one would hope that *this* concept, if anything from The Laws of Disruption[4], would work its way into the public consciousness! Being that the book is only a couple of years old at this point, you're likely to be able to find it in your local bookstore, but the on-line big boys currently have it at a deep discount, and *new* copies can be had from the new/used guys for as little as a penny (plus the $3.99 shipping, of course). This was an interesting read, and I'm glad to have taken in the information, but it's not something that built up a lot of enthusiasm in me ... perhaps it's my wariness over messing with Intellectual Property rights, or my general distaste for anything having to do with the legal profession ... but this is one that I'd only recommend if you have a specific interest in the topic.

Notes:

1. http://btripp-books.livejournal.com/128546.html

2-4. http://amzn.to/1XnmIm5

Monday, April 16, 2012[1]

Perhaps in some other universe ...

As I've previously noted, I will, from time to time, get queried by any of a handful of publishes (on whose radar I apparently appear) as to my interest in getting a review copy of an upcoming book. This one came from such a communication by the good folks at Ten Speed Press, the home of the Bolles' "Parachute" job-search book empire. It's been a while since I'd read any books *specifically* about the job search, and was, frankly, feeling a bit guilty that I was letting down my readers over on The Job Stalker[2] by only bringing them "societally important" or "business trend" books in recent months, so I was quite open to adding this to my "to be read" pile.

Had my reading over the past half year or so trended more to job-search topics, I might have taken a bit more discerning look at Quentin J. Schultze's Résumé 101: A Student and Recent-Grad Guide to Crafting Resumes and Cover Letters that Land Jobs[3]. First of all, *The Job Stalker* is largely focused on those "in between jobs", meaning that I'd assume that most of my readers there would have at least a modicum of professional background to work with on their resumes. This, being quite directly targeted to those in or recently out of college, has an entirely different focus ... which, additionally, really didn't "speak to me" much, given how long *I've* been out of college! Secondly, there's the old joke about *opinions*, and how they're like certain bodily orifices in that "everybody's got one" ... this adage is perhaps *cubed* when it comes to the subject of resumes.

I can not begin the count the number of *wholly contradictory* opinions (often presented as Universal and Unquestionable Truths) I've encountered on the subject of resumes in articles, books, webinars, lectures, workshops, and consulting sessions ... the only consistent element is that each disagrees with the others, frequently *vehemently*. I, of course, have my own thoughts on the subject, and my resume reflects an amalgam of assorted approaches ... and it has garnered reactions from folks doing "resume reviews" from total snide dismissal as *"hopeless"* to *"looks good, I wouldn't make any significant changes"* (I would like to point out that I've gotten this latter reaction from a number of places *who make their money* writing resumes, so I feel that's a particularly strong endorsement).

I wanted to set up this context for my review of Résumé 101[4], which started off quite strong (in my opinion) and then "fell completely off the table" for me. Honestly, there is stuff in here that goes 180° from much of what I've recently *paid* to hear about resume development that it boggled my mind ... the one defense that I can come up with for Dr. Schultze here is that he is a college professor working with college students who, generally speaking, have "nothing to say" (professionally) on their resumes yet need to say *something*. He also makes recommendations for preparation of resumes that, were I to do these things in *my* job search, it would double my time devoted to getting out applications, and probably cut down the number of things that I *could* apply to by a factor of 10 or more!

Again, this started off well in the introductory chapters where the author is dealing with the *philosophy* of the resume, I felt that the first two of these were particularly good examples:

> {in comparison to a "sales piece"} … in a résumé you leave out as much as possible, because the employer is reading your résumé to see if there's any excuse for screening you <u>out</u>. Put in one or two sentences too many, or mention something that you think might <u>eventually</u> "sell" you but is misinterpreted on a piece of paper that an employer spends about eight seconds scanning (typically), and you're toast.
>
> …
>
> {A}n authentic résumé is far more than a list of jobs. A résumé is "you" in a particular written format. A résumé is "you" on paper or on a computer screen. A résumé is what you offer to an employer – somewhat like what a restaurant menu offers its customers. … Your résumé is like your personal, specialized menu of what you offer your customers – your potential employers.
>
> …
>
> The big three aspects of your life story – your skills, knowledge, and traits – are the keys to transforming your life experience into a standout, interview-generating, career-opening résumé. Why? Because every employee is a person, not just a worker. And because employers seek employees who have the right combinations of skill, knowledge, and personality.

This last quote is where the book veered off into unreality for me. In the *vast* majority of cases, no "employer" is going to see your resume. It's going to be scanned by a machine, and if that machine finds the right key words/phrases that it's programmed to look for, it might get routed to an *intern* who's been given another set of filters to look for as they take those 8 seconds or so that they'll spend looking at your resume … as noted above, the goal of the resume reading process is to *ELIMINATE* as many would-be candidates as possible … and unless you're *very* lucky and your resume ends up in the dozen or so that get handed to the actual Hiring Manager, all that touchy-feely stuff about your "potential" as an employee is just "noise", and probably rejection-generating verbiage at that.

In discussions I've had with various recruiters, most are looking for a very specific profile, which I envision as being an exact multi-sided polygonal shape ... if you're a circle, a square, a triangle, you're shot down at the first view, after that it's a matter of counting your sides and measuring your angles. If you pass *that* inspection, you might get called in to see if they can fit you into the exact polygonal hole they're trying to fill. Most of this book *ignores* this reality, and attempts to make the best of slim achievements, but in reality, unless an employer is looking for somebody who can run and talk at the same time they're *not* going to care if you played soccer and were on the debate team!

My reactions aside, the book is very well structured, taking the new job seeker from the very basics through a lot of details on crafting one's resume, getting references lined up, developing cover letters, etc., with examples, tips, and recommendations (and stories from the author's own experiences, which I found charming), all through the book. The *most useful* part of this, however (and I'm extrapolating to what I'd guess college kids would find most handy), is the last quarter of the book where Schultze presents check lists, worksheets, editorial guides, word lists, and lots of examples of resumes and cover letters.

Obviously, I "had issues" with Résumé 101[5] ... but I'm a long way from college and have been fighting the job search out in the trenches of the real world for *years*, so I'm probably taking a more reactive view than most would on this. I don't doubt that this would be a reasonably handy guide for a college kid to get out their first resumes and start building up the scar tissue they'll need out there, but from where I sit, its view of what "lands jobs" is pretty Pollyanaish. It's brand new, so should be available at your local book vendor, and, of course, the on-line big boys have it at a discount from its quite reasonable cover price. This drove me nuts reading it, but if you're a college student looking to get started on the long, brutal, soul-crushing job search, it might very well be a good first toe in the minefield.

Notes:

1. http://btripp-books.livejournal.com/128861.html

2. http://jobstalker.info/

3-5. http://amzn.to/1SgHLjo

Wednesday, April 18, 2012[1]

Some splainin' about human origins ...

This was another of those delightful dollar store finds ... always a treat to discover a nice hardcover, in perfect condition, *for a buck*! The randomness of the dollar store books is one of the most attractive (well, aside from the $1 price, of course) parts of the find, as these will, obviously, not be things that I went out looking for, but often are quite interesting, and expand my reading outside of its habitual ruts.

Not, of course, that paleoanthropology is a particular *stretch* for me, my having read many books on the subject ... it's just one that I don't typically go out *looking* for. So, Donald Johanson & Kate Wong's (he's the paleoanthropologist, she's the co-author who happens to be the Editorial Director of ScientificAmerican.com) Lucy's Legacy: The Quest for Human Origins[2] was a particular treat to discover some weeks back at one of my periodic trips to the dollar store.

As I was coming to this "by accident", I didn't have much preconceived expectations of the book, and found that it was a very interesting interweaving of Johanson's personal reminisces and current research into the early predecessors of *Homo sapiens*. Johanson, of course, is a major player in the unfolding of the story of that research, having been the discoverer of "Lucy", the famed fossil remains of a young *Australopithecus afarensis* female in the Hadar area of Ethiopia's Afar region back in 1974.

Lucy's Legacy[3] follows his career, from the early '70s up through when the book was published in 2009, with much of the "action" happening in Ethiopia, from the later days of Haile Selassie's reign, and resuming in the 1990's. One is tempted to assume that the writing division here is Johanson providing the "boots on the ground" material, and Wong filling in the scientific background, as the narrative swings in and out of "what was happening" and into "what it means".

One certainly gets an interesting look into the day-to-day activities of a working camp in a fossil-rich area, with all the inter-disciplinary work that's involved on dating finds, etc. There is also quite a bit of drama involved with the changing political landscape ... as the Marxist military regime that ousted and succeeded Selassie was varying in how it related to "outsiders", and for the better part of a decade forbidding *any* paleoanthropological research in the country. Later expeditions were also saddled with military escorts, but these were more in a "protective" role (despite having the predictably dampening role to open investigation) with active rebel activity in the regions Johanson and associates were working, as well as having significant *tribal* issues to deal with (at various times they needed to maintain close, or at least *cordial* relations with two tribes that were on either side of *generations* of hostilities).

The main thrust of the book is the efforts to figure out the "family tree" leading from our *Australopithecine* predecessors (in various manifestations, the relation of which are still very much under debate) on up the assorted branches of *Homo*, leading to our current *sapiens* "humanity". One fascinating point is presented late in the book:

> Geneticists believe that sometime around 140,000 years ago, the founding populations of modern humans underwent a catastrophic event that slashed their numbers from around 12,800 breeding individuals to a mere 600. Those 600 people gave rise to the modern humans that would one day leave Africa and colonize the rest of the world.

I'd read about "population bottlenecks" before (like the Toba event about 70,000 years ago), but this is the lowest number I'd seen for "surviving population"! Needless to say, with these sorts of realities in the mix, it's no wonder it is sometimes difficult to "connect the dots" between numerous sets of fossils.

I'm not going to even *try* to summarize the over-all paleoanthropological info from the book here … just suffice it to say, that this is not a "dry" presentation of the theory of Human Origins, but a tapestry of stories from the field, reminiscences from academia, and solid background information that only occasionally directly relates to the narrative (not a bad thing, it fills in the gaps that Johanson didn't specifically work on).

If you have any interest in this field, I'm pretty sure you will find Lucy's Legacy[4] quite an engaging read. It is still available, in a new paperback edition, although the hardcover can be had (at Dollar Tree, if you're lucky) in "very good" condition via the new/used on-line vendors for under a buck (but with $3.99 shipping, of course). I suspect that even more "general readers" might appreciate the "story" here, and I'd certainly recommend it as both informative and a good read.

Notes:

1. http://btripp-books.livejournal.com/129263.html
2-4. http://amzn.to/1XnkI7Q

Saturday, April 21, 2012[1]

"Put the glasses on! Put 'em on!"

I don't know why these books never crossed my radar back when they were coming out ... they sold tons of copies, and I guess got lots of ink, but I was oblivious to them until much later. In fact, I tried to get an interview with Lois Weisberg, the Chicago Commissioner of Cultural Affairs, some years back (related to a job opening I'd seen), having seen her mentioned in a magazine article, and I got a note from "her people" saying that ever since appearing in *The Tipping Point*, she was so swamped with requests that she just couldn't do any ... and I had no clue! So, although I came late to the books of Malcolm Gladwell, I've been catching up ... in this case, with Blink: The Power of Thinking Without Thinking[2].

This book is a collection of stories from a wide array of contexts and settings, all dealing with the way our perception works. From the instant "read" we might have on something (in the first piece here, a forgery of a statue), that can be more accurate than expert study, to how our unconscious can mis-read the "truth" in a situation, and to how this can be managed and even trained.

There is an awful lot of individual bits and pieces of research, background, and narrative here, so it's not something where I can sketch out the "story arc", instead, I've pulled out a few quotes that I think give a taste of what's in here.

First is a thing that deals with looking at which doctors get sued, and which don't. Contrary to what one would expect, this has very little to do with their competence or track record. Even odder, the research leading into this was based on studying couples with an eye to which were going to break up or not.

> {The researcher} listened to {the study's} tapes, zeroing in on the conversations that had been recorded between just surgeons and their patients. For each surgeon, she picked two patient conversations. Then, from each conversation, she selected two ten-second clips of the doctor talking, so her slice was a total of forty seconds. Finally, she "content-filtered" the slices, which means she removed the high-frequency sounds from speech that enable us to recognize individual words. What's left after content-filtering is a kind of garble that preserves intonation, pitch, and rhythm but erases content. Using that slice – and that slice alone – {she} did a Gottman-style analysis. She had judges

> rate the slices of garble for such qualities as warmth, hostility, dominance, and anxiousness, and she found that by only using those ratings, she could predict which surgeons got sued and which didn't.

So, from less than a minute of meaningless speech patterns, signals came through which allowed accurate predictions of which surgeons were sued ... how? It turns out that the *attitude* of the doctors, which came through all this reduction, was the key element ... those that were treating patients like *a case* and not like *a person* were the ones that ended up being sued if things went wrong.

There were other experiments that showed that subtle elements could change results dramatically ... asked to think of professors or soccer hooligans before taking a test, the former (randomly selected) group of subjects got 55.6% right while the latter got only 42.6% correct ... a *huge* difference just from thinking of a particular "type" before the test! More dramatically, a study of Black students showed that the group asked to fill out a questionnaire before the test that had a place to identify their race, scored only *half* as well as a similar group whose pre-test form did not have that question.

> The results from these experiments are, obviously, quite disturbing. They suggest that what we think of as free will is largely an illusion: much of the time, we are simply operating on automatic pilot, and the way we think and act – and <u>how well</u> we think and act on the spur of the moment – are a lot more susceptible to outside influences than we realize.

What was striking here was that the pattern of influence was evident in a wide swath of studies, quizzes full of items about senior citizens had their college student subjects moving far more slowly and hesitantly on their way out of the testing center than peers who didn't have those cues ... people "primed" with word scrambles that either had "rude" or "polite" entries in them acted out the programming in a subsequent "accidental" encounter, with 82% of the "polite" subject *never* interrupting in an structured inconvenient situation. It makes you wonder how close movies like *They Live*[3] are about the messages being fed to us!

On the flip side "they" don't necessarily have a firm grasp on all this ... there's a section dealing with "sensation transference" where product *packaging* totally overwhelms things that one would expect to be top difference-makers, like taste or brand name ... or situations where our "gut reaction" has *five times* the accuracy than when we're asked to *analyze* why we prefer A to B. One of the issues raised here is that people are rather change averse, and "different" is often taken for "bad":

> The problem with market research is that often it is simply too blunt an instrument to pick up this distinction between the bad and the merely different.

> ... {in initial testing of <u>All in the Family</u> and <u>The Mary Tyler Moore Show</u>} Viewers said they hated them. But, as quickly became clear when these sitcoms became two of the most successful programs in television history, viewers didn't actually hate them. They were just shocked by them. And market researchers at CBS utterly failed to distinguish between these two very different emotions.

The challenge is to find out what is just so new that it shocks, but then is embraced, and what is actually *bad* and will never find a wide audience. There's also a test you can try at home ... do a blind "sip" test between Coke and Pepsi, and many (but by no means all) can pick which is which, but throw in a *third* cup, and a second serving of one of these, the average success rate drops to 1/3rd – right at chance – and Gladwell reports that when he tried this on a group of his friends, they *all* failed to make the correct identifications!

Finally, as though to validate the "happy smiley", "fake it till you make it" people, it appears that just trying to *look* a particular way effects the whole body/mind complex ... suggesting that those (irritating) people who go through the day smiling like they're having a great time, are actually ending up *happier* than those of us with a firmer grip on reality ...

> {Researchers} gathered a group of volunteers and hooked them up to monitors measuring their heart rate and body temperature – the physiological signals of such emotions as anger, sadness, and fear. Half of the volunteers were told to try to remember and relive a particularly stressful experience. The other half were simply shown how to create, on their faces, the expressions that corresponded to stressful emotions, such as anger, sadness, and fear. The second group, the people who were acting, showed the same physiological responses, the same heightened heart rate and body temperature as the first group.

Again, this is just a small sampling of what's covered in <u>Blink</u>[4] ... it's an amazing collection of things that will shake how you see the world, and maybe even change the way you go about things (I know that the next time I need to take a test, I'm going to start making a list of "genius things" before I go in!).

Despite being out for seven years, <u>Blink</u>[5] is still in print, available in both hardcover and paperback, so it should be available in the brick-and-mortar stores, but the on-line big boys have it at about 1/3rd off of cover, and the new/used vendors have "very good" copies of the hardcover for as little as a penny (plus shipping). This is one that is such a "shock to the system" that I really wish everybody would read it ... it's in the intersection of a good read, an interesting study of human psychology, and a satori-like unfolding of an unsuspected reality. If enough folks read this, maybe we won't need George Nada's sunglasses to see the "obey" and "consume" signs[6]!

Notes:

1. http://btripp-books.livejournal.com/129404.html
2. http://amzn.to/1SgGKYv
3. http://www.imdb.com/title/tt0096256/
4-5. http://amzn.to/1SgGKYv
6. http://goo.gl/GOYB5A

Sunday, April 22, 2012[1]

"Who controls the present ..."

I heard Erik Qualman do a presentation on Socialnomics: How Social Media Transforms the Way We Live and Do Business[2] at the December 2009 meeting of the Social Media Club of Chicago (along with Shel Israel talking about his Twitterville[3]), just a couple of months after it came out. I suppose it's a testimony to the book's popularity (and my on-going poverty) that I was unable to get connected with a "reasonably priced" used copy until just this January ... notably, getting to it *after* I'd read his new book Digital Leader[4].

While this is a very good book for its time (it's amazing how a book that's not quite 3 years old at this point can feel "dated" already), but it suffers from the author's evident excitement over Barack Obama (whose campaign, admittedly, *did* make significant use of Social Media tools) ... were the Obama election just *one* case study among many (it gets its own chapter, and the Obamas have more mentions than *anything else* in the index), it would be less of a problem here, but, as it is, this imparts to Socialnomics[5] something of the same "irrelevant" feel that most political books have within a year or two of their publication.

The book starts off with laying some groundwork about word-of-mouth information distribution, and how communication systems are changing ...

> We have shifted from a word where the information and news was held by a few and distributed to millions, to a world where the information is held by millions and distributed to a few (niche markets). ... While {the} traditional mediums were still trying to grasp how to handle the upshot of blogs and user-generated content, social media suddenly came along, causing yet another significant upheaval in the status quo.

Once this basis has been established he moves into "behavior", outlining two types, "preventative" and "braggadocian". The former of these can be brought down to the phrase *"Live your life as if your mother is watching."* ... and is, basically, the herald of the recent dystopian "self-edit *or else*" vibe that one needs to *conform to social norms and expectations* or be indelibly branded a pariah (since, as he also notes: *"What happens in Vegas stays on You Tube"*). The latter is the trend to documenting one's existence via Social Media tools, and how various "generations" interact with these. In both of these chapters there is a lot of "what's good for society" at the expense of the individual, side-by-side with case studies from various businesses. This segues into the political chapter:

> In 2008 ... several companies gave away freebies on Election Day. Generally most marketers steer clear of anything political, but in this case, the brand marketers wanted to be a part of a community, and the community in this instance, thanks to social media, was the American community. ...This is the sense of community that human beings long for, and it is something that isn't lost with social media. In fact, it is part of the reason for social media's meteoric ascendancy in our lives. Face-to-face interaction still can't be beat, but social media does help you feel part of a community. It is even able to help keep an intimate community feel on a national or global level.

This at least had an interesting bit about how search engine traffic can serve as a predictive measure of future events, from emerging pop stars to patterns of flu outbreaks (before they're recognized as outbreaks). There is a rather dystopian spin here too, talking of ways the government could become more involved in our daily lives. The next sections are about how people prefer to get recommendations from peers rather than marketing messages from companies.

> The 30-second commercial is being replaced by the 30-second review, tweet, post, status update, and so on. Not all great viral marketing ideas need to originate in the marketing department – businesses need to be comfortable with consumers taking ownership of their brands. The marketers' job has changed from creating and pushing messages to one that requires listening, engaging, and reacting to potential and current customer needs. And it's not just marketing that changes; businesses models need to shift. Simply digitizing old business models doesn't work; businesses need to fully transform to properly address the impact and demands of social media.

Again, most of the illustrative stories here are specifics of how various companies did or did not succeed in using Social Media and associated web technologies ... the details are interesting in context, but really not suitable for extracting as examples here ... ultimately, the over-all tone of Socialnomics[6] is very much that of an introductory volume for business people who may not have *any* experience with Social Media, but are quite conversant with advertising and marketing challenges.

As much as the assorted business "snapshots" here provided fascinating illustrations of how Social Media affected the success or failure of numerous companies, I was disturbed by the "meta" implications of some of the over-riding *themes*. Qualman keeps returning to the at least the *suggestion* of personal sublimation to the Society ... he refers to "The Death of Social Schizophrenia" positing that having a private self and a public self is a symptom of a *disease* and that one needs to make one's personality and activities "transparent" and congruent, "for the good of society" ... with the obvious implication that if one's personal orientation, attitudes, behaviors, and beliefs are *not* "approved", one will be shunned by the less-individualistic masses (or at least their HR department keepers).

Admittedly, I suspect that most people reading this book wouldn't even notice the "dystopian meta themes" running through Socialnomics[7], but they were ongoing "nails on a chalkboard" to my Libertarian sensibilities. Unlike many of the Social Media books I've read, this is very much oriented as a business "primer", so the feeling was less that of enthusiasm for the new technologies of communication and interaction, and more looking at how these could be brought to bear on beating the competition. As noted, it's been very popular, and is currently widely available in a paperback edition. This certainly has worthwhile material in it, and I'm sure that I'm an extreme "outlier" in my visceral reactions to the societal spin I found implied in it, but I don't think this would be near the top of my recommended Social Media reading list for general audiences, although it might be an ideal intro book for MBAs and fans of big government.

Notes:

1. http://btripp-books.livejournal.com/129703.html
2. http://amzn.to/1SgFCEu
3. http://btripp-books.livejournal.com/95428.html
4. http://btripp-books.livejournal.com/125867.html
5-7. http://amzn.to/1SgFCEu

Monday, April 23, 2012[1]

Holey moley!

I suppose that I *really should* read the descriptions of the books being offered in the LibraryThing.com "Early Reviewers" program more *carefully*, but in my defense, the only indication that this was a *kids' book* was an offhand thing saying "children and adults alike", so I was surprised to find that it was a book targeted for the 9-12 age range. Ooops. I suppose that I *have* looked at other science-books-for-kids previously, so the "Almighty Algorithm" might have taken that into consideration when matching me with this, but frankly, I think there were *better* matches among the several I'd requested in the February batch.

Fortunately, I happen to have a 12-year-old handy, and cajoled her into reading the book, and providing me with *her* review of Carolyn Cinami DeCristofano's A Black Hole Is Not a Hole[2], which follows below. I must admit, however, that I found the book delightful, even from a perspective of having read numerous books which have dealt with the subject. At no point was the science *trivialized*, although being brought down into language and "idea units" targeted for a Junior High audience. One of the great strengths of the book is its gorgeous and quite informative illustrations, helping to envision some of these difficult concepts much better than most of the "general reader" books on black holes have done.

Before I end up "stealing her thunder", let me plug in here the review that my daughter Claire wrote about this, as it's, obviously, more germane to the book than *my* opinions:

> A Black Hole is NOT a Hole
> By Carolyn Cinami DeCristofano
> Reviewed by Claire Tripp
>
> "A Black Hole is NOT a Hole" is all about explaining the qualities of a black hole. Although it may sound like you are about to read a text book, that is not true! The author was very uplifting and explanatory on the topic. She kept the reader informed and entertained by being very creative in her writing. She also balanced the book out with the history of science and how people approached the topic of outer space, stars, gravity, planets, etc.
>
> One of the main qualities that surprised me was that not for one minute was I bored or, well, reading a science textbook! I do not really enjoy science, but this book was very enjoyable and fun! The way she approached the topic was clear and kid-friendly, she also included connections to our day-

> to-day lives as kids! The illustrator, Michael Carroll, also did an amazing job at creating clear and beautiful pictures. They were very accurate to the book.
>
> The author also had little "chat bubbles" that had little sayings such as "Then what is it?" in reference to the title. This was another example of her creativity in her writing. Overall, the book was very fun and exciting while it was still educational and informed me on the topic.

While I wish she was more interested in Science, I think it's telling that she was as enthusiastic about A Black Hole Is Not a Hole[3], and I was pleased and surprised that she got her review written up and into my hands with only the barest minimum of reminding (she had put it off until her History Fair project was presented at the Regionals).

Anyway, as I said, this is a remarkably informative and comprehensive look at the current theories involving black holes. Obviously, the author was challenged by the nature of her target audience to step things back to very basic levels, and so the book starts with looking at the Solar system, and the concepts of really big numbers, then comes up with a parallel of a black hole and a whirlpool, and explains that it's "kind of" like that, but not exactly … which then sets up a discussion about *gravity* (complete with a sketch of an apple bouncing off of Newton's head), with the basic concepts spun out along with some tables of how much various things of a particular size would weigh (a "snowball-sized" black hole would weigh more than 10 earths!). This leads to the *very* difficult concept of the "event horizon", which then proceeds into a look at the life cycle of stars, and how stars of various sizes end up doing quite different things when they die.

At this point the book shifts a bit back to some basic astrophysics, looking at how light behaves in assorted contexts (and why it can't get out of a black hole, thus making it "black"), how we can *find* black holes out in the universe, and lots of pictures of galaxies, etc. in which they've determined there are black holes. Finally, they get to the "thought experiment" part with the obvious question about "what happens to stuff falling in?" and getting into Relativity and non-Newtonian space. I had sort of expected them to get into the "hole in space/time" diagram earlier, but it comes in at this point as a final look at "a hole". The book concludes with a very interesting timeline (from Newton on), an illustrated glossary, and the author presenting (in a very conversational mode) her sources for the information in the book, along with a more standard list of resources.

Considering the difficulty and complexity of the subject, and the age of its audience, A Black Hole Is Not a Hole[4] does an *amazing* job of making this understandable, while not (in my daughter's words) making it like reading a textbook. While I might not have learned anything *new* per se here, I certainly picked up good "images" of how to frame the concepts (like the snowball-sized chart noted above), and I can appreciate the efforts of the illustrator to make these things visible to us terrestrial-bound life forms!

This has only been out a couple of months, so it should be available in the bigger book stores, but (of course) the on-line guys have it, with a discount that would make it cheaper (assuming you add it to other stuff to get free shipping) at this point than getting it from the new/used vendors with their shipping add-on. Again, this is a really remarkable book, and a *tour de force* in making something very challenging both accessible and entertaining. It's a volume every kid (especially those *with* an interest in science) should get a hold of.

Notes:

1. http://btripp-books.livejournal.com/129798.html
2-4. http://amzn.to/1GRRsP4

Wednesday, April 25, 2012[1]

Paraphrasing from the Persian ...

This is a perfect example of why I love picking up those Dover Thrift Editions to fill in holes in my education ... now, *of course* I knew *of* The Rubáyát of Omar Khayyám[2], and certainly was familiar with the more famous excerpts from it, but I'm pretty sure I'd never *read* it, and I certainly didn't know *about* it, at least to the extent I do after reading the introductory materials here.

While the *source* material of the book originates with an 11th century Persian "mathematician, astronomer, and philosopher" (who was *not* known as a poet during his life, but it seems that the core writings of this were in his papers, and over the centuries more and more material was "attributed" to him). What is an eye opener in Edward FitzGerald's The Rubáyát of Omar Khayyám: First and Fifth Editions[3] is that its translator was actually more of an *interpreter* of the material, and that what we know as "The Rubáyát" (which pretty much is Arabic for "quatrains") is really FitzGerald's "take" on the original rather than an attempt to make a literal translation, making the "classic" work an expression of 19th century English composition instead of an work of Sufi poetry the likes of Rumi.

It at first seemed odd that this slim volume would contain *two* editions of FitzGerald's work, the first edition (1859) and the fifth edition (1889), but by including both it allows one to take a look at what was happening here. First of all, when this initially came out, it was an anonymous translation, purporting to be Omar Khayyám's writings ... in fact, FitzGerald's hand in the "translation" did not come to light until 1875, prior to the fourth edition in 1879. FitzGerald died in 1883, but he had "marked up" a copy of the fourth edition, and this served as the basis of the posthumous fifth edition.

There are *significant* differences between the first and the fifth editions, with the former having only 75 quatrains, and the latter 101. Of these only 12 were the same (with only punctuation and capitalization changes) between editions, and 3 of the first's are missing (or sufficiently "spread out" over other quatrains as to be unidentifiable), #37, #38, and #45, with 28 "new" quatrains in the fifth edition (two of the fifth's, #83 and #87 use half of the first's #60, thus bringing the total up to 101). Most of the new material appears between #38 and #53 in the fifth (which come in a gap between the first's #36 and #39), with most of the fifth's 60's new (but for #63 which is a version of the first's #26).

Many of the quatrains are only slightly changed between the versions, with (as noted) 12 being basically unchanged, and another 20 having only 1 line out of 4 differing, and only 10 exhibiting changes to all four lines. However, one would expect that if this were a *translation*, especially by the same person, there would be a lot more consistency. It seems that FitzGerald was more interested in having the poems "live" than having them express exactly what the Persian sources *said*, and so there was a lot of trying to create a poetic expression that was over-riding any literalism.

To take an example, here's a quatrain that probably provides the most famous line from The Rubáyát[4] ... *"A Jug of Wine, a Loaf of Bread – and Thou"* ... in both its versions:

> *I – 11*
> *Here with a Loaf of Bread beneath the Bough,*
> *A Flask of Wine, a Book of Verse – and Thou*
> *   Beside me singing in the Wilderness –*
> *And Wilderness is Paradise enow.*
>
> *V – 12*
> *A Book of Verses underneath the Bough,*
> *A Jug of Wine, a Loaf of Bread – and Thou*
> *   Beside me singing in the Wilderness –*
> *Oh, Wilderness were Paradise enow!*

Obviously, with a book of this vintage and renown there are many free versions to be found (just do a Google book search), but I found the juxtaposition of these two editions here quite charming, as they do provide a window onto the reality of this "paraphrasing" by an English writer of the medieval original. Of course, one of the other "charming" things about the Dover Thrift books is that they're so *inexpensive*, this has a cover price of a mere $2.00 ... which is *very* handy when one's on-line order is not quite at $25 to get free shipping and you're not wanting to throw in another "regular" book! Aside from those concerns, the poetry itself is quite enticing, as FitzGerald really did a very nice job of making the quatrains "live" in English. It's something you should keep in mind for that next order.

Notes:

1. http://btripp-books.livejournal.com/130146.html

2-4. http://amzn.to/1M6ZnPZ

Friday, April 27, 2012[1]

We all need control.

Another Dover Thrift Edition, another "hole" in my education plugged. Here's something you may not know … the term "robot" is derived from a word in a Czech dialect meaning "forced labor" or "drudgery", and was coined by a Czech writer. Now, I had some idea about the broad strokes of this, but hadn't encountered the writer, nor the book in which the term had been introduced previously, so I was thrilled to pick up Karel Čapek's R.U.R. (Rossum's Universal Robots)[2].

As widespread and persistent as the idea of robots have been in popular culture (let alone their less-glamorous, but more productive, non-anthropomorphic cousins on factory production lines), it is fascinating to take a look at where the word originated. The idea of the automaton or other artificial being had, of course (be it Dr. Frankenstein's re-animated corpse, or the *Golem* of Jewish folklore, etc.) preceded this depiction, but I believe that Čapek introduced the idea of industrially manufactured beings. Interestingly, Prague was the scene for the most famous *Golem* narrative, and it was in Prague that Čapek published, in 1920, R.U.R.[3] I should say published *and staged*, as this is a *play* (something that had not filtered into my mental file on the work, and something that I certainly did not expect).

The play features the daughter of some government head, who is on a trip visiting the Rossum factory, where she meets with the factory director, and eventually with various of the department heads there. What is quite interesting is that the process for making the robots is *organic* and that they are artificial *biological* creatures, rather than mechanical devices. This has a key element to play in the course of the plot (and, by the way, if you're "allergic to spoilers", you may want to quit reading as I'm going to discussing all the major points here).

Anyway, this young woman arrives and meets with the factory's director, who gives her the background on the development of the robots … a scientist named Rossum (derived from "reason") had come up with "artificial living matter" that he could coax to differentiate into various tissues and forms … but it wasn't until his son, an engineer, got involved that they were able to make artificial humans. Once developed, factories could be set up to make the new workers in whatever quantities were necessary.

As one would expect, this quickly turns into a dystopian vision, with the robots causing unemployment, and then being armed and turned into fighting forces that eventually turn of their creators and seek to destroy the humans. This happens between acts one and two in the play. In the latter part of the book (ten years after the first act) the remaining humans are trying to figure a way to survive. At one point the main character, Helena, *burns* the files that end up containing the only formulas for making the materials from which the robots are made.

This, of course, becomes inconvenient as nobody else has been able to independently figure out what was involved in producing this, and without it there will be no new robots, and the robots have been doing a fairly efficient job of eliminating the humans. The robots are shocked to find that the few remaining humans in the factory can't discover how to recreate the formula, and are facing their own extinction (they, like the Replicants in *Blade Runner* only last a certain amount of time, about 20 years). However, the stress of this situation appears to be enough to *evolve* the robots, and two of them start exhibiting *emotional* behavior (in trying to protect each other), and eventually become a new "Adam and Eve" at the very end of the play.

This is a very short work, under 60 pages, so there's not a lot of room for "fleshing out" a lot of the finer details or filling in too much of the wider "historical" story arc. Most of the *action* (in terms of wars and massacres, etc.) happens off stage and in vague reports. The actual dialog is presented within a few rooms in the factory complex with a 10 year span happening between. Because it *is* a play, most of the story line is carried forward by discussions and interactions between the main characters, so there isn't much opportunity to detail the happenings beyond those walls.

Needless to say, R.U.R. (Rossum's Universal Robots)[4] is a fairly quick read, but an entertaining one that does closely hold one's interest. There were certainly parts of this where I would have *liked* to have had more information on what was happening in the wider world, but, within the context of the play, one is limited to the sources the characters have available to them, so there's not much temptation to get cranky about not having long descriptive passages inserted into the dialog.

As you would expect for a book from the 1920's, it can be found free on the web[5], however, the Dover Thrift Edition of R.U.R.[6] has a mere $2.50 cover price, so is one of those things you should keep in mind when ordering from the on-line big boys where free shipping kicks in at twenty-five bucks, and one often finds your order is just a buck or two shy of that. I enjoyed reading this, and feel like I've added a "key piece" to some part of the puzzle of recent culture in having read it!

Notes:

1. http://btripp-books.livejournal.com/130435.html
2-4. http://amzn.to/1GROdXU
5. http://ebooks.adelaide.edu.au/c/capek/karel/rur/
6. http://amzn.to/1GROdXU

Saturday, April 28, 2012[1]

the sky tumbling down

As I have no doubt mentioned previously, until my recent job search, I had never been given to reading "business books". Over the past several years, however, I have read quite a number (due in large part to my writing *The Job Stalker* blog over on Chicago Now), so one would think that I would be past "old biases" towards the genre ... still, I had approached Groundswell: Winning in a World Transformed by Social Technologies[2], by Charlene Li and Josh Bernoff, a bit hesitantly as it was from Forrester Research, and published through *Harvard Business Press* ... I mean, how *boring* a read was I setting myself up for? Well, I'm happy to report that it's quite an engaging book, and while it has its *moments* of going into more details than I felt I needed to know, it never drags itself into an "MBAs Only!" zone.

I suppose to start off, you're wondering, *"Uh, what's this groundswell thing, anyway?"* ... I had the same question, although it didn't start bugging me until I was several chapters into the book. Here's their definition:

> *A social trend in which people use technologies to get the things they need from each other, rather than from traditional institutions like corporations.*

Yes, I think that's pretty vague, but I guess they were going for a broadly inclusive frame to include a varied range of particulars. On its surface, this echoes Napster and the demise of the entertainment industry, but that's the "blunt instrument" manifestation of the concept, and the dynamics of this "groundswell" weaves its way through more subtle channels as well, manifesting as blogs, forums, ratings, reviews, wikis, and the "live" channels such at Facebook, Twitter, and Google+, among others.

Structurally, Groundswell[3] is in three sections: "Understanding the Groundswell", "Tapping the Groundswell", and "The Groundswell Transforms" ... with most of the heavy lifting done in the middle section which looks at strategies for, listening to, talking with, energizing, helping, and embracing the groundswell. In each of these (well, all throughout the book, actually) there are specific cases discussed, frequently companies that Forrester was working with, but also others who had made public mistakes or successes. One of the latter was Unilever's Dove skin-care brand, which had, in 2006, a video released to YouTube that went viral ... and ended up driving *more than twice the traffic to their website* than their 2006 *SuperBowl commercial* did. Cost of placement of the video: zero; cost of placement of the ad: $2.5 million! That's obviously an impressive "ROI" for working *with* the dynamics of the groundswell.

While this is interesting, accessible, and even entertainingly written, it's at base a book for the business reader, and it helps to keep that in mind.

Here's what seems to be the basic call to action:

> You're about to fundamentally change how your company relates to its customers. This will require not only fortitude on your part but difficult negotiations with other people throughout your company. We've identified some mistakes you may make, and you'll probably find a few we haven't thought of. At this point you might ask yourself, "Why should I bother?"
>
> Here's why.
>
> You cannot ignore this trend. You cannot sit this one out. Unless you are retiring in the next six months, it's too late to quit and let somebody else handle it. The groundswell trend is unstoppable, and your customers are there. You may go a little slower or a little faster, but you <u>have to move forward.</u> There is no going back.
>
> We will leave you with this: <u>there is no one "right way" to engage with the groundswell.</u>
>
> While there are plenty of wrong ways to join the groundswell – not listening, for example, or trying to fool people – there are also many effective strategies. Each company must adopt the tactics that are right for its customers and its way of doing business and adapt as the technologies change. Copying others doesn't work because your company, your customers, and your goals are not the same as anybody else's.
>
> So it's time to engage with the groundswell. Your company will be better for it.

The book is robust in delivering its message, with numerous examples that run the gamut from extremely specific to broad-strokes overviews, leaving the reader with the impression that they've been toured through an entire tapestry of how these technologies are impacting businesses.

I do have one fairly substantial gripe, however. The notes point to a place on the Forrester website for a LOT of supporting material (and additional resources) with the address groundswell.forrester.com/site#-# ... but they've apparently changed the directory structure, and this ends up at a "server not found" page. Since the forrester.com domain is certainly still active, having all the links in the book be *bad* is almost unforgivable ... and not only are the links not working, there's no *trace* (that I could find) on the forrester.com site. Now, I have a copy of the 2008 hardcover edition, and there is an "Expanded and Revised Edition" paperback that came out in 2011, which I assume has updated links (I would *hope*), but it's a big "slap in the face" to anybody who is reading the original version that there's not even a page on their site that the links from this would go to that would explain that the info was someplace else. I tried to get an answer from them via Twitter today on this issue, but have not heard back … there may be something out there, but it certainly isn't easy to find (and I went looking for anything that would provide those links, even through archive.org's "wayback machine")!

Anyway, I found Groundswell a very engaging and informative read, and would recommend it to anybody with a business interest in the new communications technologies (with the caveats above). As noted, there *are* two versions of this kicking around out there, the 2008 hardcover (which is what I have), and an updated paperback. There are "like new" copies of the hardcover available through the new/used vendors for as little as 14¢, but, given the abandonment of the supporting materials by Forrester, I'd probably have to recommend getting the paperback. I very much enjoyed the "groundswell experience" until I tried checking out the links … and really feel "cheated" that I was unable to follow up on that information, and find it somewhat inexplicable that, in the obvious case of the directory structure having no good reason to be *gone*, there shouldn't have been the absence that there is of those!

Notes:

1. http://btripp-books.livejournal.com/130660.html

2-4. http://amzn.to/1OHcuYF

Sunday, April 29, 2012[1]

Her name is written on the Clouds

This was another of those Dollar Store finds ... and I actually went back to pick up another copy to pass along to a friend, so I guess that says something. Swami Ramananda's Bliss Now!: My Journey with Sri Sri Anandamayi Ma[2] is certainly not the typical fare for the dollar store, and, I have a hard time imagining that this was remaindered off of the Walmart shelves, given its subject matter, but it's over at Dollar Tree in *quantity*, yet is still available on-line.

Bliss Now![3] is a "spiritual autobiography" of Swami Ramananda (on who I was unable to dig up any biographical information, beyond what's in the book, so I can't even give you his "real name"). In his youth, he had recurring dreams of a lady, who was encouraging him to come to India, and he managed to follow this and come in contact with his guru, the famed Sri Anandamayi Ma.

This book owes an inspirational debt to Ram Dass' *Be Here Now* from 1971 ... a relationship that Ramananda is certainly cognizant of, mentioning it on a number of occasions. There is a connection, as Ram Dass' teacher, Karoli Baba, is one of the figures here, but I'm pretty sure that the "look" of this book isn't *accidentally* evocative of the older one (and there's a quote here suggesting that Bliss Now![4] completes a trilogy, with Bhagavan Dass' *It's Here Now, Are You?* being the middle expression).

This is one of those books that likely has less to do with the author's *history* as it does with his inner journey. There is a lot happening within its pages, but not so much in its text. Ramananda (or whatever his birth name was) has visions, convinces his family that he needs to go to India, gets there and (in the narrative) almost immediately hooks up with his first teacher, Swami Shankarananda Giri, and begins traveling visiting various holy men. His teacher decides it's time to part ways (he believes it's his time to die), and begins the long walk to Benares ... leaving Ramananda behind, but also set up as his dharma successor. The author begins to wander, when suddenly a car lurches through the forest he's in, and who happens to be there, but Sri Anandamayi Ma, who "recognizes" him from previous lives and tells him to get in the car.

Now, obviously, one has to either have experiences that include these sorts of belief systems or be able to "suspend disbelief" a lot here, as there is a recurring element of "spiritual recognition" going on from "past lives" (and it seems that the author and his main teachers seem to hold that he's a reincarnation of the 15th century Indian saint, but not to be confused with *other* teachers concurrently going by the same name). There is also a lot of "spiritual experience" being presented as literal happenings (people "glowing", etc.) which likewise requires a cognitive jump for most folks.

One thing I wondered about here was the timing of the book ... Sri Anandamayi Ma died in 1982 at age 86, but the autobiographical part of the book only tracks up to that point. Yet Bliss Now!⁵ did not come out until 2002 ... when Ramananda got his PhD (in Indian Philosophy and Yoga, from a U.K. university). Following his guru's death, Ramananda goes back to the US, and begins to be a Yoga teacher ... but there is scant info on that. The second part of the book is a collection of pictures of and devotional poems about Sri Anandamayi Ma, which is then followed by his explaining about the various types of Yoga that his teachers practiced, the obvious Bhakti Yoga (focusing on devotion to the deity), Japa Yoga (using mantras), and then a long section on Hatha Yoga featuring him demonstrating (in photos) a couple of dozen poses (which, one has to ask, are of what use here? ... one can hardly do a practice out of a single picture and a paragraph of description!), before getting into Karma Yoga, with a lot of diet and housekeeping suggestions, and finally discussing building communities. The book closes out with suggested reading and web sites, and a fairly extensive listing of Sanskrit terms and their definitions.

Frankly, it feels like Ramananda really wanted to do *two* books here, one the autobiographical part up front, and the other the explanatory material in the back. I think this would have been better had he been able to flesh out the first section of the book to more than the 54 pages he applies to his spiritual journey. I'm sure he has *fascinating* stories to tell about many of the spiritual teachers that he largely only name-checks there. Ramananda keeps falling back to his theme of "bliss" rather than talking about the who/what/when/where of the situations, which may be sort of the point, but "I was at this place with this person and it was *so blissful*" only goes so far as literary structure.

I did enjoy Bliss Now!⁶, however, and found a number of things that will be interesting to follow up on. I should probably note that I have never "gotten" the Bhakti Yoga path, and that's *clearly* the central element here, so there's a lot of the *essence* of the book that I just wasn't connecting with ... but that's likely to be more me than him. As noted, this is still available via the big on-line companies (Amazon has it at a whopping 60% discount), but if you have a Dollar Tree handy, you might well be able to find a copy for a buck out there ... the one I went to today had a dozen or more copies on hand, so I'm guessing it's out there pretty broadly at the moment!

Notes:

1. http://btripp-books.livejournal.com/130903.html

2-6. http://amzn.to/1M6dxdV

Friday, May 18, 2012[1]

Anachronistic advice?

This was another Dollar Store find, and it's probably a good thing, or I would have been having "buyers' remorse" otherwise. Although the book did redeem itself to a certain extent by the time it was over, it was a long strange trip (and not in a good way) through a lot of very anachronistic advice!

As regular readers of this space know, I read quite a lot of social media, web, and other "digital space" material. Being that much of this is "bleeding cutting edge" at the time of composition, it frequently has a less than stellar shelf-life, and I've frequently commented that "a book that's seven years old, might as well be seventy years old". Well, Bette Daoust's Networking: 150 Ways to Promote Yourself[2] hails from 2005, and, for most of it, reads like it might as well have been written in the 1940's!

Now, I've been in a seemingly unending job search, and make a point of getting out to 2-4 networking events per week, so the subject of this book is certainly of interest to me. However, the tone here is more "your grandfather's networking" than anything that I'm familiar with. Of course, I live in downtown Chicago, and much of the advice here seems targeted to Mayberry ... and certainly appears aimed more at insurance salesmen or aluminum-siding reps than the job seeker, or tech start-up partner.

Frankly, as I was reading through this, I kept trying to imagine *who* the audience was for the book, or *why* it read the way it did. Stylistically, it has the pontificating tone of Napoleon Hill's books back in the early parts of the last century ... lots of "you *must* do this" or "you should *never* do that" sorts of instruction ... all reflecting a business world that I've not seen a trace of since the 70's, unless you count the stories of my father-in-law!

As one might guess from the subtitle, this has 150 entries, each just under a page in length, assembled into ten subject sections: Event Marketing, What to Join, Strategic Alliances, Announcements, Speaking Engagements, Relationships, Power Pad *{note: this is not some tech item, but a note-taking system the author concocted}*, Business Card Marketing, Web Relationships, and Printed Networking ... each with fifteen individual "chapters". I wasn't exactly keeping score, but I think she mentioned the web, or the internet, or even e-mail only 2-3 times before she got to the ninth section there ... this in a book that was written a *full decade* after I'd launched my first e-commerce web site ... as I noted above, this was a bit like reading a book from the 1940's that had been re-written with a few updates in 2005 to give a nod to that "new fangled" stuff!

Even outside of the section on business cards, she spends a lot of time fixated on the subject, and is very proud of her own (as she frequently reminds the reader: *"Some people have even said it is the most professional and great looking card they have ever come across."*), and quite dismissive of others that she doesn't consider being up to snuff. Given her attention to micro-managing instructions for the subject, she'd evidently never heard of VistaPrint, which had already been around for ten years when she wrote this!

Again, the focus here seems to be on the guy out there trying to move a few extra pallets of widgets, or sell a few more insurance plans than it is for "networking" per se., and the setting is certainly in a small town or suburb (this is especially evident when she talks about doing out-reach to the press). That somebody, even seven years ago, could write:

> Whether you understand it or not, the Web is likely here to stay; those businesses that do not yet have a web presence, or at least e-mail addresses, are likely to get left in the dust.

with a straight face is pretty amazing! Sure, that statement is true, but by 2005 who *didn't* have e-mail??? She elsewhere declares: *"a website is like an electronic brochure"*, putting the sensibilities of that aspect of the book squarely in the mid-90's.

I'm not saying that Networking: 150 Ways to Promote Yourself[3] was a *useless* read (there were several points that made me think, or led to considering a couple of new approaches), but it was *bizarre* in the context of the chronology of its composition. I suppose if you have a small business-service operation in small-town America, this might be your business-building bible, but in other settings it's a bit like trying to take a WW2-era business book for your template ... good luck with that!

Incredibly, this appears to still be in print (although Amazon has it at nearly 2/3rds off the cover price), but, as I said, it's currently showing up in the dollar stores. Needless to say, unless you fit the profile I'm suggesting is the plausible target audience for this, I'm not exactly recommending it, but if you *do* stumble across it for a buck, you might consider picking it up.

Notes:

1. http://btripp-books.livejournal.com/131302.html

2-3. http://amzn.to/1PFxazn

Saturday, May 19, 2012[1]

A book from a book ...

This is a perfect example of a "dollar store find" that if it hadn't been there for a buck, I would *never* have connected with it. How to describe Jan Karon's A Continual Feast: Words of Comfort and Celebration, Collected by Father Tim[2]? The term "meta" certainly comes to mind. The book, despite the title, etc. on the dust jacket, purports to be a journal of Father Timothy A. Kavanagh, and, once the dust jacket is removed, appears to be just that, with a faux lizard cover, and his gold stamped name on the front, with no other identification on the book.

I take it that "Father Tim" is the main character in a series of books that Jan Karon has written in the "Mitford series", books about an Episcopalian minister in the small mountain town of Mitford, NC. Needless to say, "Christian Fiction" is *not* high on my list of things to read, but this is not a fiction book, but a book that *relates* to the books, being a journal kept by the protagonist ... similar, I suppose, to the Quidditch rule book that was out in the wake of the Harry Potter movies.

The book is set in a hand-written font (I had initially thought it had been hand-written and scanned, but after 20 or so pages, I realized there were too many identical characters to not be a font), in both blue and black ink, with an occasional "insert", both "post-its" (not particularly well executed in grey), or typed pages "taped" in (and in some cases with "smudges" under the tape), and even the particulars of the very old-style typewritten pages (it seems that Fr. Tim has a problem with typing "ii" instead of "i" a lot of the time) ... the sort of detail that is quaint here, but might be "meaningful" in the stories. I'm guessing that some of the names, etc. that crop up in these (notes to send things to particular people) would also be familiar to readers of the series.

Most of the book are quotations ... about half coming from the Bible, and half from other sources ... just enough balance to not have it feel *too* "preachy". There's also some subtle humor, like the "post it" that says: *"God sings!! remind choir"*, and the occasional note about a birthday, or something that needs to be bought, or even a recipe ... all breaking up the flow of quotations. I could have done without the sermons (several of which are typed up and "taped in" here), but I guess that goes with the territory in context of the "meta" aspects

of the book. There are also a few sketches in here, very convincingly looking like they'd been done in pencil.

One thing that drove me *nuts* here was the lack of page numbers, so I could never tell where I was, or how I was progressing (I'm terrible with the OCD habit of figuring out what percentage of a book I'm at, or have just read, etc.), which reminds me with one of my main gripes of reading e-books, which was a bit of a revelation to me (i.e. that I'd like e-books better if I had page counts).

Oddly, this doesn't stand alone ... there's at least another collection of quotes *and* a cookbook in the series. However, if you appreciate collections of quotes, A Continual Feast[3] will probably appeal to you. The sources range from Founding Fathers to modern authors, the classics to religious figures, and, of course, the Bible.

This is still available (Amazon has it at 60% off), so this must have been something "slipping through" to the dollar stores from Walmart, etc. ... used copies (of the paperback, not the hardcover) are also out there for a penny (plus $3.99 shipping, of course) as well. I'd certainly recommend this as something to keep an eye out for if you're at the dollar store, but "your mileage may vary" as to how much you'd be interested in paying for it. I enjoyed it, but liked it almost for its quirkiness than anything else!

Notes:

1. http://btripp-books.livejournal.com/131375.html

2-3. http://amzn.to/1ZVH6JD

Sunday, May 20, 2012[1]

"Does a dog have Buddha-nature?"

I'm not sure how The Big Moo: Stop Trying to Be Perfect and Start Being Remarkable[2] got on my radar ... it probably showed up on one of those Amazon lists of books I might like. It's a follow-up to Seth Godin's Purple Cow[3], and is credited to "The Group of 33", and edited by Godin. It's a collection of essays from *"33 of the world's smartest business thinkers"* including Malcolm Gladwell, Guy Kawasaki, and Mark Cuban. Oddly, there are 72 essays here, and none of them are attributed to individual writers, so one figures that there are multiple essays from most, but no way to tell for sure. There are a few that sound very much like authors whose work I know well, but, again, it's all attributed to the "group" (and all the proceeds were donated to charity).

The pieces range from a few sentences to about 7 pages (with most being 2-3 pages long), so are easy to blow through fairly quickly. However, there's little coherence in theme or subject, and the reading swings from one place to another ... at one point you're reading a scant half-page piece about a button that top Sarah Lee execs were wearing to get across a message, and at another you're reading a "play" of a borsht-belt routine which illustrates three principles of being remarkable.

While I enjoyed reading this, I didn't hit *anything* while in it that I was driven to bookmark, which, in my reading style, is fairly unusual. While I take it that these pieces were produced specifically for this book (*"they distilled their best secrets for creating sustainable and shared remarkability"*), there isn't *that* much that's particularly remarkable in any of these.

Frankly, not knowing who wrote what was a significant irritant ... I mean, in some cases you could *guess*, but it really was quite a jumble of voices, points, and approaches ... with most so short that it would have been helpful to have the "background" of knowing where that person was coming from. Also, I assume that the 72 essays are unevenly distributed across the 33 authors ... with my guess being that *most* just weighed in with one piece, so who wrote the rest? Did Godin seed this with his own bits? In the Introduction Godin writes: *"We {didn't credit the individual contributions} because it makes it easier to read the book as a whole, to avoid being interrupted by the noise your brain makes as it shifts gears from one voice to another."* ... I feel he's wrong here, and that the *unavoidable* shifts between voices are *more* distracting when they happen "in the flow" of the book, without having the *context* of knowing who's currently at the mic!

It could be argued that Godin "does the heavy lifting" up front here, and the rest of the book is just a series of footnotes illustrating the main points. Interestingly, he also *encourages* copying of material from the book, since it's all done pro bono, so in that spirit, I think I'll pass along a chunk of the Preface where he pretty much defines his terms:

> Let's begin with ... two things that are true:
> 1. The only way to grow is to be remarkable.
> 2. The only barrier to being remarkable is your ability to persuade your peers to make it happen.
>
> In the old days, showing up was 95 percent of success. If you offered a good product at a good price in a reliable way, you'd be fine. Being local was a good thing. Having a long track record helped. Decent quality and personal service mattered as well.
>
> No longer. Good enough isn't good enough, because now <u>everything</u> is good enough. Our expectations of quality are unrealistic – and are being met every single day. We don't just want to be satisfied, we want to be blown away.
>
> Not only that, but today everything is a click away. Being local isn't good enough either.
>
> {detailing various depressing business scenarios} ... <u>But wouldn't it be better to leave that fear behind and grow instead?</u>
>
> You will grow as soon as you decide to become remarkable – and do something about it.
>
> Remarkable isn't up to you. Remarkable is in the eye of the customer. If your customer decides something you do is worth remarking on, then, by definition, it's remarkable. ... Remarkable is not in the eyes of the marketer. It doesn't matter one bit how hard you worked on something or how cool you think it is. It's up to the consumer. If the consumer thinks it's worth remarking about, then you've got a purple cow. ... A big moo is the extreme purple cow, the remarkable innovation that completely changes the game.

Godin goes on to say *"This is a book about how and why to grow. It is not a book of facts or logical reasoning. ... My colleagues and I are intent on slipping some subversive ideas into your subconscious ..."*, and perhaps this is why the book seems to be such a cacophony – it's going for a non-linear impression.

I enjoyed reading The Big Moo[4], but it's hardly my favorite Godin book. It's still in print, and the on-line big boys have it at about a third off of cover, but the new/used vendors have "like new" copies going for a penny, plus the $3.99 shipping (which is how I got my mine), so that would likely be your best bet. This is good if you're looking to be a Godin "completist", or if you've got the "remarkable" fetish, but it's not exactly one I'm recommending for "all and sundry".

Notes:
1. http://btripp-books.livejournal.com/131670.html
2. http://amzn.to/1M69FcS
3. http://btripp-books.livejournal.com/108106.html
4. http://amzn.to/1M69FcS

Monday, May 21, 2012[1]

More as branding than as a quality statement...

One of these days I'm going to swear off "resume books", but they keep coming my way (thanks to my penning The Job Stalker blog over on the Chicago Tribune's "Chicago Now" site), and I keep reading them. As regular followers of this space will appreciate, after spending the first 25 years of my professional career between two gigs that I only left because the companies folded, I have since been through an unending scramble ... essentially a full decade of on-and-off looking for work (with a few years of scattered employment in various entrepreneurial settings which also went out of business). I have worked with "career management" groups, various "coaches" and consultants, and a whole parade of seminars, workshops, trainings, support groups, along with the assorted recruiters "slumming" around in those settings. The one constant of all this is that everybody you talk to has a fairly particular concept of what a "proper resume" should look like, but they are all *different*, and all in deep disagreement with one another.

Given this background, I was, obviously, not the most open-minded place for a review copy (kindly provided to me by the good folks at Ten Speed Press) of the The Damn Good Resume Guide, Fifth Edition: A Crash Course in Resume Writing[2] to end up. I know it may sound cruel, and snarky, and unkind, and mean (yet I assure you that it's true), but one of the *best* things about this book is that it is *very short*, getting to the point without much fluff or posturing. It has 10 pages of introduction, 26 pages of instruction, 36 pages of sample resumes, and 12 pages to cover five appendices.

This book at least has an interesting back-story, its (late) original author, Yana Parker, had started this as a handout she'd provide to clients and others, eventually charging a couple of bucks for a print-out, and then landing a "real" publishing deal. Parker died in 2000, and the most recent previous edition came out two years later ... this one has been updated by Beth Brown, who had been a writer for Parker's newsletter. Obviously, a lot had changed in the world in the decade between the 4th and 5th editions, but I still don't think it's "up to speed" with the ugly realities of the current economy. The 5th edition still clearly operates under the assumption that "real people" will be reading one's resume and *thinking* about it, when the likelihood is more that a computer will do a key word search and summarily reject the vast majority of the resumes submitted to any job, totally unread by a human, and the remaining smattering that made it through *that* cut will be handed over to an intern to further filter (and "round-file") this remnant down to a handful that will actually be *considered* by a hiring manager. It's nice to think that there's somebody on the receiving end of your resume who *cares* about it, but it's been my experience that there are a LOT of machines and people whose <u>sole function</u> is to find an excuse, *any* excuse, to throw resumes out ... basically unseen and unread beyond the most mechanical and cursory review.

Anyway, the "meat" of The Damn Good Resume Guide[3] is the 10-step process to take a job seeker from a helpless newbie to a polished presentable candidate.

> Step 1: Choose a job objective
>
> Step 2: Find out what skills, knowledge, and experience are needed to do the target job.
>
> Step 3: Choose a resume format that fits your situation.
>
> Step 4: Make a list of past jobs you've held.
>
> Step 5: For each job, list your skills and accomplishments.
>
> Step 6: Describe each accomplishment as an "action statement".
>
> Step 7: Arrange your action statements in your resume format.
>
> Step 8: List your education, etc.
>
> Step 9: Write a summary.
>
> Step 10: "Polish and proof" the document.

Each of these has its own section in the book, with further instructions, and "cute" responses to commonly raised objections. This 10-step approach is at least consistent, comprehensive, and (reasonably) easy to implement. It is aimed more at new-to-early-career job seekers, with a lot of advice on how to bring "non-job" activities into play within the context of one's resume. I'm guessing that Beth Brown had to "walk a fine line" in updating The Damn Good Resume Guide[4] for this 5th edition, as there are elements here which are quite dated (seeming more apropos to the 3rd edition, fifteen plus years ago, than they are now), such as spending time on the *look* and graphic presentation of your resume. In the past 3 years of *my* job search, I have sent out a *physical* paper-in-envelope resume less than five times, one of which was somewhat as a joke to a tech-industry contact who does almost *nothing* on paper – just to stand out. Obviously, you do want to have a resume that is clean, well organized, and *proofread* to perfection, but in nearly all job applications it will be parsed by a machine, *or* you'll be asked to cut-and-paste in a text-only version. Fonts and visual styling are not concerns except in the hard-copies that you'll bring to interviews or job fairs.

There is a web site associated with the book, http://damngood.com[5], which is the career service company for which the book was developed, and they offer resume writing and critiquing services (surprise!), counseling, coaching, and vast numbers of sample resumes (whole books full of them). This book has 25 sample resumes, each with a little note (which I thought was *very* useful!) indicating *why* the various resumes ended up with the format and the particular information that they had.

The book finishes up with five appendices, one on "action verbs", one about "informational interviewing", one on Social Networking, one on "customizing" your resume, and finally one on cover letters and e-mail. It's odd that something that is frequently seen as "essential" like cover letters ends up in the last appendix, but, as noted, any two books on resumes are likely to be in strident disagreement about any number of points, and here this seems to be an afterthought.

As I said, [The Damn Good Resume Guide](http://amzn.to/1ZVDnf9)[6] is short, to the point, and presents a consistent "system" for developing resumes; it would no doubt be a good place to start for somebody who hasn't been massaging theirs for decades. The focus is definitely on the lower end of the career ladder (featuring sample resumes that target jobs such as line cooks, cashiers, retail sales clerks, various types of "assistants", etc.), more so than I can recall in any other resume book I've plowed through ... so that's something else to keep in mind. It's inexpensive (the on-line big boys currently have it discounted to under ten bucks), so if you, or somebody you're handing out advice to, is in need of a starter resume book, this might be what you're looking for. Be careful, though, when ordering it, as copies of both the 4th and even *the* 3rd editions are still out there, and you'll want to have the version that's as up-to-date as possible (and this 5th edition officially goes on sale *tomorrow*!).

Notes:

1. http://btripp-books.livejournal.com/131965.html

2-4. http://amzn.to/1ZVDnf9

5. http://damngood.com/

6. http://amzn.to/1ZVDnf9

Tuesday, June 12, 2012[1]

So tempting to quote Hamlet ...

One of the great advantages of the Dollar Store source for books is that it provides me with the opportunity to justify taking a chance on something which I'm pretty sure that I wouldn't buy at full price. Now, as regular readers of this space may realize, I *will*, from time to time, read some humorous books, so picking up Samantha Bee's I Know I Am, But What Are You?[2] is not *totally* out of character, albeit representing a minority segment of my library, to be sure.

As is usually the case with dollar store acquisitions, I had only the briefest consideration about picking up the book ... this is both a strength and a weakness, a strength in that it pushes me into reading things that had a fairly low probability of getting poured in my head if it wasn't sitting there for a buck, but a weakness in that I, generally speaking, will launch into the reading without much preconception of what I was getting into.

I'm not a huge fan of *The Daily Show* or the *Colbert Report*, but The Wife is, so I'm reasonably familiar with Samantha Bee as one of the characters from that particular universe. From this, I obviously surmised that the book would be a humorous take on *something* and most of the jacket copy referred to "essays". What I *wasn't* expecting that the book is, or at least purports to be, an *autobiography* of sorts, tracking Ms. Bee's life history from early childhood through a reasonably recent period.

However, as I read through it, my credulity was more and more challenged. Either she has had a *remarkably* bizarre life, or this is wholly made up, perhaps peppered with actual events to give it a feel of plausibility. Of course, the same haziness is the stock-in-trade of the Stewart/Colbert media empire, with only the vaguest of lines separating what presents itself as news and outright broad buffoonery. While this certainly "works" in the realm of the mock-news comedy show (and in print with *The Onion*), it creates a uncomfortable zone here where one can't get one's bearings as far as how to *process* what's being detailed on the pages.

Much like the X-Files' Mulder, on some level "I want to believe" that the stories here are her reminiscences of a deeply strange upbringing, but it keeps pushing the envelope just far enough that the BS meter in the back of my head would be red-lining "nahhhhhh". The most egregious section for this was her tale of her "criminal career" where she and her Croatian boyfriend would steal cars ...

> "We drove carefully, so as not to raise any red flags with the police, and took great road trips anywhere we wanted to go. Then, guided by inner voices that would tell us when the car was getting too danger-

> ous to continue using, we would abandon it on a busy street and walk away. Of course, not before selling off any valuable parts, which he would do, and then I would rent a hotel room under an assumed name, and we would throw a big party."

I mean, yeah, this was in *Canada* and twenty years or so back, but *still*, it sounds highly unlikely as an on-going *plan*. This comes in about half-way through the book. Of course, she describes her parents as pretty close to post-hippie counter-culturalists (she was largely raised in this by her grandmother), so if *that* part is really as it plays out here, maybe the rest just spins out, however improbably, from that. Much to her parents' horror, her grandparents managed to get her hooked on Jesus ...

> It wasn't easy being so Catholic around my parents. They were forcefully nonreligious, but they hadn't really been in the picture when my grandmother had done all the decision making about my education. If either of them had had their way, I would have gone to the Atheist School for the Children of Heretics and Pagans.

(Come to think of it – that sounds like where *I'd* have like to have sent my kids!).

Again, maybe it's just me, but I spent a *lot* of the reading of I Know I Am, But What Are You?[3] trying to fit the stories in here into a plausible human existence. There are certainly hilarious bits, some of which "feel" realer than others (like when she was "headlining" a live Sailor Moon stage show in which she ended up meeting her husband), and I guess that pretty much *is* the recipe for this sort of humor, but the *uncertainty* kept reining in whatever sympathetic rapport I might have been developing for the character.

Oh, by the way ... not that this is an issue for *me*, but there are also plenty of "blue" parts here, so be warned if you're the easily-mortified type.

Reading this was an enjoyable respite from my usual "serious nonfiction" fare, only tempered by the believability issue. As noted, it's floating around the dollar store channel at the moment, which would certainly be your best bet for grabbing a copy ... but it's also still in print, with the on-line big boys having it for a whopping 60% off of cover, and the new/used vendors (predictably for something that's made its way to the dollar stores) are offering copies for as little as a penny (plus shipping). This certainly isn't an "immortal work of literature", but it's a fun read, and if you're a fan of Samantha Bee from her cable "humor news" work, you should probably look into picking up a copy.

Notes:
1. http://btripp-books.livejournal.com/132273.html
2-3. http://amzn.to/1LJxMIY

Wednesday, June 13, 2012[1]

Do-it-yourself Psychology!

This was another good Dollar Store find ... showing that you never know *what* will filter through that strange retail channel (as I've noted here previously, I've been told that they buy bulk "shelf turn-over" from the big discount stores, so frequently the books are just last month's "titles du jour" at those limited-item departments). The Next Ten Minutes: 51 Absurdly Simple Ways to Seize the Moment[2] by Andrew Peterson, EdD is a bit of an odd thing to have been out there anyway, being various exercises to change how you approach things in your life.

The book is "dedicated to two propositions": 1st - *"Big changes in our lives start with small shifts in our state of mind."* and 2nd - *"The seeds of change are embedded within the most ordinary activities of daily life."*. And, as one might surmise from the title, the (51) exercises in it are designed to be able to be worked through in about 10 minutes. I showed this to a therapist friend of mine, who was *quite* impressed, saying that he could run a whole weekend retreat off of the stuff in here, which I take to be pretty high praise.

There is a lot of humor involved here too ... in fact, most of the exercises are pretty ridiculous on their surface ... to pick a few for illustration: "Go into Another Room", "Stare at the Wall", "Do Something", "Misuse an Object", "Pose a Threat", "Plug Your Ears", "Retrace Your Steps", "Stand Up", and (the final one) "Do Nothing". Many of these are *almost* as odd as they sound. Another interesting feature of the book are its two appendices, "How Are You Feeling" and "How Would You Like To Feel", which list a few dozen feelings and make suggestions as to which exercises to try for them.

Generally speaking, the exercises in this book are ways to mindfully, consciously, do things that one might do anyway (such as "Stand Up"), or might do if one was so inclined (like "Plug Your Ears"). In these Peterson coaches for things to look for in one's thoughts and physical reactions, both directly, and in variations. I found the following alternative (from the first, ironically placed, "Procrastinate" exercise) particularly interesting:

> **Do it, but only halfheartedly.** *A final way to vary this exercise involved harnessing your capacity for passive-aggressive behavior. Don't procrastinate, but don't do the task well either. We all do this at times, but usually we do it more or less unconsciously. Try bringing full awareness to a task while you're doing a half-assed job on it. Can you stay focused on your refusal to do the task well even as you are doing it?*

This is the sort of mental "stretching" that's all through the book, along with other *"I did not know that"* (kudos to the late Johnny Carson) tidbits like "you can't speak while inhaling".

Frankly, my reactions varied widely to the exercises in The Next Ten Minutes[3], from "oh, cool – I'll have to try that" to "puh-leese", but they all seemed to have pretty worthwhile psychological ends for which they're designed. Speaking of psychology ... I felt like I just *had* to share the following digression from the "Dig In Your Heels" (#44) exercise:

> **Prescribing the Symptom**
>
> I know I'm going to get in trouble for this, but I'm going to do it anyway. I'm going to give away one of the most important secret behind this entire book. So be forewarned. If you read the rest of this section, you might not need this book (or your therapist) anymore. You might be albe to do it all on your own.
>
> It's called paradoxical intervention, or "prescribing the symptom".
>
> That's a fancy way of saying that you get put into a double blind. Here's an example: Say you go to a therapist for help in managing your fear of speaking in public. You describe to the doctor how you get paralyzed with anxiety whenever you have to talk in front of groups. You just can't seem to get it under control. At the end of the session, the therapist tells you that it's very important for the treatment that over the next week you continue to feel your fear of speaking in public. In fact, you should try to worry about it even more, to intensify your fear.
>
> You leave the session in a state of confusion, wondering if your therapist is completely out of her mind. But whether or not she is sane, you still have to figure out what to do next. If you follow her instructions, you can't help but acknowledge that you have control over how you experience your symptoms, and thus that you have the ability to improve them. On the other hand, the only way to not follow her instructions is to worry less. This is the bind. So even if you do nothing, you have already altered your state of mind. You shift from being the person who is afraid to being the person observing the fear. Either way, something has changed.

It is this "something has changed" result that these little 10-minute exercises are attempting to get at ... small shifts that end up making huge differences (and, in another story here, he had triggered a major change in one patient simply by suggesting that they sleep on the opposite side of the bed than they were used to ... which is almost getting into Edgar Cayce territory!).

Anyway, The Next Ten Minutes[4] is a very interesting read, if only to see what sorts of things could bring on major shifts in one's perceptions. It's still available out there (the on-line big boys even still have it at very near its cover price), but the new/used guys on the web have *new* copies for as little as 1¢, though you'd still do better if you could find a dollar store copy rather than one you had to pay shipping on!

Notes:

1. http://btripp-books.livejournal.com/132352.html

2-4. http://amzn.to/1LJvinJ

Sunday, June 17, 2012[1]

What a long strange trip it's been ...

This is another book that came my way via the LibraryThing.com "Early Reviewers" program ... a fact that I frequently have flogged in these introductory paragraphs, largely for the benefit if the FTC and other governmental busy-bodies. However, I'm starting with something *new* with this review, and that's including the "compliance" badge from CMP.LY ... a service that lets bloggers make it clear when they've gotten a review copy, or other consideration (all the way up to being an outright paid shill for a company) via 16 different badges (see my previous post[2] on the subject) ... and clicking on the "review" badge down below will take you to a page specific to my review of this book. It's a fairly *elegant* solution to a somewhat complex problem, and I anticipate using this on-going for situations where I've gotten promotional copies of stuff I'm reviewing here.

This book comes with a certain *gravitas* as its author is Curator of the Spitzer Hall or Human Origins at the famed American Museum of Natural History in New York City, and one would suppose that it is reflective of the most recent research, as it is only a couple of months old at this point. I suppose, then, that it's somewhat unfair of me to find myself wishing that Ian Tattersall's Masters of the Planet: The Search for Our Human Origins[3] was more *engaging* than it was.

This is not to say that the book is *boring* or "textbooky", as it's not, it's just that it seems to take a very long time to get where it's going ... of course, one could certainly argue that the hominid line itself took a very long time to get to current humanity too. As regular readers of my reviews my recall, as I read I generally put in little slips of paper to flag things I want to revisit, either choice bits to drop into one of these scribblings, or information that I want to follow up on. A book which really "grabs me" will have a forest of these sticking out of the top of the book, this had a scant few, and none of them appearing in the first 80% of the text.

My "take away" therefore is that the book spends the first 4/5ths setting up the key final bits. Obviously, in a survey like Masters of the Planet[4], the author can't necessarily assume that the reader is coming to the text with any in-depth knowledge of the subject (and I found that much of what I *have* read on the subject has, perhaps, been superseded by subsequent research), so there is a sense that Tattersall is having to fill in the first six or seven million years of hominid evolution as efficiently as he can, a challenging task given the very slim material that researchers have to work with.

It helps to keep in mind that in very many, if not most, cases, what evidence we have of previous hominids may be a leg bone here, a jaw there, a skull if we're lucky, with the occasional nearly-complete skeleton like Lucy. From these scanty remnants, the development of our species is conjectured across millions of years. What complicates matters is that it appears that, through *most* of that history, there were multiple "types" of hominids living in various niches. As we are used to being the only example of our immediate family extant in history, this is hard to get a hold of, but if you think of it in the way that there are many *types* of monkeys out there, so there were, at various points in time, multiple hominid lines existing concurrently. As you can imagine, this muddies the waters in terms of sketching out a lineage which leads to modern Homo Spaiens.

One of the things that Tattersall keeps returning to here is that, although these species were related, and similar to us in many ways, they were profoundly *different*. What qualitatively sets modern man apart from his predecessors and surviving more-distant relatives (the other great apes), is a hard-to-fossilize sense of symbolic relationship with the world. Even recent lines such as the Neanderthals, who may have even had larger brains than ours, don't seem to have had the level of symbolism which enables language and rich, rapid, cultural development. Tool-making preceded our species by several hundred thousand years but it, with few exceptions, stayed very limited, and "frozen" in form and technique generation after generation.

From genetic tracking, we know that the human genome is remarkably non-variant, with the entire of humanity having less variety than some chimpanzee populations in Africa. This suggests two things, that modern man is a very recent development, and that our population has been through some near-extinction "bottlenecks". Both the genetic markers and geology point to the most dramatic of these being the explosion of Mount Toba in Indonesia some 74,000 years ago, which appears to have created a "volcanic winter" in which the hominid line that was going to emerge as modern Homo Sapiens was reduced in number to the extent where they *all* could have been seated in a large football stadium. The fact that the variation we see in humanity today came out of adjustments from that small pool of genes and in that short period of time is amazing.

The other thing that is suggested here is that, for whatever reason, there was a change in these hominids, and a part of the brain began to develop called the "angular gyrus", which is large in our brains but small or missing in other primates. This is in an area of the brain which seems to exchange information in a new way, and may be the seat of symbolic thought. Once this ability to name objects and communicate the symbols was established, it allowed for the development of culture, and the spread of our kind across the planet (not by *design*, but by simply groups "expanding their range" by a mere 10 miles a generation).

Again, Masters of the Planet[5] is a detailed over-view of the development of our species out of its assorted primate and hominid forbearers, but is far more interesting towards the end (which, I suppose, is a better "arc" for a book than the opposite!) ... although this, admittedly, could just be *my* reaction to the material here. As one would expect for a brand-new book, there aren't many inexpensive options out there, although the on-line guys currently have this at a fairly substantial discount. As it's only been out a few months, your odds of finding it in your local brick-and-mortar book vendors are pretty good. If you're "into" paleoanthropology, or looking for an up-to-the-moment look at the current models of how we got here, this is certainly recommended.

Notes:

1. http://btripp-books.livejournal.com/132725.html
2. http://btripp.livejournal.com/1116826.html
3-5. http://amzn.to/1RmDE4y

Wednesday, June 27, 2012[1]

Vive le Roi!

As readers of my main blog may recall, I attended a presentation by Mark W. Schaefer a few weeks back and talked about it (and did *pictures*!), I also got a chance to chat with him as a TweetUp the next day, and decided that I'd reach out to McGraw Hill for a review copy of his new book Return On Influence: The Revolutionary Power of Klout, Social Scoring, and Influence Marketing[2].

Contrary to the behavior evidenced by most authors out flogging their books, Schaefer's talk was less about the book than about the context from which it arose. I was, thereby somewhat surprised to find that some key bits of his speech did *not* appear in the book (I'm guessing that we got an amalgam of his consulting pitch and his classroom lectures, with a sprinkling of soundbites for the book), and how central Klout was to the text. Of course, being that it is "name-checked" in the subtitle, I should have had a clue).

However, although using Klout as a narrative axis, Return On Influence[3] is really much more a general book on what he calls "influence marketing", and (to judge by my "how many bookmarks did I stick in this?" scale), it is chock full of fascinating information. The book is split in half, with the first part discussing "The Roots of Influence" (there's a marketing geek's dream band name), laying the theoretical groundwork for the concepts, and the second part being on "Klout and the Social Scoring Revolution". One of the main structuring elements here is spun out from a base of Cialdini's "weapons of influence": Authority, Likeability, Consistency, and Scarcity, to which are added Social Proof and Reciprocity, and then "the seventh weapon", Content. On this last point, Schaefer comes up with one of those mnemonic acronyms that he uses in his classes: R.I.T.E. - for content that is Relevant, Interesting, Timely, and Entertaining., which he suggests is a good way of making your content *"part of the signal instead of the noise"*.

Much of the second half of the book is based on discussions the author had with Klout founder Joe Fernandez. Here's a bit from a section where they're talking about how Klout developed:

> *"The importance of social networking broadly for individuals and companies has reached a tipping point, and we are in what I like to think of as an attention economy. With Facebook, people started using their real names, and as you start to use your own name online, your personal brand starts to matter. You can build your own influence like never before. All those things started happening around the same time Klout began its social credit score."*

Obviously, Klout taps into many divergent hard-wired behavior patterns, from the quantification inherent in having a numerical "score" (and the subsequent competitiveness that engenders), to pack/tribal "pecking order" perceptions. This, in the sociology spin, is the "social proof" influence, which is described thusly:

> "Offline or online, when people are in a situation in which they are unsure of the correct way to behave, they often look to others for cues to the correct behavior. Social proof often leads not just to influence in the form of compliance but also to internalized acceptance as the belief that so many others must be correct becomes stronger."

Needless to say, *this* is the element that gets the marketing community salivating ... and passing out mega goodies to those identified as being "opinion leaders" in various fields. Schaefer talks about and to many of the top Klout scorers, and notes the downside of what is, essentially, creating a "caste society" where "influencers" get red-carpet treatment and the rest of us are left hoping we'll get a "Perk" coupon we're interested in using!

Speaking of Klout Perks, there is a section here based on material from Shripal Shah, who leads one PR agency's digital practice. He describes five key benefits that marketers get via ranked-influence marketing programs: 1. Authentic Advocacy – cozying up to somebody with a high Klout score in, say, *knitting* might produce far more enthusiastic message delivery than an ad ever could ... 2. Cost-Effective Impressions – early research suggests that the CPM for these programs compare very favorably to traditional advertising, but with more "influence" ... 3. Fresh Marketing Channel – most brands aren't going to *drop* their other vehicles for the "social scoring" platforms, but it adds another way to effectively reach consumers ... 4. Consumer Feedback Loop – since social media is done largely "in public" and is trackable, it's much easier to get accurate fixes on how products, etc., are being perceived by various audiences ... and, 5. Brand Buffer – companies marketing through the Perks program have their messages pushed through Klout and not directly to the consumer, so are less intrusive and typically seen more as a "pull" on their part.

Both halves of Return On Influence[4] are filled with "case studies" and stories of how people have developed and wielded Influence, as well as how numerous companies have implemented marketing programs based on Twitter, Facebook, Klout, PeerIndex and other platforms. There is also a section on "How to Increase Your Klout Score", which is not as helpful as one might have hoped having read the chapter heading (it basically boils down to three steps: 1 – develop a network, 2 – create great content, and 3 – suck up to other influencers ... none of which are quick or easy), although it does included advice from numerous key players (such as Fernandez, who should know, chiming in with *"You only have a high Klout score if you're creating good content"*). My own Klout score (not that I'm blaming Schaefer) has slipped from the "magic number" of 50 (pretty much the dividing line for "being influential") down to 46 since encountering this material, so it's certainly no "magic wand"!

In the penultimate chapter, the author "hands the mic over" to a selection of leading lights in the Influence Marketing game, letting them prognosticate on "The Future of Social Scoring", along with his own thoughts, continued into a summary in the final chapter. The book closes with two *very useful* appendices, "The Social Media Primer" (which I suggested would make a nice promotional e-book) which gives late-to-the-game readers a general overview of the field, and a quite handy and informative listing of "Platforms that Measure Influence" (a surprising 19 of which are discussed).

Obviously, Return On Influence[5] is not for *everybody*, but if you have an interest in marketing, or are a Social Media enthusiast, this is probably something that you'll want to get a hold of. Not only does it shine a rather detailed light on Klout, it provides solid philosophical contexts for the development of the field, and the seemingly "unfair elitism" which comes with it. This just came out a few months ago, so is likely to be in your local brick-and-mortar book vendor, and the on-line big boys have it at nearly 40% off of cover. I really enjoyed this one, and felt that I learned a lot, but the combination of social media and marketing put it one of my "sweet spots", so, in the classic quip of Dennis Miller: *"your mileage may vary"* if these aren't "your things".

Notes:

1. http://btripp-books.livejournal.com/132936.html

2-5. http://amzn.to/1LET8B0

Wednesday, July 11, 2012[1]

The Transmedia Process ...

This is another book that came to my attention via an event put on by the folks at BIGfrontier[2] (who had previously brought in Mark W. Schaefer to talk about his Return On Influence[3]). In this case, I thought ahead to contact the publisher in time to get a review copy, read it, and get the review out before going to the talk (just barely, it's tomorrow morning!). Anyway, that's how I ended up reading Andrea Phillips' A Creator's Guide to Transmedia Storytelling: How to Captivate and Engage Audiences across Multiple Platforms[4].

Frankly, I wasn't too sure what to expect with this. My own experience is tied into the publishing world, and very much colored by my previous work with a Second Life developer, and a long-term project involving WireWax interactive video. While I'd been *aware* of "external bits" of some TV shows and movies (like the web site for the paper company where the bad guy in *Heroes* worked, or the S.H.I.E.L.D. "recruiting site" that accompanied one of the Marvel movies), I'd never been enough of a fan to spend a lot of time chasing after these leads. I've also never been a "gamer" (although I have become a bit more familiar with the genre via my elder daughter's enthusiasm for the assorted "Arkham" Batman games), and this seems to be the main background of Ms. Phillips ... so there was something of a disconnect for me there.

However, A Creator's Guide to Transmedia Storytelling[5] does make an effort to be an encompassing over-view of what's come to be called "Transmedia" (a term that I can't quite disassociate with Genesis P-Orridge's mid-'90s project). The book, which is laid out in a landscape orientation, is divided in five fairly even sections, "Introduction to Transmedia", "Storytelling", "Structure", "Production", and "The Big Picture" which walk the reader through the process, touching on many media and scales.

Much of the take-away (for me, at least) here is that the "industry" of Transmedia Storytelling is only in its infancy, because it still is unable to get a substantial audience. This creates a dual threat to its viability, the big well-funded programs for movies and such are tied to beancounters' determination of ROI, and boot-strapped small productions are having to fight for every set of eyes. One point came up here which I've seen time and again in books on "new marketing" and Social Media – that the currency of today's (and certainly tomorrow's) market is *attention* ... people only have so many hours to dole out across an ever-increasing universe of information and entertainment entities that *need* attention to survive. Phillips has an interesting graphic illustrating the challenge here, based on the classic 80/20 rule (that 80% of whatever you're measuring comes from 20% of the things measured), and in this case 80% of "your audience" is passive, and might only be peripherally aware of what you're doing, 15% are "engaged" with your project (to whatever extent) and only 5% are "super fans" who *really care* what you're doing. All through the book are cautionary tales of top-tier producers who still have to keep their day jobs, and corporate projects that unceremoniously get cut, leaving their Transmedia talent pool suddenly on the street (this was an all-too-common happening in Second Life, where massively popular builds were suddenly closed because of some line-item decision on a marketing budget at a sponsoring corporation!).

Despite this, Phillips goes back to basics, theater, fiction, the roots of storytelling, even using *Romeo & Juliet* as a case study for what might be possible in various types of Transmedia narratives. She looks at how different media use different methods for pointing out what is important or not important for the continuing story, and shows how not conforming to certain patterns is likely to confuse the audience, leading to a loss of interest. Of course, in games and other open-ended digital forms, the possibility for "clues" is nearly endless:

> *This is a form that delights in hiding information in the subtlest, tiniest ways: Mysterious film credits and Morse code in the background of an audio file. Hidden links in source code. Significant clues left out of focus in the background of a photograph, which is only one of many photographs in a Flickr stream.*

Unless you're doing a game where the "coded stuff" lights up to show you to interact with it, what can you do to keep the story going? I know that I've been *very* frustrated by video games (one of the main reasons I'm not tempted to play them) because all the stuff I want to check out is either a place the character can't get to, or isn't coded to be interactive (what *is* in those file drawers???).

One of the advantages, however, with only having 5% of your audience hyper-involved in your project, is that it makes it, assuming you can identify *those* users, much more efficient for getting out "special" materials. One item pictured in the book is a "scent chest" that was developed for the *Game of Thrones* show (that had to be *painfully* expensive to produce), which was distributed to key bloggers in that fan universe, including materials that would prove to be key bits of information in the Transmedia aspects of that program. Obviously, the major studios can afford this, or major Facebook ad campaigns (for the Marvel projects), but the small guys have to try harder with low-cost or free vehicles. One thing that's mentioned here, in various permutations, are a series of Twitter projects. I was surprised to read this, as I've spent a *vast* amount of time on Twitter over the past five years, and these never came to my attention ... clearly illustrating the difficulty in reaching outside of that 20% that's engaged, or perhaps even the 5% that's enthusiastic!

Over-all <u>A Creator's Guide to Transmedia Storytelling</u>[6] was a very informative read, and if one was a web developer/designer, a writer, a film buff, or a gamer, this would be an excellent guide to what Transmedia production is about, and what's promising and worrisome in the field. This has only been out a month or so at this point, so should be available at the larger brick-and-mortar book vendors. However, the on-line big boys have it at about a third off of cover.

I enjoyed reading this, and, obviously, was fascinated by how different my experiences had been from the other side of the field (I can think of several *book* projects that could easily fit into the author's definition of "Transmedia" productions ... including one I recently reviewed here: A Continual Feast[7] which is an "artifact" from Jan Karon's "Father Tim" books). If you have any interest in working on the cutting edge of media storytelling, you might find this book of great use.

Notes:

1. http://btripp-books.livejournal.com/133211.html
2. http://bigfrontier.org/
3. http://btripp-books.livejournal.com/132936.html
4-6. http://amzn.to/1LjgY3C
7. http://btripp-books.livejournal.com/131375.html

Thursday, August 23, 2012[1]

Rewiring the brain ...

For those following along at home, it's been *quite* a while since I've knocked out a book review. As noted elsewhere, one of my consulting projects has expanded to a full-time gig, and, being a start-up, "full time" has been running 12-18 hours a day!

I almost wrote a review for the current book a month or so back, but the cover (as you can see in the "double" pic, this came to me as an ARC - advance reading copy) asked to not run reviews before the on-sale date, which was earlier this week. This was one of the LibraryThing.com's "Early Reviewer" program books, and, instead of cranking out a review for the LT site, and *sitting* on it for a month, I put it aside, but figured out of the *dozen* books that have gone un-reviewed over the past month or so, I'd get this out first.

Anyway, the #1 take-away from Daniel Coyle's The Little Book of Talent: 52 Tips for Improving Your Skills[2] is that it is, indeed "little" ... of the 52 sections, only one (at 7) is longer than 4 pages, and many feature under a half-page of text (the shortest is a mere 3 lines). The book is structured in three thematic sections, "Getting Started", "Improving Skills", and "Sustaining Progress", plus interesting introductory material and appendix. Needless to say, it is rather a fast read.

Coyle had previously produced a book, *The Talent Code* which involved him traveling around the world researching places where talent and training came together to produce excellence:

> ... a new view is being established, one in which talent is determined far less by our genes and far more by our actions: specifically, the combination of intensive practice and motivation that produces brain growth.

As he visited these various schools, centers, etc., he kept jotting down notes that he felt would be useful at home, and that is the basics of what is in this book.

It's hard to summarize the book *in detail* as the material arises from such a wide spectrum of sources, but, in general, it follows a general theme expressed as: "Small actions, repeated over time, transform us." So, this goes from the very basics like "buy a notebook" or "end on a positive note" (that's the topic of the 3-line chapter), to fairly specific regimens like the one that recommends practicing something, taking a 10-minute break, practicing it again, taking another 10-minute break, and then practicing it again ... which the National Institutes of Health suggest is an optimal pattern for brain retention.

One thing that I found particularly fascinating was the appendix dealing with research into the Myelin sheathing in the nervous system:

> *Every time you perform a rep or a reach, your brain adds another layer of myelin to those particular wires. The more you practice, the more layers of myelin you earn, the faster and more accurately the signal travels, and the more skill you acquire.*

Also:

> *Action is vital. Myelin doesn't grow when you think about practicing. It grows when you actually practice – when you send electricity through your wires. ... Studies have linked practice to myelin growth and improved performance in such diverse skills as reading, vocabulary, music, and sports.*

Although one is very tempted to *assume* when encountering the number 52 that this book is set up for a weekly exercise, Coyle doesn't suggest that, and (as noted) some of these things are so basic (the notebook) that it's hard to imagine one *practicing* it for a week to get that particular tip set as a habit. But there is that structure that moves through definite stages. I found the utility of the things in here all over the board, from ones that I felt were brilliant to one that seemed a bit too "process" for general use. Overall, however, it's a very inspirational book, and I'm planning on getting a copy of its predecessor.

As The Little Book of Talent[3] has *just* hit the stores, you should be able to find it pretty much anywhere ... although its cover price is fairly steep for such a thin volume. The on-line big boys have it for a substantial chunk off of that, so you might want to consider ordering it if you want to save several bucks. I do recommend this highly, though, as the suggestions in it are likely to be helpful for anybody to improve on whatever they're attempting.

Notes:

1. http://btripp-books.livejournal.com/133409.html
2-3. http://amzn.to/1Ps3qa8

Saturday, August 25, 2012[1]

Two Sides to the Social Media Coin ...

Scott Stratten is one of those guys that I "know" from Twitter ... we've only briefly met, never talked on the phone, but I have had enough on-line exchanges with him that I don't consider myself a stranger. His previous book _Unmarketing_[2] is one of my favorites of the "social media genre", and I was excited to hear about his writing another. I contacted the good folks over at Wiley, and was sent an ARC of it. The book has an interesting design feature in having _two_ covers, with one part of the book reading in from the front and one part of the book reading in from the back. Since I'm not sure how this is going to work in the edition as released, I'm going with the Amazon graphic over there which shows both _parts_ of the book in one image.

One could describe Scott's previous book as a "philosophical approach" to social media marketing, which makes it the gem that it is (in that anybody can pick it up and get quality info from it). His new one The Book of Business Awesome: How Engaging Your Customers and Employees Can Make Your Business Thrive / The Book of Business UnAwesome: The Cost of Not Listening, Engaging, or Being Great at What You Do[3] is more an _application_ of its predecessor's philosophy to business settings, and is very much written to a business audience. This will no doubt mean that it will have a better reach into companies of various sizes, but at a cost of over-all accessibility (as there are a lot of people enthusiastic about social media who really couldn't care less about its use by business, as long as they're not getting spammed).

Again, this is structured as _two_ books, one about people "doing it right" and another about people "doing it wrong", and is largely built around case studies of these. If you've heard Scott speak, or follow his blog, some of these will be quite familiar (so familiar that in one case I thought he was repeating from _Unmarketing_), but they're all interesting and informative. Most of the chapters feature an example, and then some lessons to take from that. Here's one from Scott's experience at a Phoenix Suns game:

> ... This is where most customers sit, in the static mode. They are just there, not overly pleased, not overly angry. They just exist. Letting them sit there is the wrong mentality for brands to take. We shouldn't be looking at how many customers we have but at how many ecstatic customers we have. Static customers come and go very easily, not angry enough to tell you why they're upset – and not happy enough to have any loyalty. When we do things to shift them into being ecstatic, loyalty increases. Ecstatic customers are also more willing

> to tell you when they become upset, giving you an opportunity to keep them from leaving. Instead of a revolving door of static customers, create ecstatic ones and they'll bring people in the door for you.

There are a few bits here which I did not much care for ... in three or four sections he, essentially, "hands the mic over" to somebody else, with reprints of other people's looks at similar material ... these "break the flow" of the book, and make, at times, a radical shift in tone, without adding enough to justify their inclusion. I'm sure the author felt that these "were covered so well" in the included pieces that it was better to insert them than to paraphrase and otherwise spin them out in his style, but in nearly every case it felt like having to take a detour on the highway (especially the *eight pages* about a haunted house's web site).

Not everything here is based on case studies, Scott also goes off on a tangent or two, most notably on public speaking (which, of course, he does quite a lot of). I'd even suggested to him that he take the truly remarkable "Thirty Tips for Speakers" and make a promo piece out of it, only to discover that he'd already spun it off as an article on some other web site.

Obviously, there are two ways to approach this, either starting with "Awesome" (which I did, since that was where the copyright, etc. info was, so seemed more "the front"), or "UnAwesome" ... and I suspect the reading experience is somewhat different depending on which end of the book you start out. The "UnAwesome" side is certainly a more, uh, *visceral* ride, with various levels of horror, *Schadenfreude*, and slapstick all weaving themselves in with the telling of companies and people who simply "were doing it wrong". These go from the various abuses of Facebook (from invitations to events that you are thousands of miles away from to Zynga spam), to abuses of corporate/HR attempts at micro-managing social media, to idiotic misuses of QR codes (billboards on the highway or mail on the phone).

Speaking of QR codes, there are quite a few in the book, offering more info at the end of many chapters. I wish I could tell you what is on the other side of those, but most of the ones in the ARC lead off to a video that Scott made indicating that those were going to be put in right before the book went to press, so as to have as up-to-date info as possible in them. There are some, however, which go off to other videos and stuff ... which I *was* able to watch. I've been hard on books previously that included QR or MS-Tag codes (especially before *I* got a smart phone), but I think the penetration of the technology needed to read them has gotten to the point where it's useable ... and at least here most of the codes are accompanied by text versions of the URL.

While I don't feel that The Book of Business Awesome / UnAwesome[4] is quite the classic that its predecessor was, it certainly is an entertaining, informative, and highly worthwhile read. This just officially came out a week or so back, so it should definitely be available via your local brick-and-mortar book vendor carrying business books, but (as usual) the on-line guys have it at a deep discount. There's a certain guilty voyeuristic glee in reading this (especially on the "UnAwesome" side) that should amuse anybody with an interest in the Social Media sphere, so I guess you really wouldn't *have* to "be in business" to enjoy it.

Notes:

1. http://btripp-books.livejournal.com/133717.html
2. http://btripp-books.livejournal.com/101421.html
3-4. http://amzn.to/1RQGSy8

Sunday, August 26, 2012[1]

Not the book I would have liked it to be ...

Sometimes a book might *sound* like a good idea, but isn't, and sometimes a book was never even intended for publication, but get published. Jeanne de Salzmann's The Reality of Being: The Fourth Way of Gurdjieff[2] appears to be one of these sorts of books.

As regular readers of this space will not doubt recognize, I have plowed through quite a lot of the Gurdjieff and other "Fourth Way" material, and, being interested in this line of study, I'm always keeping an eye out for books I've not previously encountered in it. When I read of Madame de Salzmann's book, I was, understandably, quite enthusiastic about getting a copy, as she had been the student to whom Gurdjieff had passed along responsibility for the teachings, even "forbidding" her to die prior to reaching the age of 100 (she lived to 101). Her background had been in music, and became a dancer and then teacher with Dalcroze's school, where she met her husband, Alexandre de Salzmann, an artist and theatrical production designer. Both of the de Salzmanns became students of Gurdjieff, and she was instrumental in the presentation of the "movements" from the Work.

However, The Reality of Being[3] is not so much a book *about* the Gurdjieff work (as I had hoped it would be), but a collection of Madame de Salzmann's journal entries on her *practice* of the Work. I had brought up the topic of the book one time when I was visiting the Chicago Gurdjieff center, and was told that it was materials that really *hadn't* been intended for publication, but that, with the passing of her son, the estate had moved down a generation, and a decision had been made to make use of these writings as a book, some 20 years after her death.

Needless to say, my *first* reaction to hearing "this material was never intended for publication", was to be quite excited about the prospect of getting "inner teachings" or some other sort of long-secret scuttlebutt about the dynamics of the Gurdjieff group. However, this was not the case, instead, this is very personal, and quite specific, reflections of *one person* (albeit as closely connected to the source of the material as one could hope to find) on their experience with putting these teachings to use in her own life.

In an age where people keep their journals out in public where anybody with an internet connection can delve into their inner life, it's hard to reach a level of *shame* for this sort of voyeuristic engagement, but I frequently felt uncomfortable in the way one might having randomly encountered somebody's diary, and set to reading it.

Also, the writing is very reflective, it's *not* written to address an outer audience, but is constantly Madame de Salzmann's inner dialog being set to paper. As such, it has very little *flow* or structure to it, beyond the fact that there are 140 entries assembled according to "theme" into 12 non-chronological sections by "a small group of her family and followers".

Now, I don't want to say that the book is *useless*, as there are some truly remarkable insights floating around in its pages, and I do suspect that a more "touchy-feely" reader would delight in immersion in the author's inner dialog, but what can you, practically, do with:

> *When I become aware of the movement of breathing in and redistributing this fine material in me, I realize that I can, by my attitude, allow it to take shape according to pathways and centers of gravity particular to it. I become sensitive to feeling this attitude, and in practicing this I see that a very close relation is created between my body and this fine material. I can feel this substance of "I" in the body. It is of another order. But for now it is without its own force, powerless, without material. I need to have a more lasting awareness of it as at totality. Later, crystallized, it will have power over my manifestations.*

... I could have picked any paragraph, and it wouldn't be much more, or less, dense, cryptic (or, inner-experience specific), or amorphous that this ... and that's the case for virtually *all* of its 300 pages.

I'm usually a reasonably fast reader, but this book took me over 3 months to plow through. Despite being fairly well versed on Gurdjieff's teachings, I was unable to get any traction here, because it was like climbing down a ladder into de Salzmann's head and being swept along with her thoughts, feelings, and efforts in trying to achieve these aims that were left to her.

Again, I'm sure there are a lot of people who the idea of immersion in the inner working of Jeanne de Salzmann's mind would be a wonderful experience, so "your mileage may vary". I ended up with a modicum of bookmarks sticking up out of the top of my copy, so there were things in there which I found enticing enough to want to go back and see what I could extract from them ... but there's no "teaching" here, just peeping into the inner workings of one of Gurdjieff's primary students.

The Reality of Being[4] has been out a couple of years at this point, but is put out by Shambhala, so probably hasn't disappeared from the brick-and-mortar stores, and, of course, the on-line guys have it (and currently at about a third off of cover price). This was a real chore for me to get through, but I do feel that I got worthwhile insights from it, but it might be something you'd enjoy more.

Notes:

1. http://btripp-books.livejournal.com/133926.html

2-4. http://amzn.to/1LjffeF

Thursday, August 30, 2012[1]

An interesting half a book ...

This was another of the LibraryThing.com "Early Reviewer" program books ... although, I must admit, this is closer to something that I might have actually picked up to read than what I typically end up with from that program (you can get the details of LTER here[2]). Michelle Boule's Mob Rule Learning: Camps, Unconferences, and Trashing the Talking Head[3] is, as one might gather from the title/subtitle, about new modes of learning and information exchange, ranging across a spectrum of formats, approaches, and philosophies (I was amused to find that she'd name-checked the Ignite seminars here, as I was reading this the same week as I was doing a presentation at Ignite Chicago[4]).

I was very interested to get into this book, as I have, aside from Ignite, attended or followed assorted "alternative" conferences over the years, and the first half of the book did not disappoint. However, this is very much *two* books, one that follows pretty close to the sub-title, and one that veers off into what one might describe as "educational philosophy". The shift is quite abrupt, and where I was quite engaged with the material in the first half, I was not so much in the second part. Having been in the publishing biz, I had to wonder if Ms. Boule was shopping around a hundred-page topical look at trendy conference formats, and was told that she needed to come up with something additional (I did this with one of my authors as a prerequisite for considering his book)... resulting in the second half, looking at school applications.

Anyway ... the first part focuses on "camps and unconferences", terms that the author opts to use interchangeably, which she defines as being *"exemplified by (a) distinct lack of structure"*. Much of the concept behind these comes from the theory of OST – Open Space Technology (where "technology" is used in the anthropological sense of *"anything that changes the way a society behaves, constructs, or is structured"*), dating back to the early 1980's.

> OST is a belief system that has changed the way some people approach meetings of all kinds. It hinges on the belief that a group of people, given a purpose and freedom, have the ability to self-govern, self-organize, and produce results. A meeting or conference using OST will have little or no agenda, no predetermined out-comes, and no predetermined leaders. Individuals gather together with an idea and then are set free. This freedom can often produce unexpected and wonderful results.

> ...
>
> *There are four rules of principles that govern OST gatherings. These rules are not meant to bind, but to set free. These four principles are:*
>
> *1. Whoever comes is the right people.*
>
> *2. Whatever happens is the only thing that could have.*
>
> *3. When it starts is the right time.*
>
> *4. When it's over, it's over.*

Obviously, there is a lot of potential chaos in this ... chaos that is *highly unappealing* to many traditionally-structured organizations, and how these sorts of dynamics can be infused into those types of structures in a significant theme here. Several situations are discussed where, for instance, "unconferences" were run before the start of an official associations meeting to get a different level of involvement rolling before the (as she refers to it) "Talking Head" part began, or how these were used in situations where there was no time to organize something more formal (as one can surmise from the four "rules" above, this model can be rather spontaneously held).

Perhaps the most *useful* part of Mob Rule Learning[5] is the almost step-by-step (if one can have that for something so loosely structured!) description of how these would work in theory, along with numerous examples of ground-breaking camps and unconferences. I don't think it would be an exaggeration to say that if one read carefully through the first half of this book, took good notes, met with a handful of co-organizers, one could reasonably expect to be able to set up a successful "unconference" in a matter of days. However, trying to implement these modalities within the context of a large corporation or association might be a very uncomfortable process.

Speaking of uncomfortable ... there's the second half of the book, where the author takes the broadest theoretical strokes of the first part, and turns her focus to the *classroom*. This felt a bit like a "bait-and-switch", to me, although I've certainly read other "future of education" books (the better bits here reminded me of Larry D. Rosen, Ph.D's Rewired: Understanding the iGeneration and the Way They Learn[6]), and am not *uninterested* in the topic ... it just seemed like "oops, said all I can say about *that*, how to fill up another hundred pages?" here! Unfortunately, if one isn't a *teacher*, the second half of the book is very hard to get, it's full of stuff about classroom approaches, heavily laced with context-specific acronyms (that I had to keep looking up to figure what the heck she was talking about), and seems to be primarily based on her own college experiences (and, as opposed to the case studies in the first half, many of the "examples" she looks at here have long since been discontinued by the institutions offering them).

Fortunately, the first half of this is pretty much worth picking it up (and, of course, if you're a *teacher*, you'll no doubt find the second half of interest). It's been out since last fall, so you may or may not be able to find it in the brick-and-mortar stores, but the on-line big boys have it, and at a bit under the cover price. Obviously, from all the above, this isn't something that I'd recommend "for all and sundry", but if you're interested in the "unconference" movement, or are a teacher looking to move your classes into a new model of education, this should be something you consider finding.

Notes:
1. http://btripp-books.livejournal.com/134353.html
2. http://www.librarything.com/er/list
3. http://amzn.to/1hMuQZs
4. http://ignitechi.org/
5. http://amzn.to/1hMuQZs
6. http://btripp-books.livejournal.com/96964.html

Friday, August 31, 2012[1]

Exploring the darkness behind 9/11

This was another of those occasional dollar store finds. Unlike some others, this did not scream out the question "why is this here?", as it is a rather niche book ... but a fascinating one. Penned by two journalists, Yosri Fouda, an investigative reporter from *Al-Jazeera*, and Nick Fielding, who's with the London *Sunday Times*, Masterminds of Terror: The Truth Behind the Most Devastating Terrorist Attack the World Has Ever Seen[2] takes a ride through the festering underworld of Islamic extremists. Fouda, of course, was the key to this access, being a Muslim employed by an Arab TV network. A mere seven months after the 9/11 attacks, he had been contacted, at the new London offices of *Al-Jazeera*, by a member of the cabal responsible for those atrocities. It turns out that Fouda had done coverage on his show that al-Qaeda leadership felt was "balanced", and they reached out to him as a way of furthering their message. In fact, following the initial vague phone calls was a highly-detailed 3-page fax, outline what they *wanted* him to do for a follow-up report (on the anniversary of the the attacks).

Fouda was a bit shaken by this, but followed up with the contacts, and was invited to come to Pakistan for his research.

> From now on it was all going to be about survival. Getting back home in one piece was his main concern. If he got a reasonable story on the back of the trip, that would only be a bonus.

Although it isn't specifically split out, one assumes that the "research" parts here are from Fielding, and the "narrative" parts (as well as materials leading to the research) are from Fouda. The book swings back and forth from uncomfortable descriptions of Fouda's time among these most notorious of terrorists, and in-depth looks at the background of various "main players".

Obviously, by this point, the "foot soldiers" of 9/11 were long since dead, but the book digs as deep as possible into their backgrounds, with particular attention paid to Mohammad Atta, from his youth in Egypt, his school years in Hamburg, and the shadowy path into the heart of al-Qaeda. It is chilling to see how little, even with a middle-class upbringing in a major urban setting, and a technical education in Western colleges, Western values effected Atta. He was cold to the entire culture from the start, and only became more hateful as he mixed with the outer fringes of Islamic extremism.

However, by the time Fouda was contacted, Atta was gone, and the main focus of the book is on the activities of Khalid Shaikh Mohammed and Ramzi Binalshibh, two of the main *planners* of the attacks, and their circles of influence. Again, it is disturbing how hostile these people are to the West, totally taken up with a mythology of the time of Mohammed, and the periods of past Islamic conquest.

> The 'Hypocrites', as the half-hearted supporters of Islam were called, had long been a thorn in the side of the Muslims. It is a moving and commanding section of the Koran and Ramzi was entranced by it. In a fearful, shaken but beautiful voice, Ramzi wept as he went on reciting more of the same surah:
>
>> Lo! Allah hath bought from the believers their lives and their wealth because the Garden will be theirs: they shall fight in the way of Allah and shall slay and be slain, It is a promise which is binding on Him in the Torah and the Gospel and the Koran. Who fulfilleth His covenants better than Allah? Rejoice then in your bargain that ye have made, for that is the supreme triumph.
>> (Surah 9, Verse 111)
>
> It was this very surah, it has since become known, that the hijackers were instructed to recite as they carried out the hijackings on 11 September ...
>
> ...
>
> Irresistibly, this period in the history of Islam has a unique flavor of magnetic nostalgia: its own aroma, rituals, myths, visions, metaphysics, and even its own vocabulary. People are rigidly divided, according to this way of thinking, into believers and disbelievers, and hypocrites. No one can have a personal philosophy, for there is no such thing as philosophy.

Needless to say, this is somewhat bizarre to the Western eye, as though a substantial sub-set of Christianity was still trying to live as the romantic vision of knights, combat and all. Interestingly, this form of Islam, is described as "almost heretical" in its reliance on dreams, visions, and borrowings from the time of Mohammed.

Masterminds of Terror[3] attempts to trace an intentionally murky web of connections across several continents and years of development, and does a very respectable job of this. The authors should be congratulated for their efforts here, as not only was this *dangerous*, but certainly frustrating. Fouda was faced not only by a violent, secretive, and unpredictable organization, but one that appears to have been facing internal divisions, as there was a constant back-and-forth regarding a set of video tapes that he had been initially supposed to have been provided – that ended up being repeatedly made unavailable as different power centers in al-Qaeda influenced control.

This is a fascinating look at the "other side" in that tumultuous first year following the 9/11 attacks. It's not a particularly *pleasant* read, being a view into a world that would wipe out our way of life and replace it with a brutal medieval theocracy, but sketches a perspective into a blood-thirsty subculture that few other books that I've encountered provide. It appears to be out-of-print currently, but the new/used guys at the on-line vendors have both hardcover and paperback versions available for as little as a penny (plus shipping). If you have an interest in trying to make sense of September 11, this, while uncomfortable, is quite a unique resource.

Notes:

1. http://btripp-books.livejournal.com/134497.html

2-3. http://amzn.to/1LjdJcB

Saturday, September 1, 2012[1]

The commercial conversation ...

I'd seen this one recommended various places on the web, as well as being continually featured in the WordOfMouth.org newsletter (the author runs that group, which is not to be confused with WOMMA[2], which he used to head), and decided to request a copy from the good folks at Greenleaf Press. Just in case you didn't recognize his name, Andy Sernovitz pulled in some "big guns" for the Foreword and Afterword of Word of Mouth Marketing: How Smart Companies Get People Talking[3], with Seth Godin and Guy Kawasaki providing those sections, respectively.

This book is both practical and theoretical, setting up frameworks for *thinking* about WoM, and then providing tools to put it into action. It's a bit of a "firehose", with material coming fast at the reader, but not necessarily in depth. There's a lot of "this is what it is, and this is how you do it". Physically, the book is noteworthy, from the rounded-off outer corners, to the "taped up paper bag" look of the outside, and the taped, paperclipped, and coffee-stained conceits on the internal design, which add up to a rather distinctive reading experience.

I've been trying to figure out a good way to summarize the information here, but its structure makes this difficult, so I think I'm going to highlight some particulars, and leave it up to you to get a copy and fill in the details:

> The Four Rules of Word of Mouth Marketing
> Rule #1: Be Interesting
> Rule #2: Make It Easy
> Rule #3: Make People Happy
> Rule #4: Earn Trust and Respect
> ...
> The Three Reasons People Talk About You
> Reason #1: You – They Like You and Your Stuff
> Reason #2: Me – Talking Makes Me Feel Good
> Reason #3: Us – We Feel Connected to the Group

In this latter section there's an interesting addendum on "how to *stop* Word of Mouth", with three no-no's: "Prizes and Rewards" (I recently had to "go to the mat" with a client to fight against inflating a "fun facts" quiz into a full-fledged "knowledge" contest in their niche), "Overexposure", and "Forgetting Why People Talk About You" (the case study they used was Krispy Kreme when their donuts were everywhere at retail, and no longer just hot and gooey off the line).

The Five Ts of Word of Mouth Marketing
1. *Talkers – Find People Who Will Talk About You*
2. *Topics – Give People a Reason to Talk*
3. *Tools – Help the Message Spread Faster and Father*
4. *Taking Part – Join the Conversation*
5. *Tracking – Measure and Understand What People Are Saying*

There's also a bit about *ethics* here as well ... obviously, "word of mouth" can be interpreted (in its non-marketing version) as *gossip*, which can be quite nasty. There is a two-page ethics checklist, and this set of rules:

The Rules of Honest Word of Mouth Marketing
1. *Word of mouth isn't stealth.*
2. *Fake word of mouth doesn't work.*
3. *Oppose all deception.*
4. *Follow the Honesty ROI.*
   - *Honesty of Relationship.*
   - *Honesty of Opinion.*
   - *Honesty of Identity.*

Sernovitz makes a very good case that WoM is the best marketing, but because in the days before Twitter, Facebook, etc., it was very hard to measure this, plus:

> ... word of mouth usually doesn't cost anything. If we don't have a budget for it and we don't have staff assigned to it, we usually forget to add it to our reports about sources of new customers. On top of that, it screws with our spreadsheets, because you can't write a formula to figure the return on a zero-cost word of mouth campaign. So most of us skip it.

In the introductory material there's a section recommending how the reader should approach the book, including taking time to "think about the philosophy" in the "Deep Stuff" section, which presents:

Six Big Ideas
1. *Consumers Are in Control – Get Used to It*
2. *Marketing Is What You Do, NOT What You Say*
3. *The Permanent Record*
4. *Honesty Is the Essence of Word of Mouth*
5. *The Math of Customer Satisfaction*
6. *Word of Mouth Marketing Makes More Money*

That, along with a 13-point Manifesto, takes us up to the half-way point, where defining WoM gives way to sketching out *how to do it*. This is rather dense with lists, sample forms, worksheets, and nuggets of wisdom relating back to all the preceding "theory". While not exactly being a graduate school course on the subject, it does walk the reader through a plan of action, which should be implementable in most companies and organizations. There are key points that stand out, such as *"Start asking, "Would anyone tell a friend about this?" in every meeting, in every department. If you don't get a resounding "Yes!" then you need to add something."* and *"You need the pass-in-the-hall test."* where the topic should be formatted as simply as *"You should try X, it's Y."*

Additionally, Word of Mouth Marketing[4] looks at B2B WoM, dealing with *negative* WoM, and how to track the WoM you're generating. The book closes with a list of 16 "sure thing" WoM techniques, and an 8-point "action plan" (there are also downloadable versions of all these on the book's companion web site). This edition (they don't really mention that this is a "second edition" except in the course of a "note to the reader", talking about what's new in it) just came out this year, so it is likely to be available via your local book vendor, but the big on-line guys have it at about a third off of its (very reasonable) cover price. Obviously, this is not a book for "all and sundry", but if you do have an interest in marketing, and new communications platforms, this is a great introduction/manual for the topic.

Notes:

1. http://btripp-books.livejournal.com/134737.html
2. http://womma.org/
3-4. http://amzn.to/1khnOxV

Tuesday, September 4, 2012[1]

Once upon a time ...

This was another of those pleasant dollar store finds ... a nice National Geographic book, full of pretty pictures, for a buck. Now, as regular readers know, I'm a sucker for almost anything with an archaeological spin, and there, on the back cover, was a real sweet winter shot of the "Cliff Palace" ruins at Mesa Verde ... so there was no way that I *wasn't* tossing a copy of this into my cart!

I must admit, however, that Robert Fisher's America A.D. 1000: The Land and the Legends[2] would not have been very high on my to-read list if not for that. This is a "story" format anthropological work, with content aimed at (what I would guess to be) a high school interest level, that takes a "day in the life" look at individuals from five Native American cultural groups ... arctic, eastern woodlands, great plains, Pacific northwest, and the canyon lands of the southwest ... across North America at approximately 1000 AD.

Each section paints a word-picture of one tribal member and uses that to present a wide spectrum of data in a story format, creating a somewhat forced (some of the details are clearly "shoehorned" in to provide "educational" value about specifics of the culture) narrative of that group. Of course, there are pages and pages of photography, but not many "archaeological artifacts" (maybe a half a dozen), most of the focus being on "nature" shots, landscapes, animals, etc. There are several very interesting "historical" photos here as well, but I think they went sparingly with those in order to not suggest that the early photographic images were realistically representative of the tribes' appearances 8-9 centuries before photography. In addition, there are quite a number of illustrations of various activities, from a market day in Chaco Canyon, to an aerial depiction of the Etowa site in its prime, and to a 3/4th submerged image of a whale being brought back from the hunt.

In "People of the Aurora" we are presented with the story of an Inuit seal hunter. At first this covers the hunt for a seal, but then spins out to describe other hunts, from whales, to bears, to caribou, and even birds. In each case the technology (as far as we know it) is described, the sorts of tools and weapons used, etc. This then switches to the culture itself, with "daily activities", how the community is laid out and what sort of houses there are, etc., and eventually to the religious beliefs of the people.

In "People of the Fire" we are presented with a little girl from the Mississippian culture at Cahokia. The story presents cultural elements from her perspective, and things here, because of this, sort of "spill out" of the narrative into details that she would have been unlikely to have either known or been particularly interested in ... resulting in this being a bit more "cinematographic", making her surroundings more the feature than the girl herself.

The author manages to get in politics, commerce, agriculture, religion, science, etc. in the telling of the little girl's meanderings around the city.

In "People of the Bufflao" we are presented with a Hidatsa grandmother. Here the main character is generally reminiscing about various elements of her life, which allows Fisher to insert the same broad swath of info about the culture. An interesting, but odd, addition here are paintings by George Caitlin, who visited with the Hidatsa in the 1830's ... which at least implies that what he painted then was representative of how the characters lived nearly a millennium before.

In "People of the Rugged Coast" we are presented with a Makah shaman. Now, one would hope that this would be focused on the spiritual/religious aspects of the culture, but it really (again) just provides a pair of eyes of somebody who would be "out and about" through the village. There are perhaps a bit more elements here of magic (like how a whaler's wife is doing sympathetic magic emulating the whale at home while her husband is off on the hunt), but these also fall into the "how do we know that?" realm, as cultural details like that are hard to extrapolate from data so far removed in time.

Finally, in "People of the Canyon" we are presented with an Anasazi astronomer. This attracted my attention both for being about sites that I've visited, and "technologies" that I've read about. The character here is an astronomer responsible for monitoring the movements of light "daggers" across carved glyphs, but his main function seems to be a discussion of how the culture expresses itself across the calendar.

Again, America A.D. 1000[3] is very much a "picture book", full of great photography, that, generally speaking, only has a peripheral connection with the text. While quite a lot of cultural detail is presented, it comes through as a narrative, so is not very specific, although I suppose (in cases like how a doll is made, or a harpoon barbed) the details are drawn from artifacts from these cultures. Of course, this isn't about in-depth analysis of artifacts, but (having read quite a lot of material that is), I found the "story" format a bit less than engaging ... however, I figure that my 14-year-old self would have liked this quite a lot.

I'm not sure if this is out of print or not ... Amazon doesn't have it, except via the new/used guys, but B&N does have it "at retail" ... yet I wasn't able to dig it up over on the National Geographic site. In any case, the new/used guys have "good" copies (and I wonder how beat up a heavy-photo-paper hardcover gets – my copy from the dollar store would have rated "like new") for as little as a penny, plus shipping, which is probably your best deal unless you stumble over it like I did. Again, I'd say this would be great for a middle-school kid, less so for folks who've read a lot on the topic.

Notes:
1. http://btripp-books.livejournal.com/135164.html
2-4. http://amzn.to/1LiSCXT

Thursday, September 6, 2012[1]

I dropped the good brain, Master ...

As I have previously noted, one of the functions that the dollar store's book section has in my life (aside for being a source of $1 books, of course) is seeding in the random, serendipitous, bits of reading that I would be *highly* unlikely to actually seek out. This is certainly in that class.

The author, A.J. Jacobs, is an editor-at-large for *Esquire* magazine, and writes for several other established bastions of old media. He is, however, possibly better known for his extreme "experimental" book projects, including *The Year of Living Biblically* where he journaled his attempted to delve into *all* the myriad restrictions on behavior found in the Bible, and *The Know-It-All*, which tracked his cover-to-cover reading of *Encyclopedia Brittanica*. Obviously, The Guinea Pig Diaries: My Life as an Experiment[2] is in this vein, albeit in more "bite-sized" pieces. The book covers nine "experiments" which run from on-going runs of a particular sort of research, to behavioral challenges, to trying to break through personal boundaries. Since these are, for the most part, free-standing on their own, I guess I'll just give a synopsis of each:

"My Life as a Beautiful Woman" - In this, he is trying to set up his kids' very attractive nanny. He convinces her to try on on-line date service, and works with her to set up a basic profile, but then he *takes over running it*, fielding all the traffic, trying to act as he would assume the nanny might, and occasionally presenting her with a filtered list of "approved" suitors. In this he presents a rather (for a guy) unsettling view of how most of our camp looks in these situations. After a few less-than-stellar dates, the nanny opts out of the experiment leaving him with mixed feelings about the whole thing.

"My Outsourced Life" - Here he takes on not just one, but *two* "personal assistants" from India to help him with various projects. If you're like me, you've *read* about using these services but have never quite been able to figure out how to make that work enough to justify the not-insignificant expense. He uses them in some predictable ways, like asking questions about his cell phone bill, or finding a hard-to-find toy for his kids, and also some industry-specific manners (he has them respond to a source of frequent, yet inappropriate for *Esquire*, news releases with what he describes as *"the best rejection notice in journalism history"*). However, this then progresses into making his regular weekend call to his parents, apologizing to his wife (!), and even reading a bedtime story to his son. The piece ends with him getting bored with the project, and outsourcing the end of it to them as well (although he did say he kept one on a $10/month retainer on-going if needed)!

"I Think You're Fat" - In pursuing a piece for the magazine about a group called "Radical Honesty", he gets hooked into actually *trying* it ... just saying whatever he *actually* thinks of things, people, etc. ... pretty much to the point of expressing every random thought that floats through his head (including telling Rachel Ray that he'd just tried to look down her shirt). Needless to say, this does not go well on a lot of levels.

"240 Minutes of Fame" - It appears that Jacobs looks a bit like the actor Noah Taylor (who was briefly a hot item following the release of the movie *Shine*), who was skipping the Academy Awards, and the editors at *Entertainment Weekly* wanted to get an "inside view" piece and convinced him to attend *as* the actor. He chats up stars, *does interviews*, signs autographs, and is pretty much in a "celebrity whirl" until he runs into Taylor's co-star Geoffrey Rush, who, as one would expect, *does* realize that this is not the actor (although Rush opts to just fade into the crowd rather than making a scene and calling security). Obviously, Jacobs gets quite an exposure to what fame feels like ... and he even got a call from Taylor's agent after the fact saying that he'd been *thrilled* to have "been there" without having to actually attend!

"The Rationality Project" - This one is a whole lot like a condensation of a dozen or so "brain science" books, where he's trying to avoid any of a dozen or so "logical fallacies" which leaves him acting a good deal like Star Trek's Spock, much, of course, to the irritation of all those around him.

"The Truth About Nakedness" - At *Esquire* he's trying to get actress Mary-Louise Parker to write a piece about what it feels like to pose naked. His editors insist that he convince her to, yes, pose naked for the article. She agrees, but with one caveat: he needs to pose nude as well, and she gets to pick which shot goes in the article. He goes along with it, and deals with all his inner turmoil around the experience.

"What Would George Washington Do?" - A factoid that had seemingly slipped my social studies and history education was that George Washington had a list of rules of behavior (originally presented by a 16th century Jesuit, so you know they're not *"hard and beer, in the clear"* sorts of adages) that he lived by ... *110 rules* ... and (much like his former Biblical adventure), Jacobs tries to live according to them for a number of weeks.

"The Unitasker" - OK, I've seen the cognitive theorists too, all saying that multi-tasking is bad ... and here is the author's experiment with only doing one thing at a time (better him than me!). He tries blindfolding himself when on the phone, taking meditation classes, convincing his wife that they can have dinner without the TV *or conversation*, and various other approaches, without a great deal of success. He finishes the piece on a manual typewriter.

"Whipped" - In what his wife describes as his *"best experiment in, well, ever"*, he spends a month doing exactly what she wants him to do ... from extensive lists of household chores to agreeing with her on everything, to increasingly extreme requests. She even gets to write the follow-up.

Interestingly, for a book of this type, it has some very useful appendices, all *eight pages* of George Washington's rules, and six pages of various "cognitive biases" that played a part in "The Rationality Project". Kudos for their inclusion. Also interesting is that The Guinea Pig Diaries[3] appears to still be in print (despite being 3 years old and moving through the dollar store channel), with the on-line big boys having it in stock ... you can, however, get "like new" copies of the hardcover for as little as a penny (plus the inevitable $3.99 shipping) if you feel so inclined. I bought this a number of months ago, so it's probably no longer out there for a buck, but you might find it worth what the new/used vendors are getting for it.

Notes:

1. http://btripp-books.livejournal.com/135241.html

2-3. http://amzn.to/1PrsbDd

Friday, September 7, 2012[1]

Beauty and suffering ...

Yes, another of those charming little Dover Thrift Editions, which tells you that I was a buck or so short of getting to the free shipping on an order. Of course, I have tried to "kill two birds with one stone" when it comes to these, picking books that fill holes in my education, and, as I really didn't read any philosophy in college, adding some Nietzsche to my head seems like a good decision. This one, The Birth of Tragedy[2], was quite a pleasant surprise. I recall thinking while reading this *"Hey, this is the sort of thing that gives philosophy a good name!"* ... which does imply that I typically approach these sorts of books a bit the way the cliché kid would the proverbial spoonful of cod liver oil ... figuring it's going to be good for me, but not looking forward to the experience.

I don't know if this is a particularly engaging piece of Nietzsche's writing, or if the translator (Clifton P. Fadiman, in a 1927 publication) did an especially attractive job at rendering it into English (I know that I liked his versions of parts of it more than an on-line version[3] that I referred to in passing along bits of this to a friend), but I found the book a *delight* to read, and even bothered my elder daughter (who had the misfortune of being stuck waiting for buses with me while I was in the midst of this) with out-loud readings from it.

This is, primarily, Nietzsche looking at the arts, traced back to "Tragedy" in ancient Greece. He defines two polarities, the Apollonian (typified by restraint and control), and the Dionysian (typified by passion and the irrational), with much of this being contrasted with the state of the German culture in the 1870's. That culture is returned to frequently here (this even has a Foreword specifically addressed to the famed composer Richard Wagner), and, frankly, this was the *first* time that I "got" where the Nazis were inspired by Nietzsche.

There were a few passages that I found particularly notable, such as:

> ... The story of Prometheus is an original possession of the entire Aryan race, and is documentary evidence of its capacity for the profoundly tragic. Indeed, it is not entirely improbable that this myth has the same characteristic significance for the Aryan genius that the myth of the fall of man has for the Semitic, and that the two are related like brother and sister. The presupposition of the Promethean myth is the transcendent value which a naive humanity attaches to fire as the true palladium of every rising culture. That man, however, should not receive this fire only as a gift from heav-

> en, in the form of the igniting lightning or the warming sunshine, but should, on the contrary, be able to control it at will — this appeared to the reflective primitive man as sacrilege, as robbery of the divine nature. And thus the first philosophical problem at once causes a painful, irreconcilable antagonism between man and God, and puts as it were a mass of rock at the gate of every culture. The best and highest that men can acquire they must obtain by a crime, and then they must in turn endure its consequences, namely, the whole flood of sufferings and sorrows with which the offended divinities <u>must</u> requite the nobly aspiring race of man. It is a bitter thought, that, by the <u>dignity</u> it confers on crime, contrasts strangely with the Semitic myth of the fall of man, in which curiosity, deception, weakness in the face of temptation, wantonness,— in short, a whole series of preeminently feminine passions, — were regarded as the origin of evil. What distinguishes the Aryan conception is the sublime view of <u>active sin</u> as the essential Promethean virtue, and the discovery of the ethical basis of pessimistic tragedy in the <u>justification</u> of human evil — of human guilt as well as of the suffering incurred thereby. The pain implicit in the very structure of things — which the contemplative Aryan is not disposed to explain away — the antagonism in the heart of the world, manifests itself to him as a medley of different worlds, for instance, a Divine and a human world, both of which are in the right individually, but which, because they exist separately side by side, must suffer for that very individuation. In the heroic effort towards universality made by the individual, in his attempt to penetrate beyond the bounds of individuation and become himself the <u>one</u> world-being, he experiences in himself the primordial contradiction concealed in the essence of things, that is, he trespasses and he suffers. ...

Nietzsche goes into various cases of the Apollonian and Dionysian polarities, both in their Greek originals and in "degraded" examples from his current world, and eventually turns to Socrates as a pivot point, of the introduction of the "theoretical man" which appears in this telling to be the mark separating the ancient and modern world views. He describes what Socrates brought forth as an *illusion*

> ... This illusion consists in the imperturbable belief that, with the clue of logic, thinking can reach to the nethermost depths of being, and that thinking can not only perceive being but even modify it. This

> *sublime metaphysical illusion is added as an instinct to science and again and again leads the latter to its limits, where it must change into* art*...*

He then continues:

> *If we now look at Socrates in the light of this idea, he appears to us as the first who could not only live, but — what is far greater — also die by the guidance of this instinct of science: and hence the picture of the* dying Socrates*, as the man raised above the fear of death by knowledge and reason, is the sign above the entrance-gate of science reminding every one of its mission, namely, to make existence seem intelligible, and therefore justified: for which purpose, if arguments are not enough,* myth *also must be used, which I have just indicated as the necessary consequence, as the very goal of science.*

This is certainly heady stuff, although I will admit that the materials about music and dramatics (really the backbone of his thesis here) did lose me on several occasions. However the "meta" themes such as the "one world being" were fascinating on a deeply involving level.

Again, The Birth of Tragedy[4] *is* available through various web archives, if you just want to read the text. As noted, I found this particular translation quite agreeable, however, and the cost of this volume is only $2.50 ... ideal for capping off an on-line order that's a bit shy of the $25 free-shipping promised land. However, due to the very low cover price, the odds of finding a copy of this in any but the *largest* brick-and-mortar stores is probably pretty low, so you may just want to keep this in mind for a shipping-saving throw-in to another order.

Notes:

1. http://btripp-books.livejournal.com/135617.html
2. http://amzn.to/1PrqmpX
3. http://records.viu.ca/~johnstoi/nietzsche/tragedy_all.htm
4. http://amzn.to/1PrqmpX

Wednesday, September 12, 2012[1]

How do you know who to trust?

While I don't make a *habit* of this, from time to time I'll see a book discussed on the web, or referenced in another book, and hit the publisher up for a review copy. Generally speaking, these are cases where I'm *interested* in the book, but only marginally so, making it unlikely that I'd go buy a copy, but I do want to know about it as background, context, or counterpoint for the original source that brought it to my attention. Unfortunately, this also occasionally results in my not having all that much to say about a book when I get around to reviewing it, and that seems to be the case with Bruce Schneier's Liars and Outliers: Enabling the Trust that Society Needs to Thrive[2], which was very kindly provided to me by the good folks over at Wiley.

This is, of course, not to say that this is an *uninteresting* book, but it is in a niche (Sociology) which has never much grabbed me, and when I sat down to produce this review I was having a hard time bringing to mind what exactly it had been about. Now, part of this comes from my schedule over the past 3 months (I finished *reading* this 11 weeks ago) which, until just recently, was taken up with a project that was leaving little "free time" in my days. I realize that this is significantly "unfair" to the book and the author (I do recall that I was impressed with some of the themes in this), but that's the way it is. So please excuse any vagueness here, which is no doubt more due to my recall than to the book itself.

Liars and Outliers[3] has a fairly straight-forward presentation arc, starting with the natural world and moving into the evolution of human society in the first part, "The Science of Trust", of the book. Here basic groundwork is laid in predator/prey relationships, and "The Red Queen Effect" which addresses population balances and adaptations in those. As humanity emerged from the crowd of earlier hominid species, our intelligence seems to have been the advantage-giving adaptation, although as noted here there appears to be a link between intelligence and violence: *"The more murderous a species is, the greater the selective benefit of intelligence; smarter people are more likely to survive their human adversaries."* ... with data suggesting that as many as 25% of prehistoric males died from warfare.

Obviously, this is an awfully high percentage to maintain for a slowly-maturing, low birth rate, species, which led to the development of assorted interaction strategies. Here the terms used are "cooperate" or "defect", which play into assorted "game theory" scenarios such as hawk/dove, which show that it's a matter of degree on every level, and that there are likely to *always* be "defectors" from the social norm, and the question is at what level can this be best tolerated. Among the coping strategies arise altruism and reciprocity, but these, except where explicitly dictated by the group, tend towards paleolithic patterns:

> ... We're evolved for the trust problems endemic to living in small family groups in the East African Highlands in 100,000 BC. It's 21st century New York City that gives us problems. ... Our brains are sufficiently neuroplastic that we can adapt to today's world, but vestiges of our evolutionary past remain. These cognitive biases affect how we respond to fear, how we perceive risks ..., and how we weigh short-term versus long-term costs and benefits.

Schneier references some of Dunbar's work (beyond his famed "number"), on group size and "emotional distance", from the 12-20 person "clique" or "sympathy group", to the 30-50 person "camp", to the well known 150 person "band" (our basic "Rolodex" of known persons), to the 500 person "megaband" and on up to 1,500 person "tribe" that Dunbar suggests is the maximum number of faces that we can recognize.

With the onset of agriculture, the small manageable groups could no longer just move on if crowded, and so institutions arose to add another level of social pressures to the "moral" and "reputational" controls of smaller groups. The second part of the book, "A Model of Trust" addresses Societal, Moral, Reputational, and Institutional pressures, along with "Security Systems", discussed via various "societal dilemma" examples, mostly based on game theory.

> Morality is a complex concept, and the subject of thousands of years' worth of philosophical and theological debate. Although the word "moral" often refers to an individual's values – with "moral" meaning "good," and "immoral" meaning "bad" - I am using the term "morals" here very generally, to mean any innate or cultural guidelines that inform a people's decision-making processes as they evaluate potential trade-offs. These encompass conscious and unconscious processes, explicit rules and gut feelings, deliberate thoughts, and automatic reactions. These also encompass internal reward mechanisms, for both cooperation and defection.
> ... Belief that voting in the right thing to do, and that murdering someone is wrong, are examples of moral pressure ... Natural selection has modified our brains so that trust, altruism, and cooperation feel good, but – as we all know – that doesn't mean we're always trustworthy, altruistic, and cooperative.

The third part of the book addresses "The Real World", looking at Competing Interests, Organizations, Corporations, and Institutions. As you might expect, this is full of real-life cases, of which most deal with commerce, handling crime, etc. Of course, in society, nothing is ever particularly free standing, here's an example where government, no doubt trying to reduce risks, actually *increases* risks when they meddle in commerce:

> Any company that is too big to fail – that the government will bail out rather than let fail – is the beneficiary of a free insurance policy underwritten by taxpayers. So while a normal-sized company would evaluate both the costs and benefits of defecting, a too-big-to-fail company knows that someone else will pick up the costs. This is a moral hazard that radically changes the risk trade-off and limits the effectiveness of institutional pressure.

This has obviously been shown in both Wall Street and Detroit in the past decade, and I'm pretty sure that government hasn't learned anything from the chaos.

The final part of the book is "Conclusions", with "How Societal Pressures Fail", "Technological Advances", and a look at "The Future".

> The lesson of this book isn't that defectors will inevitably ruin everything for everyone, but that we need to manage societal pressures to ensure they don't. We've seen how our prehistoric toolbox of social pressures – moral and relational systems – does that on a small scale, how institutions enhance that on a larger scale, and how technology helps all three systems scale even more. ... The interplay of all the feedback loops means that both the scope of defection and the scope of defection society is willing to tolerate are constantly moving targets. There is no "getting it right"; this process never ends.

Liars and Outliers[4] just came out earlier this year, so it should be available in the brick & mortar book vendors ... the on-line guys, however, have it for more than a third off. There's lots of fascinating stuff in this (I've really just hit the broad strokes here, there was tons of detail in terms of groups, populations, theories, etc. that I didn't every try to convey), but it's in a reasonably narrow band, and if you're *interested* in the subject of trust in an over-all cultural context, this would be a great book for you, but (in the words of Dennis Miller) "your mileage may vary" depending on your focus.

Notes:

1. http://btripp-books.livejournal.com/135823.html

2-4. http://amzn.to/1MN0BPf

Tuesday, September 18, 2012[1]

Auschwitz and unemployment?

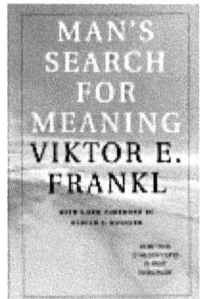

OK ... so I'd heard about this many times in the past, but it was always just as an "inspirational" book, and, well ... that's not necessarily one of my preferred genres. However, a month or so back I'd seen it referenced, found that it conveniently made an on-line order reach free shipping, and added it. Which seems to have been a good thing, as it was sitting there when my most recent employment situation imploded, leaving me with some fresh emotional scars.

As most people recognize, Viktor E. Frankl was the psychotherapist who was sent off to the Nazi death camps in WW2, survived, and went on to form Logotherapy. His famous book, Man's Search for Meaning[2] is primarily his story of survival, and the development of his main thesis that *"The one thing you can't take away from me is the way I choose to respond to what you do to me. The last of one's freedoms is to choose one's attitude in any given circumstance."*

While the main part of the book is based on the author's notes from the war, which he published initially in 1946, various bits and pieces have been added on over the years. The edition I have (a 2006 paperback from Beacon Press), includes the 90-page "Experiences In A Concentration Camp" from 1946, a 38-page "Logotherapy In A Nutshell" essay that was added in a 1962 edition, an 18-page Postscript from 1984 (based on a 1983 lecture), a Preface to the 1992 edition added by the author (prior to his death, in his 90's, in 1997), plus a Foreword and Afterword added in the 2006 edition. In business this sort of thing is often referred to a "mission creep", and, while each add-on is certainly interesting and brings context and framing to the main piece, what is presently "the book" is certainly much more rambling and less focused than what was originally published as *A Psychologist Experiences the Concentration Camp*.

The story in the main part is, of course, horrific. While culturally we are aware of the camps, and the broad strokes of what these entailed, it is quite the eye-opener to hear the daily details laid out by a survivor. Oddly, Frankl had the chance to have *not* gone to the camps, as he had been approved to emigrate to the U.S., but due to various circumstances, including not wanting to leave his parents behind (and having a serendipitous "message" from scripture come to him when deciding this, which spoke of duty to one's parents), so he and his family stayed, all to be taken to the camps.

The arrival there is a rather chilling tale, not only was there the basic "sorting" between the ones to be outright killed in the gas chambers, and those to be, essentially, worked to death, but there was the removal of *everything* that connected the prisoners to their previous existences. Frankl had a manuscript on his person representing years of research, and this was summarily taken from him, and (of course), any thing of value was appropriated by the guards. This was a key element in the arc of life in the camps, as the main theme of Frankl's "Logotherapy", extrapolating from Kierkegaard, is that humanity's search for *meaning* is the central motivating force (as opposed to Adler's focus on a Nietzschean concept of power, or Freud's focus on pleasure). Without connections to one's previous life, many had a very hard time finding "meaning" in their dire situation.

On one level, Frankl's experience in the camps served as a lab for his developing Logotherapy, and he talks about hoarding random bits of paper on which he could keep notes towards rebuilding his paper on the subject. *This* was his "meaning" that kept him going. I found the following passage of interest:

> On entering camp a change took place in the minds of the men. With the end of uncertainty there came the uncertainty of the end. It was impossible to foresee whether or when, if at all, this form of existence would end. ... A man who could not see the end of his "provisional existence" was not able to aim at an ultimate goal in life. He ceased living for the future, in contrast to a man in normal life. Therefore the whole structure of his inner life change; signs of decay set in which we know from other areas of life. The unemployed worker, for example, is in a similar position. His existence has become provisional and in a certain sense he cannot live for the future or aim at a goal. Research work done on unemployed miners has shown that they suffer from a peculiar sort of deformed time – inner time – which is a result of their unemployed state. Prisoners, too, suffered from this strange "time experience". In camp, a small time unit, a day, for example, filled with hourly tortures and fatigue, appeared endless. A larger time unit, perhaps a week, seemed to pass very quickly. My comrades agreed when I said that in camp a day lasted longer than a week. How paradoxical was our time-experience!

I, obviously (for those not following along at home, I've been searching for a new "full time" job for over three years at this point), noticed Frankl's comparison of the concentration camp experience with that of being unemployed – people who have not fought through long-term joblessness don't understand what a torture it can be ... elsewhere he writes: *"being jobless was equated with being useless, and being useless was equated with having a meaningless life"*, which certainly plays out in the abysmal emotional impact of the endless grind of churning out resumes.

Again, in *the* current editions of Man's Search for Meaning[3], the story of his wartime experiences is only one part of the book, and much of the rest of the book is, as noted, providing more material about his theories. This is from the section on these:

> *Every age has its own collective neurosis, and every age needs its own psychotherapy to cope with it. The existential vacuum which is the mass neurosis of the present time can be described as a private and personal form of nihilism; for nihilism can be defined as the contention that being has no meaning. As for psychotherapy, however, it will never be able to cope with this state of affairs on a mass scale if it does not keep itself free from the impact and influence of the contemporary trends of a nihilistic philosophy; otherwise it represents a symptom of the mass neurosis rather than its possible cure.*

Evidently Frankl did feel that his approach was the "Third Viennese School of Psychotherapy", and was supplanting its predecessors with this new "meaning" centered modality.

Anyway, this is widely available, with the mass-market paperback edition being well under ten bucks, and you're likely to be able to find that at your local brick & mortar book seller. Given that there are "more than 12 million copies in print worldwide", it's also available via the used channels, but with the very low cover price, you might as well go local. Personally, my "take-away" on this book was that I didn't get the enthusiasm that is so widely shown for it, and while it certainly had profound insights, it was, for me, "interesting", but hardly "life-changing". But, I'm a cynical guy with a lot of emotional damage, so you might find this just *wonderful*.

Notes:

1. http://btripp-books.livejournal.com/136125.html
2-3. http://amzn.to/1GNoY8Q

Saturday, September 29, 2012[1]

Brutal ...

This was a "win" from the LibraryThing.com "Early Reviewers" program, and almost everything about it is a bit odd. First of all, of the four titles I put requests in for back in May, this was (to my thinking) the least likely to have been matched with my library (unless I'm grossly underestimating the preponderance of "rock books" in my collection vs. the other LTER members), then there's the matter of it being in the *early* reviewer book, as this is a 2003 edition, and it doesn't appear that it represents a new paperback edition or anything along those lines that might have made it surface as new. The author *did* have another book coming out this summer, but that was, well, a different book, so unless she or her publisher was simply trying to draw attention to *her*, it seems strange to have pumped a nearly decade-old book into the LTER review channel!

This is especially a pointed concern given that Natalie J. Purcell's Death Metal Music: The Passion and Politics of a Subculture[2] is very much a "snapshot" in time (and space, as well ... more on that below), and that is increasingly less germane to the topic as the years roll by. I have to admit to having glanced at other reviews for this book, and there are views all over the scale on it out there ... but I wonder if many of these are *recent* approaches to it. One element no doubt contributing to this still being in print is that it appears to be a *text book* (although I have a hard time imagining a university that would use this), with an extremely high cover price for a sub-250-page paperback.

Now, I want to point out that I did not *dislike* the book over-all ... and felt that the author did a reasonable job of balancing the "inside look" into the Death Metal subculture with the "formal research" aspects here ... where many other reviewers have taken it to task from one side or the other, I sort of felt *embarrassed* for her, having launched into very enthusiastic undergraduate projects myself, which no doubt were even more cringe-worthy than this. However, the role of her being a long-time metal fan, immersed in that "scene" is in constant dissonance with her endeavoring to be a "professional researcher" of that scene, and much of the thrust of the research (although, I will grant her, this could be simply *my* perception a decade later when Metal was less a news topic) appears to have been designed to "prove" that Metal wasn't the bugaboo that the likes of Tipper Gore made it out to be way back when.

One thing I found frustrating here was that there was very little biographical information about the author, either in the book or out on the web, but from what little contextual data I could dig up, it would appear that this was done while Ms. Purcell was an undergraduate (so is all the more amazing that this is surviving as a textbook). This could go a long way to explaining the insufficiencies of the research, as it would appear that it was done without any funding, and very much on an ad hoc basis with other metal fans of the author's acquaintance. One of the weaknesses of the study behind the book is that it only dealt with American bands, and those specifically from two "scenes" (New York and Florida), the ones the author was involved in. The highly influential (what would become the *iconic* form of "Death Metal") Nordic form barely registers here, except to note how attractive the female metal fans found the members of those bands.

While I do not have many "death metal" CDs, I do have a couple of Pandora channels based on certain bands in the genre, so have heard a certain amount of this music from time to time. Frankly, I would have a lot more of this in my collection if not for the convention of pairing unlistenable vocals (I typically describe the two predominant styles as "Beelzebub with a throat infection" and "squeal like a piggy") with otherwise quite engaging music ... I was quite interested to find that Ms. Purcell seemed to think of this as a *feature* rather than "*a bug*" in that it created a situation where only the "true fans" would get into the music and its "scene".

> *Given the extreme nature of Death Metal, it is no surprise that the lyrical content is equally extreme and often very offensive, disturbing, and disgusting to the average outsider. Most critics cite the lyrics of Death Metal music as their reason for condemning it. It is quite fascinating to note, however, that the lyrics in Death Metal are most frequently unintelligible, and many devoted Death Metal fans would be unable to recite the lyrics of even their favorite bands. Often, lyrics are poorly written (or even composed by foreign band members with little grasp of the language in which they write). For this reason, it is generally accepted that the lyrics in Death Metal (like album art and band photos) serve predominantly as a means for bands to promote an image that visually displays the aggression and extremity of their music.*

Again, at this point, much of the "analysis" here is forensic, because so much of the narrative is that of a fan of a particular scene deeply involved with a certain set of bands which probably have not left much of an impression outside of their particular circle. The author uses the term "brutal" to define the approach to vocals in Death Metal, and raises a point which seems to have been prescient: *"because many believe the boundaries of the genre are so explicitly defined, too much musical 'creativity' might produce great music but it would not necessarily be considered Death Metal"* ... i.e., if it's not played a certain way, and sung a certain way, it's not Death Metal, which leads listeners like me to, I think quite fairly, say "it all sounds the same!". Purcell tries to make a case of how the various bands exemplify this or that sound, but, without an easy to access library of examples, it's simply a matter of either taking her word for it, or simply putting it off as her involvement in and enthusiasm for a particular scene at a particular place and time talking.

As noted, it appears that the whole thrust of this book was to defend the author's "scene" against the "unfair" attentions it was getting from various politicians a decade ago. Much of the survey/interview materials focus on violence, poverty, and depression/suicide, which evidently are in specific response to charges being leveled at Metal at the time. The book, and the research, could be said to make a reasonable counter to those charges, but the scope of these are sufficiently narrow to *not* be a particularly satisfying look at the "subculture" per se. There is a lot of "justifying" elements of this (from claiming extreme levels of "musicianship" for bands that were all essentially following a formula to claiming that they were simply being targeted for being "extreme") subculture, which, again sounds more like the metal fan being petulant than making an argument.

In the final analysis, it is hard to recommend Death Metal Music[3] to anybody but those with an interest in semi-popular music history, although it might appear to those with a fondness for random sociology as well. Part of this is due to the very high (textbook) cover price ... nearly $40 for a 242-page paperback ... which is not much improved in the used channel (again, probably due to its being an "academic" release). Your best bet, were you interested in picking up a copy, would probably be in an electronic version, as the Kindle and Nook editions are both just over ten bucks.

Notes:

1. http://btripp-books.livejournal.com/136286.html

2-3. http://amzn.to/1MMU5YQ

Sunday, September 30, 2012[1]

Ancient Chinese wisdom ...

OK, so this is *another* book from the last "box sale" at OpenBooks[2] a year or so back, which was quite a haul. Because the deal was as many books that I could get into a box for a flat price, there were quite a few that went in there "just because", and this was one of those. In this case, it was much like adding a Dover Thrift book into an on-line order, in that it was something of interest (generally speaking) that I had no pre-existing knowledge of, that I figured would be good to add to my ongoing search of polymathism ... specifically here, ancient Chinese philosophy.

Mencius[3] (yes, a one-word title, which is also the name of the principle author/subject), was a Confucian sage in the 3rd century BCE, about a century following Confucius. Apparently, other than this book bearing his name, little is *historically* known about him. This is a collection of his sayings by his students, so is as much *about* him as it is a collection of his sayings. The book itself, in the Penguin Classics edition, is a translation by the noted scholar D.C. Lau, which was originally published in 1970. This features extensive additional material by Lau, explaining much of the context of the work, and how it came down to us.

From what I've been able to gather from this, it appears that Mencius was a "mainstream" Confucian sage at a time (a century on from Confucius himself) where there were various other schools and traditions branching off. A number of these other schools come up repeatedly, as Mencius argues against them (and, other than their appearances here, I have no idea how well known these are within what survives from that period). Mencius seems to be known best for his use of analogy, and much of the book involves his interaction with various figures of the time.

I am only peripherally familiar with Confucian thought, so it's hard for me to make much direct commentary on how Mencius operates within that tradition, but much here is set within a framework or expected religious rituals, and requirements of the various levels of society, with a whole panoply of very specific particulars, which seem strange at best from a modern cultural perspective. To give you a taste of how much of the book unfolds, here's a section (Book II – Part A - #5) which at least played to my Libertarian sensibilities, a couple of dozen centuries after the fact:

> 5. Mencius said, 'If you honour the good and wise and employ the able so that outstanding men are in high position, then Gentlemen throughout the Empire will be only too pleased to serve at your court. In the market-place, if goods are exempted when premises are taxed, and premises exempted when

> the ground is taxed, then the traders throughout the Empire will be only too pleased to store their goods in your market-place. If there is inspection but no duty at the border station, then the travelers throughout the Empire will be only too pleased to go by the way of your roads. If tillers help in the public fields but pay no tax on the land, them farmers throughout the Empire will be only too pleased to till the land in your realm. If you abolish the levy in lieu of corvée and the levy in lieu of the planting of the mulberry, then all the people of the Empire will be only too pleased to come and settle in your state. If you can truly execute these five measures, the people of your neighboring states will look up to you as to their father and mother; and since man came into this world no one has succeeded in inciting children against their parents. In this way, you will have no match in the Empire. He who has no match in the Empire is a Heaven-appointed officer, and it has never happened that such a man failed to become a true King.'

Parts of this are fascinating for their details on how ancient Chinese society was structured … with various levels of officials, down to various levels of "Gentlemen", having income from certain amounts of land, and how the land was distributed, taxed, and regulated. There is also quite a lot of "history" involved, but it is hard to track this, as the time-line in the Mencius book is not necessarily in agreement with other texts of the time (Lau goes into this in some detail), and in many cases there is only sketchy historical materials apart from these texts to go from.

Again Mencius[4] isn't exactly a "for everybody" book, but if you have an interest in ancient society, the history of China, philosophy in general, and Confucianism's development in particular, this may be of interest to you. As noted, the used copy I got is over 40 years old, but this edition is still available, with "good" used copies for as little as a penny. If this is "your thing", and you've not read Mencius yet, you will likely find this quite rewarding, but it's hardly an "all and sundry" recommendation.

Notes:

1. http://btripp-books.livejournal.com/136567.html
2. http://www.open-books.org/
3-4. http://amzn.to/1ONL8i2

Tuesday, October 2, 2012[1]

The math of making an impact ...

This one came to me courtesy of the authors ... Chris Brogan (@broganmedia[2]) had queried on Twitter whether anybody was interested in getting a review copy, and (of course) my virtual hand shot up. It's the second book from Chris Brogan and Julien Smith (@julien[3]), although it's not exactly a follow-up to their previous Trust Agents[4]. To start on a gripe, as I've noted previously, I "have issues" with mnemonic acronyms that don't immediately prove memorable or useful ... admittedly, not everything can be as awesome as the one for remembering how CSS properties are called around an object ("trouble": Top-Right-Bottom-Left) ... but so often these are more useful in *marketing* an idea than applying it, and I was, frankly, disappointed that The Impact Equation: Are You Making Things Happen or Just Making Noise?[5] was, to a certain extent, built around one of these. At least in this case I have been able to retain the word - "CREATE" - which is what is spelled out in the "equation":

$$Impact = C \times (R + E + A + T + E) \ldots \text{ where}$$

C = Contrast
R = Reach
E = Exposure
A = Articulation
T = Trust
E = Echo

(And I *did* have to go look up those – so they didn't exactly stick in my head from reading the book.)

I have a *suspicion* that perhaps the authors had come up with this "equation" as a way to *analyze* social media programs (despite their preface's *homage* to Magritte), and then extrapolated it out into a general business function. In the early parts of the book, there are several examples of charts and case study break-downs which take various elements of either hypothetical or real-world (McDonalds going into the coffee biz, Instagram's success, etc.) situations and block out these according to those six categories. However, the rest of the book is less about *analysis* and more about how to *achieve* these various elements in one's business or projects.

The book is divided up into four sections, Goals, Ideas, Platforms, and Network, with the latter three handling two each (oddly, not "in order") of the six elements of the "equation". Most of these chapters end with an analysis according to the equation of a company/example more-or-less highlighting the specific element being discussed. The fact that they ended up approach-ing the particulars in a different order than how they are set out in the "equation" I think is telling on how limiting these acronym approaches are!

Now, I realize that, considering the above, one might *assume* that I didn't much care for the book ... and this is NOT the case, only that it seemed to me that the messages of the book were being needlessly contorted to fit what was (possibly) a framework conceived in a rather different context. Obviously, all six of those elements are key for reaching an audience in the current web-connected world, and Chris and Julien (and, to their credit, the writing fairly seamlessly keeps a constant "voice") are quite approachable here. Frankly, most of the time I had the sense of sitting around listening to friends "riff" on a subject rather than being pontificated to by some "expert". The book is chock-full of recommendations for particular tools, resources, and books (I actually bought a piece of *fiction* due to their strong recommendation of it), and most of my little bookmarks ended up marking these rather than blocks of text to quote here.

However, one thing I think I want to point out is that, in the "equation" the element of Contrast stands apart, and is pretty much the defining element of that construction. As many other social/marketing writers have noted, excelling in a tightly defined niche is probably the best bet any of us can have in a world that has tens of millions of content creators all looking for a sliver of the available attention. One thing that Brogan and Smith recommend here, which plays to this, is embracing your quirks:

> We both have been recently working hard on self-actualization, for lack of a better term. We have both worked harder at being ourselves, unflinching versions of what we feel and believe. One piece of advice we have about the process: Package your quirks.
>
> What do we mean by that? There are many unique things that make you who you are. With a little bit of pruning and positioning, the parts of you that are quirky and different can often separate you from the crowd in a positive way. "Packaging" simply means putting a little bit of attention and mindfulness into the way your represent yourself to the outside world.

This hit home for me, as it's certainly in direct opposition to the voices saying[6] that you need to *"Live your life as if your mother is watching."*, self-editing and conforming until you're just another sheep in the herd!

Anyway, with the assorted caveats detailed above, I enjoyed reading The Impact Equation[7], and felt that I got quite a lot of value from it ... although I must admit that I've not gotten around to doing a few of the "exercises" presented in the text as yet. Again, this isn't a book on *theory*, and it's certainly not a *text book*, but, as noted, it's like having a long wide-ranging talk with a couple of friends who are very passionate about the way that things get presented in the ever increasingly web-centric world we live in.

However, you're going to have to wait to get this ... as its official release date is still nearly a month away ... but the on-line big boys have it for pre-order at a substantial discount. If you have an interest in social media, marketing, or the general direction that the world is going ... you are likely to get quite a lot out of reading this one.

Notes:

1. http://btripp-books.livejournal.com/136831.html
2. http://twitter.com/broganmedia
3. http://twitter.com/julien
4. http://btripp-books.livejournal.com/89349.html
5. http://amzn.to/1RL2P1w
6. http://btripp-books.livejournal.com/129703.html
7. http://amzn.to/1RL2P1w

Saturday, October 6, 2012[1]

"Anticipate the difficult by managing the easy."

This is one of those books that I'd seen being discussed out in the Social Media sphere and I decided to reach out to the publisher to get a copy. Obviously, I'd been in contact with both the author and McGraw-Hill recently for Return On Influence[2] which I reviewed this summer, so it wasn't much of a research project to get a hold of Mark W. Schaefer's (@markwschaefer[3]) new The Tao of Twitter: Changing Your Life and Business 140 Characters at a Time[4] (actually "new" isn't *exactly* the right word, as this is an updating and expansion of a previous self-published volume). The author's intent with this book was to provide "a manual" for Twitter (something he felt was lacking), which would help prevent the trend he saw of many folks signing up, messing around (ineffectually) for a bit, and eventually giving up on it. I'm, of course, coming to it from the other end of the scale (having been using Twitter for over 5 years at this point), but there is still stuff here that I didn't know!

If you've heard Schaefer speak (which I have both live and in webinars), you'll recognize a lot of the stories in this. The book is rooted in his experiences of relationships developing from the most trivial or ephemeral initial connections, that grow (with some attention) to significant professional connections. What he defines as "The Tao (the way) of Twitter" comes from three basic elements:

> *Targeted Connections*
> *Meaningful Content*
> *Authentic Helpfulness*
>
> ...
>
> *In an always-on, real-time, global world of business communications, the priority is on* human interaction *that leads to connections. Connections lead to awareness. Awareness leads to trust. Trust is the ultimate catalyst to business benefits, as it always has been.*

Some of the benefits he lists for Twitter include uses as: promotional tool, lead generator, customer satisfier, product development engine, and problem solver; and he sketches out examples of each. He quotes research that shows that *"Twitter users are the most influential online consumers"* with in excess of 70% publishing (and commenting on) blogs, and nearly as many writing product reviews and commenting on news sites monthly.

When he gets into the "how-to" meat of the book, he moves into a lot of lists, with 5 Set-Up Basics, 22 Ways to Attract Targeted Followers, and a handful of strategies for managing followers. Many of these points were new to me, with suggestions of resources for various purposes such as search and lists. An example of one of the useful tips here is #18 (of the 22) ...

> Create "tweetable moments" in your presentations. When you give a talk to a relevant business audience, include your Twitter handle at the bottom of every slide. One popular speaking tip these days is to actually spoon-feed the audience tidbits they can easily tweet along with your presentation.

I'd add to that later point "keep your slide up long enough for the audience to think about tweeting it, and get it keyed in on their phone" (speaking from my own frustrations in those situations!). He next addresses a basic starting approach to tweeting – what sort of content, suggestions for a basic "regimen", times to tweet, how to re-tweet, and how to use URL shorteners. He then gets into how to "be a good tweeter", with rather pointed suggestions such as *"Build your own tribe. Reach out to the real people on Twitter; don't just kiss up to the most influential ones."*, among other more general suggestions. Interestingly, at about the mid-point of the book he presents what might be considered a "Twitter glossary", with several pages of definitions of key terms ... obviously, this is more useful in the flow of the book, but it's odd to encounter what one is used to seeing as a separate section at the end, integrated into the main presentation. He also makes the topic of "lists" a chapter in itself, which I found useful, as this is probably *my* weakest point in using Twitter ... so it gave me several things to consider!

The second half of the book has a bit more of a "business" focus, with chapters like "20 Ideas to Toast Your Competition" and "Twitter Time Savers" with many very handy suggestions, leading into "Balancing the Personal and the Professional" which looks at the spectrum from the "unbranded" person-tweeting-for-the-company to the "anonymous logo" voice broadcasting info, and how these work in various situations (and, yes, the latter has its place out there). Next comes "Secrets of Influence on Twitter" which has some very interesting analysis of social influence, and how this is more determined by degree of engagement rather than just raw follower numbers. Schaefer has some very constructive and easy-to-implement suggestions here on how to improve one's Twitter influence.

In "Advanced Twitter Concepts" he gets into a lot of stuff that I'd either not been aware of, or had only encountered peripherally, including a very useful table of ways to structure queries for the search function to get best results. Following this there's a section on Twitter chats, and some closing thoughts on how Twitter works for different people, and how following the "Tao" can make the platform work for pretty much anybody.

Again, much of [The Tao of Twitter][5] is presented with stories from the author's own experiences, so there's a "your mileage may vary" aspect to this (I had a lot of *"how come I've never had that happen?"* moments in reading this), but it also leads to this being much less dry than what one would expect a "users manual" to be. As this new edition has only been out a couple of months, you should be able to find it through your local bookstore, and, of course, the on-line big boys have it at a discount from its already very reasonable (a mere $10) cover price. If you've been on Twitter for a long time, this isn't an *essential* read, but, as noted above, there is likely quite a lot of info here that you might not know. However, if you've *not* been on Twitter and were interested in giving it a go, this would be a *great* book to get you up to speed!

Notes:

1. http://btripp-books.livejournal.com/137157.html
2. http://btripp-books.livejournal.com/132936.html
3. http://twitter.com/markwschaefer
4-5. http://amzn.to/1LwpePg

Sunday, October 7, 2012[1]

A vision of the visual ...

I've known one of the authors of this book for a couple of years, both via the local Social Media scene, and from the late lamented Syncubator center where she had an office and P2PMicroversity[2] (a start-up for which I'm a consultant) had "desk space". Since she knew I was a book-reviewing fool, when this came up she asked if I'd be interested in having a go at it (duh!) and presented me with a signed copy at the release party last week. I also got to meet some of the publicists from Que Publishing (who I've had intermittent contact with on other books) at the party, which was down at Rockit (a frequent host for Social Media events). Anyway, this is to provide a bit of transparency to the fact that I'm not exactly coming to this book "cold".

The authors, Jess Loren (@ChiTownJess[3]) and Edward Swiderski (@ESwiderski[4]) are the principals of the Kambio Group agency, which specializes in social media marketing ... this book, Pinterest for Business: How to Pin Your Company to the Top of the Hottest Social Media Network[5] is obviously an extension of their efforts in that context. I suppose at this juncture I need to take a step back and ask, *do you know about Pinterest[6]?* ... although, in the social media world, that's about like asking if you've breathed any *air*, I realize that in the "real world" these things take a while longer to get into the common consciousness. This is a site where you create "pin boards" on which you "pin" graphics. It's been around for a couple of years, but was in an invite-only "beta" until just this past August (the book was done before this change to open sign-up) ... however, in that time, it managed to become the *third largest* social media platform (behind Facebook and Twitter), and was the fastest site to reach 10,000,000 users. There are various ways of getting graphics onto one's "boards", "pin it" buttons provided on a site, a "pin it" thing you can install in your browser, and ways to directly upload from your computer.

The key thing, however, in approaching Pinterest for Business[7] is that it *is* "for businesses" ... this is not really a guidebook for everybody, but a look at how companies can make use of this social media tool. Why should businesses want to be involved? Well, although the book doesn't really get into flinging around the data, there are figures out there which show that users are engaged with Pinterest for far longer than most other sites, and that it "converts" at a far higher rates as well. The book is structured as a walk-through, from basic explanations of what's what, and where the various bits are on the site, and how they work, to how Pinterest interfaces with other platforms. It then goes into some "psychology" of image-based messaging ... in this it also introduces the "format" for most of the book, bringing up a subject, and finding somebody (in many cases these appear to be Kambio's clients) to interview on that topic ... most of the book is set up with these brief interviews.

I must admit that I found the *flow* of the book less than ideal with this format, as there weren't a lot of clearly demarcated "topic shifts". The authors introduce a subject, bring up a company that is doing something within that general area, go into an interview (or an extensive quote) from a representative of that company, then roll right into the next thing. I felt this would have greatly benefited from some graphic/design separation of these sections, and, to a large extent, chapters 3-6 (nearly 40% of the book), is one long run of this. There is a "design element" of screencaps of various companies' and individuals' profile images from Pinterest, but these don't necessarily divide topics (frequently 2-3 interviewees are involved in one subject), leading to a bit of a sense of run-on that could have been avoided by graphic elements (lines, themed dingbats, etc.) clearly delimiting where there was a shift in subject. I found the parts of the book where the authors themselves were digesting, organizing, and presenting the information the *clearest*, as in the "interview" portions it was frequently (in a casual read) a bit unclear who was saying what about what, and why specifically one should give particular weight to their reported opinions/experiences.

Also, I suppose in a book targeted to businesses contemplating developing a "Pinterest strategy", it's not *surprising*, but I was somewhat taken aback by the heavy lean towards "professional services" suggested in the parts discussing photography and video. This is 180° from, say, Gary Vaynerchuk's approach of firing up a camera and going for "authentic", or Carl White's iPhone "redneck teleprompter" set up, and, frankly, it seemed at considerable variance from the general Social Media DIY ethic.

While I suppose that it really *had* to be in there, one section came close to invalidated much of the main part of the book ... the discussion of legal issues. The potential "Achilles heel" of the Pinterest platform is the question of intellectual property, and it is arguable that, unless you are pinning *only* content that you yourself have created, every Pinterest user, personal or corporate, is in danger of being sued. Chicago's own "social media lawyer" Daliah Saper weighs in with the following:

> *"Pinterest specifically encourages users to surf the Web and 'pin' third-party content that does not belong to them and that they may not have the right to distribute."* ... *"Additionally, Pinterest's Terms of Use requires every user to agree that any content he or she pins or uploads does not and will not violate any law or infringe the rights of any third-party ..."* ... *"If Pinterest gets sued because of the content a user posted on its site, the user, per the terms of use, also agrees to indemnify Pinterest* **(pay all Pinterest's legal fees and associated costs)**. ... *Accordingly, when building a pinboard, businesses and professionals should be careful to* **only upload content that belongs to them or pin to content that they have been authorized or licensed to use.**"

(emphasis mine) ... Obviously, this is the "800lb gorilla" in the Pinterest room, because the dollars involved are *not* trivial - another lawyer interviewed notes: *"A person who commits willful copyright infringement can be charged up to $150,000 per instance of infringement."*[1] Every time *I* read this stuff I want to rush off to delete my Pinterest account because *who knows* what the legal status is of those cute/fun/interesting things that get repinned from Facebook, Google+, or various other places on the web are – and each pin (that isn't one's own creation) is a potential legal land-mine. All the "customer involving" boards and techniques discussed earlier in the book certainly have the potential of running afoul of this.

To avoid ending the book on this downer, there is a final chapter which features interviews with a few other companies, themed to the "future", however, it's hard to get past the chief flaw of the platform. Obviously, companies developing Pinterest programs can (and, I suppose, *should*) focus on their own materials, and figure out ways to encourage the re-pinning of those by customers and other interested parties. In this case, the question of Intellectual Property rights are in the control of the business developing the boards ... but it's hard to imagine the social media managers having to *clear* each and every "found" image that they might want to include on a board (which represents the vast majority of all pins out there) with their legal department!

Admittedly, this is a caveat dealing with the I.P. reality of Pinterest itself, rather than any fault of Pinterest for Business[8] as a book. Over-all, this is a very useful survey of how to set up a Pinterest engagement program for a business, with most of the material coming from interviewees at companies who have been working with the platform (for the short while that it's been around – most of the case studies involved are only a year or so old). Needless to say, this isn't a book for the Social Media enthusiast, but for that MBA marketing person who wants to find out what this Pinterest thing they've heard of is about, and how it might help their business. The book's only been out a couple of months, so should be at your local brick-and-mortar book vendor that deals in business titles, and the on-line guys have it at a discount (and, unusually, the e-book versions are *quite* reasonably priced).

Notes:

1. http://btripp-books.livejournal.com/137299.html
2. http://goo.gl/HzjPhJ
3. http://twitter.com/ChiTownJess
4. http://twitter.com/ESwiderski
5. http://amzn.to/1LwoGc8
6. http://pinterest.com/
7-8. http://amzn.to/1LwoGc8

Tuesday, October 9, 2012[1]

Brothels for the Mouth?

So, I found this up at the dollar store. In my "previous life" in PR, I worked in the consumer products end of the food industry, and we did a lot of functions, soirees, and events involving hotels, restaurants, Chefs, etc., and part of me is always nostalgic for that world. I figured that Trevor White's Kitchen Con: Writing on the Restaurant Racket[2] would be a fun walk through those synapses, at least as presented by this author. However, being that the book *was* a "chance encounter" (and not a planned or recommended acquisition), I did the always-embarrassing skulk over to Amazon to get the broad strokes on its content, and see what other people were saying about it. I was *shocked* to find that this book was averaging a mere *two* stars, with some folks outright savaging it. Needless to say, this produced some trepidation when approaching it, but, having read and enjoyed it, I have come to the conclusion that the review page over on Amazon has become the stage for a particular piece of performance art ... with a barrage of nasty one-star reviews being countered by a couple of five-star reviews, with one by somebody who claims to have actually *married* Mr. White, and saying that the negative voices were coming from *"bitter restaurateurs, desperately trying to get their own back on a well-known food critic"* ... the author himself, in his biographical note, outright says that he was urged to seed the reviews with fake postings, which lends yet another level to the strangeness there. My guess is that it's all "theater", but I suppose it could be a mix of that *and* vindictive restaurateurs, but it's not your average review page!

This is not a book that takes itself overly seriously. It is, generally speaking, a memoir of the author's experience as a restaurant critic in the UK (where the publishing biz is a blood sport). White was a child of reasonably well-to-do parents, who sent him off to boarding school (and so gave him a grounding in really bad food), and then "forced him to eat in most of the great restaurants in France" thus providing him with sufficient experiences to recognize really good food. Beyond this, they endeavored to open a gourmet restaurant in Dublin when he was in his teens, in which he was somewhat reluctantly employed. He is constantly brushing off the suggestion that he knows *anything* about food (and certainly nothing about cooking), which sets up many of his musings on the industry as a whole. I found the following passage (originating from a story of a junket with other food critics later on) rather arch:

> *In seventy-two hours, I had acquired some allies, a delicate head, and a little understanding. In a hotel bed, alone, when all they can hear is the distant flushing of a loo, critics know what they do is more of a scam than a proper occupation. If humans*

> *earned prizes for ingenuity, getting paid to consume good food and wine would merit some special award. Cooks who moonlight as critics cannot quite believe their luck, and the rest of us think their dream will end in the morning. No wonder we're all so insecure.*

While Kitchen Con[3] does have an arc, it's not exactly a linear telling of a story. The author starts with defining a few things, talking about the history of the modern restaurant and the discussion and writing about food (with some choice bits from Samuel Johnson in the 1760's), and the development of the food business as opposed to subsistence, and then gets into *his* story, from his initial badgering of a local magazine to give him a column, on to writing for *In Dublin* and *Food & Wine*, and eventually his own not terribly successful *The Dubliner*.

The first half of the book is largely contained within the UK, and so the names being named: critics, publishers, politicians, chefs, restaurateurs, hotels and restaurants, don't have the warm fuzzy aura of recognition (for me) as were they the fabled notables of the New York culinary scene, for instance. There certainly is enough "general" dirt being dished that the exercise is not without its own guilty pleasures, but it's not as fun a ride as it might have been. Nobody comes off particularly well here, as there is certainly enough deserved snark to go around, and White is all too willing to dish this up by the ladle-full. Again, he too is subject to this, most notably in his New York years when he was pulled in on a book project marketed to the ultra-rich (or those who wished to take on those airs). This was an indulgent tumult of extreme luxe events and dining, but ultimately a failure that had him headed back to Ireland to lick his wounds and start his own project … *"There is a business with a higher failure rate than restaurants. I know because I left a well-paid job, crossed an ocean, and re-mortgaged my home in order to enter that business."* … this, of course (ask me to show you *my* emotional scars sometime), was *publishing*.

It appears at the 2/3rds mark in the book (end of Part 1) that the author had a bit of a breakdown, and he seems (the linearity here is a bit thin) to have wandered around the world as a journalist for a spell. It also seems that the remaining third of the book was composed later, and has some odd material, such as an extensive interview with Travel Channel star Anthony Bourdain, who is reported as being perfectly OK with White essentially cribbing the title of Kitchen Con[4] from Bourdain's "Kitchen Confidential". Much of the last third of the book could be dismissed as "navel gazing" by the author, but I think it would be kinder to call it "reflections on the industry" (inclusive of some rather damning tidbits about the guide book business, where visits to the places reviewed are frequently spaced many years apart, if not simply amalgamated from other sources!). Oddly enough, the book ends on something of a high note … it turns out that the last-minute desperation move of publishing a book of White's restaurant reviews became quite successful, and saved his magazine.

Anyway, this was an odd book, but an enjoyable read for me ... as I guess it would be for anybody who has an enthusiasm for restaurants, etc. Despite my finding this on the dollar store shelf, it does appear to still be in print, or at least available via the on-line guys (at a rather deep discount). If you enjoy "foodie reading" do find a copy, as it's an interesting, if disjointed, read ... and certainly *not* deserving of all those one-star reviews!

Notes:

1. http://btripp-books.livejournal.com/137528.html

2-4. http://amzn.to/1OxOM0O

Wednesday, October 10, 2012[1]

Hard advice ...

This was, as one might expect, yet another dollar store find. While I don't mind reading "motivational" books every now and again, and I occasionally like a "humor" book, it's a rare thing when I'd go search this sort of thing out at full price. However, the other day I was in a dollar store and went to check the book section and there this was. As you might guess from the title, this is one of those "calendar" sorts of books, intended to be read one "day" at a time (although the author does "give his permission" to just read it straight through). No Time for Tact: 365 Days of the Wit, Words, and Wisdom of Larry Winget[2] is by "New York Times bestselling author" Larry Winget, who I must admit I'd never heard of ... but he appears to have cornered the market on "ornery, sarcastic cuss" motivational books, with a series of titles (such as *Shut Up, Stop Whining, and Get a Life*) which aren't exactly the touchy-feely new-age pile of platitudes that is typical of the genre.

Now, folks who know what a cynical, bitter, kind of guy I can be would think that I'd *love* this book, but after 3.5 years of unsuccessfully looking for permanent employ, a lot of Mr. Winget's "get up off your ass" kind of approach is less amusing that it would have been in happier economic times. While I certainly *agree* with him on most of his general points, I found myself cringing a lot and spinning out *excuses* as to why things weren't working out. So, having blown through the 365 sections (it's set up with daily "thoughts", some being a few words, the longest being a page and a half) in three days or so, I'm feeling a bit beat up by him.

Frankly, he and I went in opposing directions in the introduction, where he says: *"I know the first thing each of you will do is go to your birthday and see what I said on 'your' day. That's how people are."* ... honestly, doing that would *not* have even occurred to me had he not made a point of suggesting it, so there was a disconnect here from the get-go between his assumptions and my thinking!

Oh, one other thing is odd with this book ... it has a red ribbon bound into the book to use as a bookmark, like a bible or something ... a pretty fancy conceit for the "Pitbull of Personal Development" hailing from Muskogee, Oklahoma, but I suppose that it sort of fits with moving through the book day-by-day.

Since there's really no story line here, I figured what I'd do was bring you a few choice bits that struck me as notable while reading through this:

> *January 21 – Sometimes you lose. When that happens, don't be a jerk about it. Then again, sometimes you win. When it happens, don't be a jerk about it.*

March 29 – Whining about your problem only prolongs the problem.

April 26 – Never say anything stupid like "It can't get any worse than this!" That is a challenge you do not want to issue. If there's one thing I have learned, **it can always get worse!**

June 24 – The ideal plan for your money:
>*Save 10 percent.*
>*Invest 10 percent.*
>*Give away 10 percent.*
>*Live on the remaining 70 percent.*

August 22 – Don't deny that a problem is a problem. People who say "I don't have problems; I only have opportunities" are idiots. Some problems are not opportunities – they are problems. Recognize them as problems and deal with them appropriately. Denial is stupid, and it doesn't do anything but prolong the pain of the problem.

September 1 – The truth hurts; that's how you know it's the truth. If someone comes up to you and says something really nice, they're probably lying to you!

November 16 – On average, people spend twenty hours per week watching television and less than two hours per week reading. Fifty-eight percent of Americans won't read a nonfiction book after high school. Forty-two percent of university graduates never read another book after college. Only 20 percent will buy or read a book this year. Seventy percent have not been in a library or bookstore in the past five years. I guess these folks think they have all the information necessary to be successful, prosperous, happy, and healthy.

Needless to say, I find that last one (although I've seen similar stats in other contexts) horrifying ... it's hard for me to imagine what sort of an intellectual wasteland those non-readers live in. Obviously, that's a "pet peeve" for me (thus making this list), you get an idea from the others up there what the tone of the book is. I'm surprised that Winget hadn't ever made it onto my radar before now (he has over a dozen books out and has done a bunch of media), although (as noted), I don't suppose that I go in search for much in the "personal development" niche.

I really can't say that I *liked* No Time for Tact[3] ... it's abrasive, pushy, and, frankly, hits way too close to home in various points ... but there was a certain *Schadenfreude* in reading this with its being 180° from the endless platitudes of books like *The Secret*, and imagining how the enthusiasts for that sort of "self-help" book would handle Larry Winget's approach. While I got my copy at the dollar store, it's only been out a couple of years and seems to still be in print. However, if you can't find a copy for a buck, the on-line new/used guys have copies of the hardcover for as little as a penny (plus the $3.99 shipping, of course), which would likely be your best bet if this sounds like the sort of snark that you want to start your day with.

Notes:

1. http://btripp-books.livejournal.com/137980.html

2-3. http://amzn.to/1WeJJU2

Thursday, October 11, 2012[1]

Uncertainty, Chaos, and Luck

This is another case of my seeing a book discussed online and reaching out to the publisher for a copy, this time the good folks at HarperCollins. The concept behind Jim Collins and Morten T. Hansen's Great by Choice: Uncertainty, Chaos, and Luck--Why Some Thrive Despite Them All[2] sounded sufficiently intriguing that I wanted to see what it was about – as I was aware that there were people and companies that had made their fortunes in very dark times, and I was hoping that I might find out some "secrets" of that sort of performance in the current economic abyss.

Anyway, the main thrust of the book is based on a study that the authors did of companies that out-performed their competition by an order of magnitude, thus being the "10Xers" of the book's terminology. They started out with a list of 20,400 companies and narrowed that down, through 11 levels of filters, to a final group of *seven* ... which had out-performed their industries anywhere from 11.2X all the way up to a whopping 550.4X (Southwest airlines, thriving in a time when their competitors where dropping left and right). The study looked at "dynastic eras" of the various companies, all ending in 2002, but starting as early as 1968 and as late as 1980, and each company is paired with a reference competitor. The list is about half well-known names (Microsoft, Intel, Progressive, Southwest), and half more obscure firms.

The "10Xers" are analyzed according to a formula graphed out on a triangle made out of four other triangles, each representing one typical behavior trait of these companies: "Fanatic Discipline", "Empirical Creativity", "Productive Paranoia", and something called "Level 5 Ambition" (this was a concept arising from another study, and generally indicates leaders who are *"incredibly ambitious, but their ambition is first and foremost for the cause, for the company, for the work, not themselves"*). Great by Choice[3] walks through these four traits, looking at the details of each.

In the "Fanatic Disciple" section, the authors introduce the concept of the "20 Mile March", a regular and focused expenditure of effort to achieve specific goals over time, with the imagery tied into what is needed to successfully make a very long-distance trek.

> *A good 20 Mile March has the following seven characteristics:*
> 1. *Clear performance markers.*
> 2. *Self-imposed constraints.*
> 3. *Appropriate to the specific enterprise.*
> 4. *Largely within the company's control to achieve.*

> 5. A proper timeframe – long enough to manage, yet short enough to have teeth.
> 6. Imposed by the company upon itself.
> 7. Achieved with high consistency.

What the researchers found surprising was that the 10X companies frequently "left money on the table", not rushing after "low hanging fruit" like their competition did ... they achieved their "20 mile" goals, and set up to reach the *next* 20 miles. This dedication enabled Progressive to achieve "underwriting profit" in 14 out of 16 years, and Southwest be profitable 30 out of 30 years.

The concept used to illustrate the "Empirical Creativity" triangle is "Fire Bullets, Then Cannonballs" and deals with innovation. Oddly, the most successful companies turned out to *not* be the most innovative, but the ones whose major pushes were best targeted. The concept here of "bullets" are ventures that are low cost, low risk, and low distraction efforts that allow the companies to *calibrate* their approaches and only fire *successful* "cannonballs". Everybody can come up with examples of *"What were they thinking?"* moments for major corporations, where some huge initiative went horribly wrong ... those would be "misfired" cannonballs. Using small test cases to see what works avoids potentially disastrous expenditures on major projects. Again, the 10X companies were typically not the most innovative, but the ones who coupled creativity with discipline. Additionally, there appears to be a "threshold of innovation" in each industry, which a company needs to exceed to be successful, but, once past that line, additional innovation has little effect. Also, what sort of spending consists a "bullet" and what a "cannonball" is highly variable between industries ... a publisher might put out a book in a new niche for a few thousand dollars, while an airline would be tying up *millions* in new aircraft.

Next comes "Productive Paranoia" and the concept of "Leading Above the Death Line" ... this is illustrated by stories of successful Everest climbs, and deadly attempts made by as experienced climbers at the same time.

> 10xers remain productively paranoid in good times, recognizing that it's what they do <u>before</u> the storm comes that matters most. Since it's impossible to consistently predict specific disruptive events, they systematically build buffers and shock absorbers for dealing with unexpected events. ...
>
> 10X companies took <u>less</u> risk than the comparison cases ... {they} took risks, but ... they bounded, managed, and avoided risks ... shunned asymmetric risk, and steered away from uncontrollable risk.
>
> ...
>
> 10X leaders remain obsessively focused on their objectives <u>and</u> hypervigilant about changes in their environment; they push for perfect execution <u>and</u> adjust to changing conditions...

Most of these leaders focus heavily on worst-case scenarios and have plans in place for what they can do if these come to pass ... like the expedition that was near the summit of Everest but opted to return to base-camp to avoid hazardous weather, *because they could*, having enough supplies and time to start over when the storm had passed.

Penultimately, there is "Level 5 Ambition", with the illustrative idea of SMaC - "Specific, Methodical, and Consistent" ... *"A solid SMaC recipe is the operating code for turning strategic concepts into reality, a set of practices more enduring than mere tactics. Tactics change from situation to situation where SMaC practices can last for decades and apply across a wide range of circumstances."* Over the time-spans looked at in the study, the 10Xer companies changed their SMaC Recipes very little, ranging from 10-20% (over more than 30 years), while the comparison companies changed theirs anywhere from 55-70%. One's SMaC should only be amended when conditions truly demand it, and should be only done with the other three elements.

One last section does not appear on the triangle-of-triangles, this is "Return on Luck" which features a fascinating analysis of what role *luck* might play in the outcomes experienced by the 10X companies. The authors note:

> *We defined a luck event as one that meets three tests: (1) some significant aspect of the event occurs largely or entirely independent of the actions of the key actors in the enterprise, (2) the event has a potentially significant consequence (good or bad), and (3) the event has some element of unpredictability.*

It turns out that both the 10X and their comparison companies had roughly the same amount of "luck", good and bad. Of course, not all luck is the same, a single instance of good luck is not likely to "make a company" in the long run, but a sufficiently disruptive bit of bad luck could destroy it. Generally speaking, the 10X companies were better prepared to weather bad luck events, *and* to not squander good luck when it came their way.

Great by Choice[4] is a really remarkable book, which takes a look at the most successful businesses and digs down to the patterns that they have in common. How one might apply this in one's own life is another question, as much of the material here is based on large organizations (although many of the illustrative stories deal with explorers, etc. and how they exhibited similar traits to those outlined here) ... but the often counter-intuitive results seen by the authors provide much food for thought. This has been out for about a year, but should certainly be at your local book vendor that carries business titles (although the online guys have it at around 1/3rd off). I don't usually recommend this sort of business book "to all and sundry", but it's such an intriguing look at what is involved in the most successful ventures, that I think most people who are interested in cultural/societal studies would find this enticing as well.

Notes:
1. http://btripp-books.livejournal.com/138173.html   2-4. http://amzn.to/1WelzrK

Friday, October 12, 2012

Don't shoot ...

I'm signed up for a massive number of newsletters on the web, ranging all over the place, with a lot of them being thinly-veiled shills for various grossly over-priced "coaching" programs, webinars, etc. One of these this summer was featuring a throw-in of a copy of this book ... which looked quite interesting ... so I picked up a discount copy over on Amazon. A project on which I consult is developing on-line training modules for various clients, among which is a prominent Chicago new age center, and much of what we'd discussed with them had a certain parallels with what's in Brendon Burchard's The Millionaire Messenger: Make a Difference and a Fortune Sharing Your Advice, although I've certainly been interested in seeing how this sort of thing might work for me as well.

I had a rather love/hate relationship with this book, on one hand, much of it was quite to the point, with clear directions on how to do A to get to the point of doing B, and how to avoid X if possible, etc., on the other hand, much of it is in that rah-rah tell-you-anything-to-make-the-sale garbage that I heard WAY too much of back when I was trying to build a side income in network marketing. The other thing that I had difficulties with this was that it's very much about picking ONE THING and running with it. The author himself built his entire speaking/training career on the story of surviving a car crash ... nothing more than telling that over and over embellished with "feel good platitudes". Anybody who reads my reviews knows that I've been a life-long aspiring polymath, and the only thing that I really *like* is variety. The concept of "picking one thing" is beyond me (or in the words of Robert A. Heinlein *"specialization is for insects"*!).

Anyway, Burchard took is "golden ticket" spiel and delved into studying all the big "gurus" of self-development, Tony Robbins, Wayne Dyer, Deepak Chopra, Steven Covey, David Back, John Gray, John Maxwell, and numerous others. As he notes, where he diverged from the typical enthusiast for that sort of ~~twaddle~~ stuff was that he kept asking himself "why can't *I* do that?", and he then jumped into a study of the *how* involved in the advice industry. Within two years he had a best-selling book, was making $25k a pop as a keynote speaker, selling out seminars at $10k per seat, and had a bunch of online businesses raking in millions. Obviously folks wanted to know how he'd managed all this, and so became the training program he sells (which is outlined in the book).

In Ch.3 - "The Expert Calling and Lifestyle" he takes a look at a number of famous speakers and the puts out a nine-point analysis of the "expert industry" and what's involved, and why it might appeal to the reader. A couple of pages are dedicated to each point, with over-view, a bit of a breakdown, and some very focused suggestions on how these can work, and be implemented.

In Ch.4 - "You: Advice Guru" he lists three types of experts ... the "Results Expert", the "Research Expert", and the "Role Model" and suggests building *all three* "consciously, strategically, and actively" on ones' topic areas. *"When all these pillars are strong and aligned, you will have reached a level of expertise and trust that makes you incredibly respected and in demand."* One thing he introduces here, structurally, is what he calls "Expert Signposts", which are open-ended sentences for the reader to add their own data. He tells the reader to stop at each of these and fill them out before moving forward in the book (yeah, I didn't do it either).

Perhaps the core of the book is Ch.5 - "10 Steps to an Expert Empire" where Burchard lays out the groundwork that needs to be done to get to the big bucks. Here they are:

> *Step 1: Claim and Master Your Topic*
> *Step 2: Pick Your Audience*
> *Step 3: Discover Your Audience's Problems*
> *Step 4: Define Your Story*
> *Step 5: Create a Solution*
> *Step 6: Put up a Website*
> *Step 7: Campaign Your Products and Programs*
> *Step 8: Post FREE Content*
> *Step 9: Get Promotional Partners*
> *Step 10: Repeat and Build the Business Based on Distinction, Excellence, and Service*

In each of these he dissects the methodology, addresses concerns, and talks action details. They each have an "Expert Signposts" section which gets down to such nitty-gritty as *"To pay the price point of this product, people must believe that ..."* (which would be one of MY biggest stumbling blocks, since I've never found a "product" in this niche that I felt was remotely worth what was being charged for it!).

Again, much of The Millionaire Messenger[3] is very much a "manual" (with illustrative material), so there's not much of a "story arc" in this, so I'm going to list some stuff here, as it's just easier than trying to paraphrase where he's going with it. In Ch.6 - "The Millionaire Messenger's Money Map" he lists *The Six Profit Pillars for Entrepreneurial Experts"*, these are: Writing, Speaking, Giving Seminars, Coaching, Consulting, and Online Marketing. Discussion of these then sets up:

> *A Million-Dollar Expert Empire in Five Steps*
> 1. *Create a low-priced information product.*
> 2. *Create a low-priced subscription program.*
> 3. *Create a mid-tier-priced information product.*
> 4. *Create a high-tier multiday seminar.*
> 5. *Create a high-priced coaching program.*

Burchard gets into detailed examples in each, although the dollar figures he quotes ($197 for a "low priced" product, $497 for a mid-tier-priced product!) must depend on the famous adage *"there's a sucker born every minute"*! Anyway, he goes step-by-step of how many of what his case study "Sally" needs to sell to make over a million dollars in a year. Pretty cold and clinical for something that purports to be all about "helping people".

Which brings us to Ch.7 - "The Messenger Mind-Set", a set of beliefs without which *"would-be experts give up early, lose focus, fail – or, worse, they never begin"*:

> *Mind-set #1: My life experience, message, and voice are valuable.*
>
> *Mind-set #2: If I don't know it or have it, I will go learn it or create it.*
>
> *Mind-set #3: I will not let my small business make me small-minded.*
>
> *Mind-set #4: Student First, Teacher Second, Servant Always.*
>
> *Mind-set #5: Mastery is a way of life.*

Supposedly this gives one *"the right psychology needed to share your message and build a real business while you are doing so"*.

So, now that you've been through "re-education", so to speak, you're ready for Ch.8 - "The Millionaire Mandates":

> *Messenger Mandate #1: Positioning*
>
> *Messenger Mandate #2: Packaging*
>
> *Messenger Mandate #3: Promoting*
>
> > *- Claim.*
> >
> > *- Challenge.*
> >
> > *- Commonality.*
> >
> > *- Credibility.*
> >
> > *- Choice.*
> >
> > *- Comparison Pricing.*
> >
> > *- Concern.*
> >
> > *- Close and call to action.*
>
> *Messenger Mandate #4: Partnering*

He then throws in a fifth, but more as an after-thought, although he calls it *"the Ultimate Messenger Mandate: Serving with Purpose"*, with warnings of not acting in bad faith because it's *"not good - not for you or for our community"* ... sounds a lot like the "unofficial Chicago motto" - *Don't Get Caught*, but that may just be my cynicism talking.

This finishes up with a section *about* the industry - "The Messenger Manifesto" (Or The Great Industry Reset) … but you'd pretty much had to have read up to that point to have context for the various "resets" he talks about in this. The final bit is called "Trusting Your Voice" which goes back to encouraging the reader to get into the expert biz, telling a "heart-warming" story and throwing in a few literary quotes … which I guess is far preferable than getting into details on how to write a "squeeze page" to suck people into providing their e-mail addresses.

Honestly, I liked The Millionaire Messenger[4] much more than one would think from my commentary here. It's a *very* cogent look at, and manual for, building up a business in the "advice business" … it's just that I see *so much* of this stuff come through my inbox, and have built up a major psychological wall against the whole industry. This is only a couple of years old at this point, and is still in print … the on-line big boys have it for about a third off of cover (which is very reasonable in and of itself), and you could find a used copy for about another third off of that (with shipping). If you've ever thought of getting into the "expert field", this would be a great book for you (I have plans for lending this to 2-3 friends), but if you just *hate* those endless video pitches for this or that program, you'll probably want to steer clear of it. As noted, I was a mix of the two, but I'm glad to have this "manual" on hand for future ventures!

Notes:

1. http://btripp-books.livejournal.com/138306.html

2-4. http://amzn.to/1gzMyzH

Saturday, October 13, 2012[1]

Reframing reality?

This is one of the books that I'd picked up at the Open-Books[2] "box sale" last spring, which had sat around for quite a while before my getting into it. I even had an acquaintance tell me that I'd love it, so I pulled it into the "actively reading" stack a month or so ago.

Unfortunately, I never quite *connected* with Stuart A. Kauffman's Reinventing the Sacred: A New View of Science, Reason, and Religion[3]. Frankly, I kept waiting for this to get to the "reason and religion" parts, and it just kept going with DNA and complexity theory, not even really approaching "the sacred" until the last couple of chapters. I can't imagine how this got titled the way it is ... as it's sufficiently off base to almost seem like "bait & switch"!

This is not to say that it's not a very interesting book ... only that my expectations of what I was going to be reading were certainly never met, and found myself plowing through very different book. Rather than being something taking down religion and replacing it with science, this is almost an anti-scientific science book, being more focused on disputing "reductionism" than the myths of bronze-age herders. One chapter is called "Breaking the Galilean Spell" which I took (before getting into this) as being a alternative for "Nazarene" ... but rather than breaking the spell of western civilization's main *fairy tale*, that chapter title references Galileo! The author's target here appears to primarily be the "facts devoid of values" approach of most of science's development, and not the delusions of the non-scientific world ... he doesn't even lock horns with the opponents of the scientific world view until half way through the book.

The book starts out bashing secularism as one of the "four injuries" detailed in the opening chapter. It then moves into attempting to debunk classic reductionism, and then spins out into the more theoretical reaches of physics to look at cases where reductionism doesn't work. Next comes an appeal to biology and how it can't be reduced to physics, which then leads into a discussion of DNA, RNA, and the complexity which can be developed within the coding of these molecules. It is within this that Kauffman starts to make an argument for complexity arising on its own ... not requiring divine intervention.

Now, I will grant the possibility that much of the arguments here are "over my head" ... the author spends a great deal of time looking at how genes can interact, and how the number of possible interactions are truly massive, and getting into how various mathematical processes applied to this data produce various complicated results ... but he goes *on and on and on* with this stuff, to no determinable (to me, at least) end.

There are three interesting concepts that come out of this part of the book ... the first of which being the idea of "critical" systems, which are poised between "ordered" and "chaotic" ... in ordered "regimes" there is very little change, and many genes are "stuck" either on or off, in chaotic regimes there is "avalanche" damage to 30 to 50 percent of genes, but in "critical" networks there are "power law" distributions based on logarithmic factors, leaving enough change in the genes, but without catastrophic amounts. He argues that this sort of distribution manifests even up to the level of cells ... "Critical networks, poised between order and chaos, seem best able to co-ordinate past discriminations with reliable future actions."

The next is the concept of the "adjacent possible" ... this is a concept of expressions that are not demanded by a situation, but are *possible* ... he spreads this from a look at molecules and genes and into global economy:

> The flow into the adjacent possible arises at levels of complexity above atoms, certainly for molecules, species, technologies, and human history. Here we must attend to the way the adjacent possible is entered. Salients are almost certainly created in specific "directions" in the space of possibilities, which in turn govern where the system can flow next into its new adjacent possible. These fluctuations almost certainly do not die out, but probably propagate in biased ways into the ever new adjacent possible.

The third of these is that of "Darwinian Preadaptations":

> One of Darwin's brilliant ideas is what is now called Darwinian preadaptation. Darwin noted that an organ, say the heart, could have causal features that were not the <u>function</u> of the organ and had no selective significance in its normal environment. But in a different environment, one of those causal features might come to have selective significance. ... Preadaptations are abundant in biological evolution. When one occurs, typically, a <u>novel functionality comes into existence in the biosphere</u> - and thus the universe. The classic example concerns swim bladders in fish. These bladders, partially filled with air, partially with water, allow the fish to adjust their buoyancy in the water column. Paleontologists have traced the evolution of swim bladders from early fish with lungs. ... With the evolution of the swim bladder a new function has entered the biosphere and universe ...

What is bizarre (to me) here is that he goes all this way with the molecular argument, then spins it into a systemic function, and *then* starts to apply this to to language, culture, economies, and even the brain:

> *The idea that the human mind is nonalgorithmic raises the <u>possibility</u> that it <u>might be acausal</u>, rather than a causal "machine", and the only acausal theory we have is quantum mechanics. Therefore, the mind may be partially quantum mechanical. ... When I suggest that consciousness is partially quantum mechanical, the idea that dives me concerns the <u>transition</u> from the quantum world of merely persistent <u>possibilities</u> to the classical world of <u>actual physical events</u> ... Currently the theory of "decoherence" is the favorite candidate to explain passage from the quantum world {to the classical world}. Decoherence is based on loss of phase information. ... I am proposing that the consequences in the classical world of the quantum mind are due to decoherence, which is <u>not itself causal</u> in any normal classical sense.*

So, at this point we're more than 80% through the text ... and we're just *starting* to get around to something that resembles the title's <u>Reinventing the Sacred</u>[4]. Again, it's been a fascinating ride, but most of it has been to pretty much just set up that complexity can, and does, arise without a "creator" making things happen. The author speculates

> *... that for sufficiently dense and diverse multiparticle quantum process systems and environments, or mixed quantum and classical systems and environments and the universe, such as a brain cell, <u>the way phase information is lost to the environment may be unique in the history of the universe in each specific case. But then no compact description of the details of the decoherence process can be available, hence no natural law describes that detailed decoherence process. Moreover, the specific way decoherence happens in detail may matter for how free will chooses under intentions and comes to have consequences for the objectively real, that is the classical, world</u>. The same would seem to be true of a persistent partially coherent mind.*

The remaining part of the book tries to circle back onto the nominal themes of the sacred, etc., but it really isn't much more accessible than what I've quoted above. It's a dense book ... and an interesting book, but it's not particularly coherent to the average reader. So many concepts are just thrown into the mix here to eventually get some sense via context (I guess the author assumes the reader is familiar with all the theories involved), and so many bits of research are referenced, but in a way that leaves the casual reader in the dust ... all in all, a highly frustrating read! This is still in print in a paperback edition, just in case you wanted to go down this particular rabbit hole ... but I have a hard time making much of a recommendation here ... I'm glad to have read it (and encountered some of the concepts that Kauffman discusses), but it was not what I was expecting it to be.

Notes:

1. http://btripp-books.livejournal.com/138722.html

2. http://www.open-books.org/

3-4. http://amzn.to/1JjcxBA

Saturday, October 20, 2012[1]

Gold, Natives & Wild West Shows ...

This was a "win" from the LibraryThing.com "Early Reviewers" program ... and something of a surprise. First of all, it was a release from the South Dakota State Historical Society Press, which certainly is a "niche" publishing house, and I doubt that I would have come into contact with it had it not been a LTER book. The book, in hardcover, has been out since this summer, but this is quite "early" for the paperback, which isn't due out until next July. While I do, from time to time, read "histories", the format of Paul L Hedren's Ho! For the Black Hills: Captain Jack Crawford Reports the Black Hills Gold Rush and Great Sioux War[2] is, I believe, quite unique in my reading, being about 2/3rds primary resources (letters reporting to the *Omaha Bee* and other newspapers) from Captain Jack Crawford, and about 1/3rd contextifying material from the editor/author.

The period of time dealt with in the book is primarily 1875-1876, the start of the gold rush into the Black Hills, in Nebraska and the Wyoming, Montana, and Dakota Territories. This region is still controversial, as the area is held as sacred to the Native American tribes, and there had (at that point) only fairly recently been established reservation lands for the Lakota and Cheyenne in the area. Where it must have seemed to the US government and many of the tribal leaders that they'd finally reached a territorial compromise, the discovery of gold brought in a large number of fortune-seekers. Initially the government made efforts to dissuade these miners ... General George Crook had posted the following throughout the gold prospecting camps:

> *Whereas the President of the United States has directed that no miners, or other unauthorized citizens, be allowed to remain in the Indian reservation of the Black Hills, or in the unceded territory to the west, until some new treaty arrangements have been made with the Indians.*
>
> *And Whereas, by the same authority, the undersigned is directed to occupy said reservation and territory with troops, and to remove all miners and other unauthorized citizens, who may be now, or may hereafter come into this country in violation of the treaty obligations: -*
>
> *Therefore the undersigned hereby requires every miner and other unauthorized citizen to leave the territory known as the Black Hills, the Powder river, and Big Horn country by and before the 15th day of August next.*

> *He hopes that the good sense and law abiding disposition of the miners will prompt them to obey this order without compelling a resort to force.*

Needless to say, the majority of the miners, etc., ignored these orders, and the military was very unwilling to "resort to force" to clear them out, especially as there was a constant stream of new folks coming into the region. This build-up, and infiltration into the lands set aside for the Sioux via the Fort Laramie Treaty of 1868 by the miners and speculators, was one of the main triggers of the "Great Sioux War of 1876", famed for skirmishes such as Custer's demise at the Little Big Horn. However, with the US still reeling from the Civil War, economic stresses such as the "Panic of 1873" encouraged many men to head west to seek their fortunes.

Jack Crawford had been born in Northern Ireland and had immigrated to the US with his family. His father had been wounded in the early parts of the Civil War, and Jack followed him into the military, enlisting when his father re-entered the army in 1864. Jack was wounded, recuperated, rejoined his unit, was wounded again, and eventually mustered out at the end of the war in 1865. During his second, extensive, hospitalization, he was taught to read and write by the Sisters of Charity. By 1875 he was presenting himself to the editors of the *Omaha Bee*, gaining employment at first as a watchman, and eventually getting an assignment to cover the Black Hills gold rush for the paper.

Ho! For the Black Hills[3] is mainly based on Hedren's research in the microfiche archives of the handful of newspapers that Crawford ended up "corresponding" for over those next couple of years. What is less clear here is how exactly Jack went from illiterate guy working in a series of jobs to the flamboyant "Scout" persona he affected in his journalistic career and beyond. The author tries to piece together the itineraries of various Wild West shows that Crawford might have encountered, and makes a good case of how these likely provided a template and impetus for his character and westward adventures. Again, most of the book is comprised of the materials that Hedren was able to dig up from the writings that "Captain Jack Crawford - Poet Scout" had submitted to the newspapers. These are largely rambling reports of what he saw, who he met, what was happening in assorted locales, what sort of gold was being produced where, how communities were developing, and even on-going reports on what basic supplies cost. This is a fascinating window into a different time and place, but it generally does not lend itself to excerpting here.

The last of the newspaper pieces comes from October of 1876, at which point Jack Crawford began moving into his new career as a Wild West show character. He had, essentially, resigned as a scout upon taking up the cause of a *New York Herald* reporter, and rushing back to civilization to get that story placed before others … netting him both the gratitude (and significant payment) of that paper, and the animosity of the US military. He had made contact with assorted notables as Buffalo Bill Cody, and eventually became part of that show, before setting out to produce his own. He died in New York in 1917.

If you're interested in "the wild west", and the period of the Indian Wars, you will no doubt find this a very attractive book. The combination of "history" and original documents is quite enticing, and it provides a very interesting perspective on those conflicts. Again, the main part of Ho! For the Black Hills[4] covers Crawford's reports over just about a year and a half, so is a very detailed look at his experiences in that time. As noted above, this is sort of between editions ... the hardcover has been out for several months, and the paperback (which is what they sent out for review) doesn't come out till next summer. The on-line big boys have copies of the former, and are now taking pre-orders for the latter. Because of it coming from a small press, I don't know how much luck you'd have finding this at your local brick-and-mortar, but you could, I suppose, order it through them, or from the publisher at http://sdshspress.com[5]. I rather enjoyed reading this, and I'd suppose anybody with an interest in any of the basic themes here would find it worth picking up.

Notes:

1. http://btripp-books.livejournal.com/138914.html

2-4. http://amzn.to/1Wc0z65

5. http://sdshspress.com/

Wednesday, October 24, 2012[1]

Being Indispensable ...

As I mention in my review of _Man's Search for Meaning_[2], it was fortuitous that it, and Seth Godin's _Linchpin: Are You Indispensable?_[3], were sitting at the top of my to-be-read pile when my brief tantalizing brush with being employed imploded at the end of August. They served as sorts of "coaching" for me to get past the worst of the initial shell-shock from the chaos of that situation. However, it has taken me a _very_ long time to getting around to _reviewing_ this, and I'm not sure why.

Possibly, it's because Seth Godin has _so many_ books on approximately the same subject, that they tend to blur a bit on recall, so, once this had been sitting on the (by that time, quite substantial) to-be-reviewed pile for a month and a half, I knew I liked it, but was getting hazy on the specifics. Oddly, this is, perhaps, my favorite of the half-dozen Godin books that I've read ... it's confrontational on a level that I find attractive, if in ways that I frequently felt to be uncomfortable. While I've _been_ the "linchpin" in many of the places I've worked, I have found getting _back_ into that type of role daunting at best, and much of what has kept me from trying to forge _my own_ venture is rather directly addressed here. However, it could also be the case that there's _so much_ here that I found, pithy, useful, and to-the-point (and there are dozens of my little bookmarks sticking up out of the top edge), that it's hard to synthesize a satisfactory overview that wouldn't run many thousands of words!

I would, if that was not a concern, have liked to have quoted the full four pages of the "contents" section up front, where Godin lists the 14 sections and gives a few tightly-focused lines on what each contains (heck, that would work pretty well as a free-standing review!). The basic concept is that there's a revolution going on in the world of work, and that aside from management and labor, there's now a third group, the "linchpins", people who _"own their own means of production"_, and _"walk into chaos and create order"_. However, it's hard to be _"brave enough to make a difference"_ and become a linchpin. In the comment to the "The Resistance" section, Godin says:

> So, why is this so hard? It turns out that it's biological. Deep within your brain lies the amygdala, the lizard brain. It sets out to sabotage anything that feels threatening, risky, or generous.

That last point is interesting ... the idea of "gifting" is fought by the "lizard brain", The Resistance ... and yet _"gifts make the tribe"_ and gifting _"is a critical step in becoming indispensable"_. Godin sets up pretty much everything that's wrong with the "traditional" world of work since the Industrial Revolution ... from how our educational systems are a "scam", _"designed to prep_ *you to be a compliant worker in the local factory"* to how in business *"the goal is to hire as many obedient, competent workers, as cheaply as you possibly can"*. He then sketches out the concept of the linchpin and "being indispensable" ... in terms that seem a bit odd from the standpoint of the standard model ... *"Linchpins are geniuses, artists, and givers of gifts. They bring humanity to the work, they don't leave it at home."*. What? We have to be *geniuses* to make it in this new model? We have to be *artists*? Sounds like a tall, and rather revolutionary, order ... except that he fleshes out that concept by pointing out how little kids are artists, poets, scientists, and entrepreneurs in the context of their worlds, before "schooling" grinds down the uniqueness, anathematizes risk-taking, and spits out compliant cogs for the "real world" machine.

There are not a lot of illustrations in this book, primarily just a handful of hand-drawn Venn diagrams, one of which I found, well, haunting. This has three circles, "Perseverance", "Talent", and "Charm", where the "Linchpin" is at the point where all three overlap, but it was very interesting what the other three 2-circle overlaps were defined as ... C+P= "Princess", C+T= "Prodigy", and P+T= "Frustration". Wow, persistence and talent combined only equals frustration? That sounds like my life! Interestingly, Godin doesn't flesh out that "charm" aspect much, but I suspect it has something to do with "community" and "gifts" (which he does go into at length). While on the topic of "frustration", I found another bit here rather telling: *"... if you're remarkable, amazing, or just plain spectacular, you probably shouldn't have a résumé at all ... a résumé gives an employer everything she needs to reject you. Once you send me your résumé, I can say, 'Oh, they're missing this or they're missing that', and boom, you're out."* ... not to be claiming to be *spectacular*, but this also sounds *very* familiar!

Again, I'm faced with a number of concepts here where Godin is working hard to re-write definitions and paradigms, which (short of replicating pages of copy) make it difficult to briefly summarize. He makes a distinction here between "the job" and "the work", where the latter is the process of doing one's "art"...

> *The job is what you do when you are told what to do. ...*
>
> *Your art is what you do when no one can tell you exactly how to do it.*

Another choice tidbit here would be the sort of thing that should keep MBAs up at night: *"The easier it is to quantify, the less it's worth."*. Speaking of quantifying ... I still find the concept of "one's art" here somewhat slippery ... as Godin links "art" to giving it away, making it a gift, and changing people with it: *"In order to be true to your art, you must sacrifice the part of it that hinders the spread of your art."* ... *"And if the ideas don't spread, if no gift is received, then there is no art, only effort. When an artists stops work before his art is received, his work is unfulfilled."* It seems somewhat counter-intuitive that in order to be "true to one's art" one has to, essentially, filter it down to what will sell (albeit to an audience that you've specifically targeted).

Two of the big concepts in Linchpin[4] are "The Resistance" and "The Daemon". As outlined above, the resistance is "the lizard brain", and this is in conflict with the daemon, which is the genius (the Roman term for the Greek *daemon*) within us that struggles *"to express itself in art or writing or some other endeavor"*. Godin actually goes into a bit on brain biology and evolution to explain how these two conflicting parts of us came to be. The resistance wants to scurry under a rock and wait for risky situations to go away ... the daemon wants to create something ... the resistance starts spewing out all those "reasonable" objections against this because *"you might fail"*, and "failure", to the lizard brain, *is* death, so it will pull out all the stops to keep you from being in situations where failure presents as an option. Godin goes into a lot of detail on how the resistance manifests both personally and institutionally in our lives, how it generates anxiety, and spins out scenarios *designed* to keep us from achieving. He introduces another concept in this, *Shenpa*, a Tibetan word which means "scratching the itch", which is another tool used by the resistance, this takes small worries, irritations, etc., and cycles them up into (potentially) full-fledged panic ... this is also illustrated in an array of examples.

The next part of the book is about "Gifts" ... which starts with the role that "giving away one's art" plays in the concept of being a linchpin, but moves into a look at pre-modern societies, the historical shift of allowing for usury, the Protestant Reformation (which allowed for the rise of the merchant class, and the development of our current economic system), reciprocity, and concepts like Dunbar's number:

> *When we meet a stranger, we do business. When we encounter a member of the tribe, we give gifts.*
>
> *...*
>
> *A lot of the stress we feel in the modern world comes from this conflict between the small world in which we're wired to exist and the large world we use to make a living.*

Godin also references the "three circles" model from the Art world, the circle of friends, the circle of commerce, and the circle of the masses. With the rise of the Internet, the third circle has massively expanded, and Godin describes this as a "gift system" where people are making videos and posting them for free, writing blogs and posting them for free, creating apps and posting them for free, etc. *"And the audience continues to grow, each person enjoying the digital fruits of the labor that others donate to the ever-widening circle."*. Of course, at this point one has a bunch of questions, and these are anticipated: *"How do I know what art to make? How do I know what gifts to give?"*, which brings us to the "map" or *"the ability to forge your own path"*, which involves the ideas of "seeing", "discernment", and the Buddhist term *"prajna"*. Again, the author is working with a lot of strings here, including ideas of equanimity, attachment, and passion. He presents another chart here, with two axes, Discernment – Attachment, and Passionate – Passive, with the linchpin being in the Passionate/Discernment quadrant, and bureaucrats, whiners, and fundamentalist zealots being in the other three. One key take-away from this section is: *"There is no map. No map to be a leader, no map to be an artist. I've read hundreds of books ... and not one has a clue about the map, because there isn't one."*.

The next couple of sections are on making the choice to become a linchpin, and "the culture of connection", which leads to the seven abilities of the linchpin:

> 1. Providing a unique interface between members of the organization.
> 2. Delivering unique creativity.
> 3. Managing a situation or organization of great complexity.
> 4. Leading customers.
> 5. Inspiring staff.
> 6. Providing deep domain knowledge.
> 7. Possessing a unique talent.

Each of these are looked at in some detail, the last one is a bit quirky as he relates it to the *Legion of Super-Heroes*, and how the "lower-rent" heroes, when being introduced, always *"had to speak up and describe their super-powers"* - Godin recommends developing something similar for when you meet people, to make the introduction meaningful, and *"If you want to be linchpin, the power you bring to the table has to be very difficult to replace. Be bolder and think bigger."*.

No doubt anticipating the complaints of the lizard brain, the book ends with a look at what to do "when it doesn't work" ... obviously, taking chances leads to failing ... what then? *"Make more art. ... Give more gifts. ... Trying and failing is better than merely failing, because trying makes you an artist and gives you the right to try again."*. At the end of this section Godin has a couple of more Venn diagrams, one for "indispensable" and one for "surrender", the point where "indispensable" comes in is at the intersection of dignity, humanity, and generosity ... hardly categories they teach at the big business schools!

Linchpin[5] has been *huge*, so it will no doubt be in print for decades, and is probably waiting for you on the shelves of your local brick-and-mortar book vendor. The on-line big boys have it, of course, in your choice of hardcover, paperback, audio, e-book, etc. I got my copy of the hardcover from the new/used vendors and this can currently be had for under a buck before shipping from those guys. Needless to say, this is another of those books that I really wish EVERYBODY would read ... it could be a cultural game-changer, and it addresses most of *my* frustrations with the "mundane world". Again, this is something that should be on your shelf and in your head, and it's out there waiting for you to pick it up and get clued in ... do it!.

Notes:
1. http://btripp-books.livejournal.com/139248.html
2. http://btripp-books.livejournal.com/136125.html
3-5. http://amzn.to/1WbZXNA

Sunday, November 25, 2012[1]

To thrive in chaos ...

I'm rather surprised that I hadn't heard of Randy Gage before now, as a note on the cover of this points out that he is an "author of 8 international bestsellers", although I must admit, on checking out his site, I hadn't heard of any of those *either* (they seem to primarily be "prosperity" and network-marketing books, not a genre that I had delved into much). I had, however, seen Scott Stratten[2] absolutely *raving* about Gage's new Risky is the New Safe: The Rules Have Changed[3] on-line, and decided to check it out (requesting a review copy from the good folks at Wiley). It turns out that Scott is one of Randy's "mastermind group", and his Unmarketing[4] is on the "required reading" list here, so there's some backstory involved there, I suppose.

Risky is the New Safe[5] is something of a dystopian vision. So much is changing, nothing is the way it's been before, but this pushes past those realities to project scenarios of animals, clones, and virtual reality taking over roles that humans have held ... and how one might meet those challenges. Gage paints a very dire future for things as we know it, but then says:

> *Every challenge creates a corresponding opportunity. Some of the greatest wealth was created during the Great Depression – just as many fortunes are created in every recession.*
>
> *When everyone is zigging, you want to be zagging.*
>
> *At the exact moment you're reading this sentence, you're living in the greatest time in human history. There has never been a better time to be alive. The speed and scope of changes taking place in the world (...) today offer unprecedented opportunities for living a life of prosperity.*

This is somewhat the thesis of the book ... how to move ahead when everything is falling apart around you. Change is coming both faster than one would think, and more all-encompassing. As a parent of teens, I certainly noticed:

> *If you're a parent who wants to help your 14-year-old son or daughter plan for the future, you're about to tackle a difficult feat. Because the best jobs of 2018 haven't even been invented yet. But we do know one thing for sure: Taking the safe path won't get you there.*

Now, again, I don't know much about Gage, but I think it's fair to suggest that he's an Objectivist, as he both quotes Ayn Rand in the book, and his "Required Reading for Risk Takers" list includes 3 of her titles out of the 12 books featured. I bring this up because a lot of what he talks about here, in terms of global situations and trends, is sure to rub the "hopey-changey" folks the wrong way ... for example:

> *"A Line Has Been Crossed"* – *In many places around the globe, we have crossed over a line that spells ominous trouble for the future.*
>
> *The people who are receiving government assistance now outnumber the people who are producing and paying into the kitty. Government entitlement programs have run amok. And once you provide an entitlement for someone, they begin to see it as their right. ...*
>
> *"Governments Have Become the New Ponzi Schemes"* – *They're the ultimate pyramid money games. If you practiced the same accounting practices your government does, you would be put in prison. ...*
>
> *Governments – even the well-meaning ones – are inherently corrupt and mismanaged. They never create prosperity – they squander or obstruct it. At best they can facilitate an environment that allows free enterprise to prosper – and only free enterprise can create true prosperity.*

Needless to say, most of what Gage advocates involves keeping government as far away from your business as possible!

OK, so things are going to hell in a handbasket ... what can we do about it? Well, Gage talks about "the new religion of *ideas*", how ideas are the currency of the future, and how current education fails in not teaching students *how to think*, and how those who have Curiosity, Discipline, Discernment, and Contrarianism, will be the best equipped to succeed. Gage presents what he sees as the trends in marketing, in branding (which he interestingly notes: *"A brand is really a meme-plex – a collection of related memes, aka mind viruses"*) and folks who are doing this right from Viper cars to Jimmy Buffet, and in commerce – ranging from Network Marketing (Gage made much of his fortune in MLM) to Virtual Worlds.

About two-thirds of the way through, Risky is the New Safe[6] turns somewhat "philosophical", looking at what common elements people who have been wildly successful have exhibited, including heaping helpings of *ego* and *selfishness* ... where he leans heavily on both Ayn Rand and Napoleon Hill (and, oddly enough, throws in a quote from Mother Teresa: *"To be able to give, you must have."*). Setting this up, he notes:

> To really step into your true potential and do something epic, you must lose the perception that ego is about vanity or self-love. Instead, understand the real ego is simply the part of your mind that controls consciousness.

Gage discusses how this applies to various examples from history, and ways one might be looking to build success in the current volatile world situation. One key piece he includes is:

> As a general rule, successful people work harder than others. They simply work more hours. But they also do something else: They manage what they do during those hours better than most. ... They practice self-discipline, keeping themselves focused on productive activities. They do this by making choices, which sometimes means making sacrifices.

Now, I'll admit, on certain points, Gage is "preaching to the choir" in my case, and much of what he goes into in the "Selfishness Is the New Altruism" chapter ring far truer to me than they might to most. A prime example of this is:

> If you tell me your highest good is serving others or even serving God, I think you've lost the plot. In my experience those running around trying to save the world are usually the most messed up people you'll ever meet. Their lives are usually driven by avoidance behavior so they don't have to deal with their own issues. They run around looking for drama, so they don't have time to face their own drama. To the casual observer they look like altruistic saints, but those who know better recognize them for the judgmental, insecure, drama-magnets they really are. ... Get yourself in a position of strength and you'll be amazed how much good you can do.

He later notes that for individuals who have reached a point of enlightened self-interest *"mediocrity is a sin"*. The book ends with a few general outlines for what needs to be done: find opportunities opened up by the new challenges, and find ways to leverage these, develop a "new and different level of thinking", which goes beyond contrarianism and into being able to recognize patterns in events and trends, and doing the inner work to move from "poverty consciousness" and into "prosperity consciousness".

Risky Is the New Safe[7] has only been out a month at this point, so it should certainly be available at your local brick-and-mortar book vendors ... but the on-line big boys are featuring it for a bit more than a third off the cover price. This is an *awesome* book, and I've been suggesting it to a lot of my friends and family, but it's not "one for everybody" since those clinging to the old world ways will want to stick their fingers in their ears and go *"la-la-la"*, and those who think that Big Government (with associated enablers) is their friend will probably bust a blood vessel in seeing their particular sacred cows gored so convincingly. But, hey, *I* liked it!

Notes:

1. http://btripp-books.livejournal.com/139274.html
2. http://twitter.com/unmarketing
3. http://amzn.to/1iH85aT
4. http://btripp-books.livejournal.com/101421.html
5-7. http://amzn.to/1iH85aT

Monday, November 26, 2012[1]

Pretty mechanical ...

OK, so if this wasn't at the dollar store, I'm pretty sure we wouldn't be having this conversation right now. As regular readers of this space will recall, I *do* read humor books from time to time, and even read *poetry* collections every now and again, but the likelihood of my making a particular effort to pick up a book of humorous haiku is very small indeed. However, there it was, with the promise of it being a fast, amusing, read that was only going to set me back a buck, so it got into my cart and managed to hit the top of my to-be-read pile.

As those with *long* memories know, I used to write a vast lot of poetry (250 pieces a year), and would occasionally spin off some haiku beyond that. Heck, I've won composition contests in the form, so I'm no stranger to it. I also wasn't expecting Ray Salemi's Robot Haiku: Poems for Humans to Read Until Their Robots Decide It's Kill Time[2] to stay close to the expectations of Classic Haiku[3] composition ... and make no mistake about it, I've penned some *awful* examples myself ... but one gets the impression that the genesis of this book was a joke that was taken to an extreme, something that would have been funny for the first handful of extemporized poems, but tiresome from then on. And that's pretty much the deal here.

Robot Haiku[4] is a quick read, of course (with each page containing just one haiku of 17 syllables), so there was a limit to how far the "ha-ha" went, and it's under 200 pages. However, there's not much creativity here, and there certainly isn't any consideration of the traditional *thematic* "rules" of the format. Pretty much anything that could be envisioned as a robot activity is spit out across a 5-7-5 syllable pattern, but only a handful come close to the sort of expression that one finds in well-written versions.

The book is broken up into five chapters, "Invention", "Robots at Work", "Robots in the Home", "Robots at Play", and "Destruction of Humanity" (have to get something in there to justify the clever sub-title, I suppose). In most, some human activity or role is re-imaged as being done by a robot, with some twist to make the "otherness" front-and-center. One gets the impression of a bunch of buddies sitting around over some beers and shooting these back and forth, writing them down, editing for syllabic pattern, and having the whole book done in an afternoon. It's also surprising to find that the author has had a 20-year career in the tech industry, with significant writing credits, as the level of the humor here (not to say the writing, constricted as it is), might be more likely coming from an undergraduate.

In any case, here are a few of the haiku that I felt were at least presentable:

> Relentless hunter
> Fires surface-to-air missiles,
> Cat-bot downs robins.
>
> Zen robot eyesight
> Sees growth in each blade of grass
> Compulsive mowing.
>
> Tic-Tac-Toe battle
> Stuck in an infinite loop
> This could take a while.
>
> Sun glints off metal
> Picture of futility
> Robot tries to tan.

Again, these were the best of the bunch, with most of the rest running the gamut from horrible to pointless. This is not to say that Robot Haiku[5] was a *chore* to read ... once the "joke" became clear, everything fell in line with at least a "heh" level reaction. There were pop culture references, from Shatner to Fonzie, to perk things up (the Shatner one almost made it into the above list), and enough "naughty" and scatological bits to provide occasional spiciness.

The book is helped out very much by its visual design. Needless to say, a single haiku per page is *not* a lot of text, and this is set up with enough various mechanical/scientific backgrounds and graphic elements on each page, along with playful typography, to not have the reading experience run to monotony.

As is often the case with things that show up at the dollar store, Robot Haiku[6] is still in print, and the on-line new/used guys have *new* copies for as little as a penny (plus the $3.99 shipping, of course). That still doesn't get you down to the $1 price I picked this up for, but it's something to consider if for some reason the activity of robots rendered into the general structure of a haiku sounds like something that would have you breaking up in laughs (some other reviews of the book found it to be *hilarious*). Frankly, the one buck was just about right for the brevity and less-than-inspiring nature of this to me. I don't regret buying/reading it, but it was a bit like sitting around while a clever, yet irritating, friend took a simple joke way beyond where it was working.

Notes:

1. http://btripp-books.livejournal.com/139660.html

2. http://amzn.to/1gDZF1S

3. http://btripp-books.livejournal.com/82142.html

4-6. http://amzn.to/1gDZF1S

Wednesday, December 5, 2012[1]

COIN for Brands

Maybe one of these days I'll have contacts at enough of the publishing houses that I'll be able to get review copies of pretty much anything that I run across that sounds interesting, and the current book would certainly have been a candidate for that. However, I ended up ordering this from the new/used guys online, rather than hunting down the particular publicist at the publisher.

I wish I could recall what specifically brought this title to my attention. While I was getting ready to decide what to review next (I'm back to having a stack of books waiting for me to triage my time for cranking out reviews), I was racking my brain for a clue of what had pointed to me to Johnathan R. Copulsky's Brand Resilience: Managing Risk and Recovery in a High-Speed World[2], but nothing surfaced. Obviously, it may very well been referenced in one of the *other* business/marketing books I've been reading of late, or it might have floated through in the Social Media channel, but *something* out there no doubt suggested I take a look at this, and with enough verve to convince me to actually go and *buy* a copy.

The basic thrust of Brand Resilience[3] is that in today's world of near-instant communications, the threats to brands are very hard to defend against, as word of some failing (real or fabricated) can explode across the web in hours, becoming "common knowledge" among the Connected before it could be brought to the attention of the C-suite. Of course, in this world, there are more brands than what define consumer products, Copulsky discusses chefs, politicians, newscasters, sports stars, authors, even *terrorists* who are their own "brand", and gives the example (at length) of Tiger Woods for what can happen when one of those personal brands (and things associated with them) takes a PR hit ... he cites a remarkable figure that seven publicly held companies who had sponsorship deals with Woods lost *twelve billion dollars in market value* the month after that story (and Wood's temporary "retirement") broke.

More and more brands are about trust ... they're a short-hand that the consumer uses to connect attributes they value with particular products, companies, individuals, movements and institutions ... and when that trust goes bad, and that trust can be *very* fragile, it can be disastrous. Copulsky goes back to the well-worn analogy of "marketing as warfare" and notes that while Sun Tzu and Clausewitz were models for the older world of business, the new lightning-fast reality of brands dealing with a connected world required a new model, and Brand Resilience[4] is structured according to a metaphor of "Marketing as Counterinsurgency", based on The US Army / Marine Corps Counterinsurgency Field Manual FM 3-24[5] (which is available as a free .pdf download at that link!).

The five "main takeaways" for brand defense from FM 3-24 are, briefly:

> 1. At first you may not recognize that your brand is under attack ...
>
> 2. Your natural tendencies to respond in a conventional manner to attacks on your brand may be misguided ...
>
> 3. When it comes to building a resilient brand, the winner is the one who learns more quickly ...
>
> 4. Some of the most effective weapons for counter-insurgents are not those aimed directly at brand saboteurs ...
>
> 5. If a tactic works this week, it might not work next week ...

Further, FM 3-24 has a "Guide to Action" appendix which presents "three pillars": Plan, Prepare, and Execute. From the material detailed there, a list of seven steps which each have a chapter devoted to it in the main section of the book. These break down as follows:

> Plan -
>
> 1. Assess brand risks.
>
> Prepare -
>
> 2. Galvanize your brand troops.
> 3. Deploy your brand risk early warning systems.
>
> Execute -
>
> 4. Repel the attacks on your brand.
> 5. Learn and adapt your brand defenses.
> 6. Measure and track brand resilience.
> 7. Generate popular support for your brand resilience campaign.

Now, of course, this is a *business* book, so most of this is focused on *brand* brands, and so you'll see lines like: *"In fact, for many organizations, the financial value of the brand exceeds any single asset class that appears on the balance sheet and is a significant multiple of revenue and cash flow."* ... Whuh? ... but there are also more general observations such as: *"Brand risk is contextual. The more valuable the brand, the higher the risk."*, with the further note that it's very likely that in *most* companies *nobody* is responsible for "brand risk", even where "reputation management" is a line in somebody's job description. However,

> *When it comes to brand reputation, social media have let the proverbial genie out of the bottle, and there is no way that you're going to get it back in. ... Social media make the entire world a potential stage.*

Now, I'm not going to walk you through step-by-step here, but wanted to point out a few highlights (that earned bookmarks as I was reading through this), for example, in Step 4 – Repel the Attacks on Your Brand, one of the case studies they look at was the Tylenol poisoning back in 1982 and the classic "crisis response" strategy exhibited then, with three elements, the "three Rs", Repentance, Remediation, and Rectification.

There needs to be a lot of flexibility and inventiveness to stay on top of things in the current environment (do they teach those things in MBA school?), and *"...constant vigilance and constant adaptation are the hallmarks of brand counterinsurgency. As a brand counterinsurgent, you know you can never fully anticipate all the dangers that lie ahead. No matter how well you prepare and how effective your early warning systems are, surprises will happen because insurgents are, by definition, constantly improvising the next form of attack."* The case studies here deal with transportation safety, both in the air and on the roads … with a "learn and adapt" approach constantly improving the numbers involved …

> *The notion of accident investigation with a focus on identifying the root causes and fixing them works for aviation accidents. It works in manufacturing plants. It works with cars. It works with failures of engineered products. And it can work for brands.*

Again, each of the seven points is fleshed out with case studies, and context returning to concepts of COIN warfare … fascinating, but a bit too expansive to walk through in this review.

While I'm still not an overly-enthusiastic fan of "business books", I did rather enjoy Brand Resilience[6], and felt that the linkage of counterinsurgency with brand defense worked quite convincingly. I've not had a chance to check out FM 3-24[7], but it's on my list. If you want to put this on your list, your best bet at this writing seems to be the on-line big boys, where the hardcover is being featured at a significant 60% off. It's relatively new (just came out last year), so you would probably be able to find it at your local brick-and-mortar book vendor as well. I liked it, and found the interweaving of the marketing challenges with the military metaphor fascinating, so if this falls within your interests, do go check it out!

Notes:

1. http://btripp-books.livejournal.com/139930.html

2-4. http://amzn.to/1gBkn2z

5. http://www.fas.org/irp/doddir/army/fm3-24.pdf

6. http://amzn.to/1gBkn2z

7. http://www.fas.org/irp/doddir/army/fm3-24.pdf

Wednesday, December 19, 2012[1]

With or without a cause ...

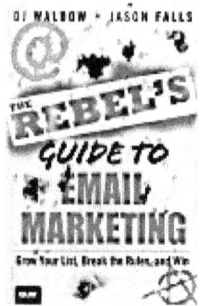

OK, so I'd seen this referenced on Twitter or Facebook or G+ (or maybe in skywriting) and it sounded interesting, so I hit up the good folks at Pearson's QUE Publishing to get a review copy, and I'm glad I did. Now, I realize that for a lot of folks a book on email marketing might be somewhere south of "great moments in paint drying", but this one *rocks*, or at least as much as a book about email marketing would likely be able to rock. No doubt this is due to the "rebellion" in DJ Waldow & Jason Falls' The Rebel's Guide to Email Marketing: Grow Your List, Break the Rules, and Win[2], as it takes a fresh approach to the subject that reminded me of what an eye-opener Scott Stratten's Unmarketing[3] was when it came out. Visually, the book has a lot of the same design feel to it as Jess Loren's recent Pinterest[4] book, also from QUE, although here it makes a bit more sense with copies of web sites, emails, and various elements thereof.

Now, I've never been in a position where email had been a significant part of the marketing mix (although I have been in situations where it had at least been "on the table"), so I have less baggage coming to this than I would for something on a subject that I've used extensively. I certainly have *opinions* on the topic, and have noticed since reading this that I have definite preferences for certain of the dozens of e-mail "newsletters" that show up in my inbox on a daily basis.

The first thing that the authors address here is the perception in some areas that "e-mail is dead", and they provide some *fascinating* numbers to illustrate how non-dead it is. First of all, there are **2.9 billion** e-mail accounts out there, compared with a world population of 7 billion. That's not *everybody*, but it's getting there! The number of daily e-mail messages is 180 *billion*, and that's not counting spam. If you figure that spam represents about 70% of all email traffic, it means that the actual volume of email is more than half a *trillion* messages a day (one note: the copy I have slips back and forth between "millions" and "billions" on these figures, and I did some research and the higher figure does seem to represent the actual numbers). That's a LOT of data ... and what's being specifically considered here is the "permission-based, opt-in" email traffic.

The book is set up in five main sections, dealing with building one's (opted-in) list, what are the main elements for a marketing email, "breaking the rules", integrating with social media, and a look to the future of email marketing. There are many screen caps of example emails from various companies and organizations, showing how some have approached the assorted elements being discussed. There is a good deal of "nitty gritty" material here, like calculations for "churn rate" (how much your list shrinks over a year) and "list fatigue", which *starts* at about 30%, and moves up depending on how well you're engaging your recipients (or not). I, for one, would never have guessed the erosion of the list would have been that deep … and it certainly underlines how important it is to constantly be replenishing (and focusing efforts on) sign-ups.

Some of the "juiciest" parts here (it is, after all, the *Rebel's* guide) is in the "Breaking The Rules" section. There are some eye-opening examples of A/B testing where a "spammy" subject line had a lower open rate (27.2% vs. 31.8% … both numbers seemingly low to my expectations) than a more "descriptive" subject line, but had sales *nearly four times higher* because the people who opened it were *very* interested in the FREE offer being hawked. Text vs. graphical formats are also examined (if one has graphics turned off in one's mail reader, an all-image e-mail is pretty invisible even if it's opened), but the inclusion of graphics and even video elements are shown to greatly increase response. One of the irritation points for most e-mail is the ability to smoothly unsubscribe (I was doing that on a couple of things just this morning!), and they show examples where the unsubscribe button is ironically a major element in the design, to ones where it's buried so deep as to be unfindable (not recommended).

There are bunches of practical suggestions that one might not have considered, such as using "lightbox" coding (where the main page is greyed out and an element floats over it) on one's web site that at least *asks* for the e-mail sign-up before the visitor gets to your content (I've since suggested this to a couple of people I'm working on projects with). They also get into the convoluted question of social media elements. I have become sensitive to this of late, as I've found that if a "share" button isn't coded for LinkedIn, it doesn't work well to cut-and-paste a link there (I never get the graphic presentation like on FB or G+, just an abbreviated link that I'm pretty sure nobody will bother clicking). I've also been irritated to find *follow* buttons where I thought there would be *share* buttons, and they discuss how these disparate (yet visually similar) pieces can be included in one's emails and associated pages. On the general subject, they present an interesting quote, that *"email is the 'digital glue' of the new media landscape".*

The Rebel's Guide to Email Marketing[5] closes with a four-step approach to successfully using the instructions in the book:

1. Grow Your List
2. Plan Your Content
3. Determine Success Metrics
4. Send, Test, Analyze, Adjust, Repeat

Again, I was surprised at just how engaging this book was, and I found it interesting and entertaining, even though I didn't have particular project on which I would be able to put this all into play. Obviously, this isn't a "general interest" book, but if you're in a situation where you're looking at building up a permission-based communication channel, this is a great place to start.

It's been out for just a couple of months at this point, so should be easy enough to find in the brick-and-mortar vendors, but the on-line guys have it at a bit over a third off of cover price. If there is one thing that I wish they'd looked at here, it would have been a "compare and contrast" over-view of the main services such as Mail Chimp, Constant Contact, etc. While some of these are *mentioned* there's not that much of "here's where you go to make all this happen", which would have been quite useful, in my opinion.

Notes:

1. http://btripp-books.livejournal.com/140274.html
2. http://amzn.to/1iF8KK1
3. http://btripp-books.livejournal.com/101421.html
4. http://btripp-books.livejournal.com/137299.html
5. http://amzn.to/1iF8KK1

Thursday, December 20, 2012[1]

In changing worlds ...

I have frequently wondered why particular books have ended up at the dollar store, but there are also ones that seem to make sense being in that channel. The current book, Geoffrey Douglas' The Classmates: Privilege, Chaos, and the End of an Era[2], is, unfortunately, one of the latter. While politics is certainly an evergreen topic, the losers of elections tend to quickly fade, if not from the collective memory (although that's certainly a possibility – I wonder how many people could come up with Dukakis' name unaided) at least from the place where anybody *really cares*.

This book is about John Kerry's boarding school classmates back in the late 1950's and early 1960's – specifically the Class of 1962 of the all-boys St. Paul's School in Concord, NH (a long-established "feeder" for the likes of Yale). One gets the impression that on some level the book really wishes that it had been about Kerry, but he turned out to be a fairly uncooperative participant in this.

The Classmates[3] has its genesis in some e-mail exchanges during the 2004 election. As one would expect, if one had a classmate who was running for President, it would be a topic of discussion, and a certain percentage of the class were participating in the back-and-forth of remembrance of events some four decades previous. That, of course, was a very different world, with a very stratified culture (of which the boys at St. Paul's were primarily "upper crust" ... if not currently from money, from long-time "position" in the northeast), and in a time where the influence of the Viet Nam conflict was just ramping up. There were echoes of this world that I was familiar with, as I had attended an all-boys school in Manhattan in my early years (admittedly nearly a generation later), one that had been established in 1628 by the Dutch West India Company, and was populated by a similar mix of 'names'. These were boys being prepared to run the world, only their world was going to be going through seismic changes over the decades ahead.

While the impetus of the book was the Kerry candidacy, the glue of the book is a character (featured pseudonymously) of another student there who did *not* fit in, and was the brunt of the sort of hazing that one can easily imagine in this sort of setting. Called "Arthur" here, his story weaves in and out of the rest of the narrative.

I think it's appropriate to note that the author, Geoffrey Douglas, was a *mess*, and was "invited to not return" to the school well prior to the graduation of the Class of 1962. Complicating matters, he was a "legacy" student, with numerous members of his family having been St. Paul products, so he is up against a mass of expectations that he can not meet. He spends much of his early adulthood in the thralls of alcoholism and gambling addictions, and the various financial straits brought on by these. Obviously, this did not help his connection with others in the class, as he wasn't *there* for much of what they recalled of their school years. His one main "vignette" with Kerry, the sharpest and most defining memory he had of their interactions while he was at the school, was not remembered by the Senator at all. There is much here that suffers from this disconnect.

Aside from the story of "Arthur" (whose abuse then and sudden death in the midst of the class' communications during the Kerry campaign is the unifying theme), there are in-depth looks at a half-dozen other classmates, discussing who they were, where they came from, and where they ended up. Some died in the war, some went to southeast Asia and came back irrevocably scarred, some found great success, others learned to manage in a drastically changing world. Add to these the chapter on Kerry, and the chapter dealing with the author, and you have the book. I'm sure this is not the book that the author envisioned writing. I'd guess that he didn't expect to get exactly 45 minutes to meet with Kerry, who had his press secretary in the room, taking notes. It took him *four years* to complete, and one has to wonder how much he had to change what he intended for it. The few folks discussed here were winnowed down from an initial group of 40 classmates, and the sense I get is that Douglas had to find a way to move this past a *"hey, we knew this guy when"* feature (perhaps in opposition to the "swift boat" sub-genre that arose out of Kerry's war contacts), and into a more general look at how America changed from the 1950's.

Again, I trail the subjects here by only a dozen or so years, so much of what's involved, as remembrances and contexts, touch me more than they might others. Each of the classmates profiled here had their own path through the changing world, and at least the author does not "beat you over the head" with symbolism relating to those changes. Their stories stand as poignant looks into lives that had certain connecting threads, and their combination leaves the impression of something of a word-portrait *Guernica* for this tumultuous half-century.

The Classmates[4] is still in print, but I suspect that it might not be easy to find on store shelves after having run through the dollar store channel. The on-line big boys have it, at as much as 60% off the cover price, and the new/used guys have new copies for as little as three bucks. This is not an easy book to recommend, as my #1 take-away was that it was a failed (or at least seriously detoured) project ... but my #2 take-away is that it, in the end, does provide a sense of how the changes in our nation made deep changes in this generation ... so if this sounds good to you, do pick up a copy.

Notes:

1. http://btripp-books.livejournal.com/140333.html

2-4. http://amzn.to/1V1OaiE

Sunday, December 30, 2012

Legendary ...

OK, so this one came to me via LibraryThing.com's "Early Reviewer" program. I've had a good run of getting books assigned to me from that, but I must admit that some are more "on target" than others, and the way these are "won" is via a matching algorithm that takes the publisher's info on the book and looks for the most compatible library among those site members who have requested copies. Obviously, I found this "interesting enough" to put in the request, but I'm pretty sure that it's the old dark corners of my collection from my college English major that put Flint F. Johnson's Origins of Arthurian Romances: Early Sources for the Legends of Tristan, the Grail and the Abduction of the Queen into my hands.

To tell you the truth, this was *not* the most enjoyable read I've had of late ... the focus is very much on digging into theses tales to prise out suggestive threads from non-surviving previous material. While the "classic" Arthurian stories come down to us from the 12th century, and the Angevan kingdom which comprised the British Isles and western France, it is based on much earlier material, and from a cultural setting far different than the continental Christian courts. The evolution of British society has always been somewhat chaotic ... from the Roman conquest in the first century CE shifting away from the native tribes, to Celtic influence, and Viking inroads, and eventually Norman control. This shifting of influence no doubt muddied the waters about whose myths and legends were preserved, but it also did much to change the language:

> *First, around AD 550 the British language shifted so significantly that the vocabulary that antedated this watershed would have become archaic and, very quickly, incomprehensible to contemporary speakers. Any bardic verse composed around AD 450 would not have been understood by around AD 600. Because of this, any literature written in AD 450 or before would not have been understood well enough to be recopied as soon as AD 600. The history remaining in that state would have been lost. In fact, it is possible that literature written only a generation before about AD 600 would have met with a similar fate. It is, after all, with the poetry of the late sixth-century bards Taliesin and Aneirin that British rhyme first emerges.*

Since the Arthurian romances date from far later, the traces of these early (and Pagan) sources were confusing to the eventual authors such as Chrétien de Troyes. Also over-laying the source materials was the fact that the surviving tales were written to please patrons, Marie de Champagne, Phillip of Flanders (whose own biography appears to have been the template for the story arc of significant portions of the Arthurian material), Eleanor of Aquitaine, etc. The book is divided into three sections, each dealing with a different story ("The Abduction of the Queen", "The Holy Object" and "Tristan"), but each structured similarly, with an introduction, various related topics for the particular material, a look at literary tools, and then concluding with the three chapters: "Motifs and Details: Clues of Celtic Origins", "The Sixth Century in {...}", and "Conclusion". Obviously Johnson is in the camp that tracks back the key elements here to a Celtic base, and explains much of the "odd" story parts to later writers not understanding the Pagan cultural substrate of that earlier time.

> *The politico-religious situation inside Celtic Britain during the fifth and sixth centuries was ... an unstable mixture of Christianity and Celtic paganism. However, throughout the period Christianity can clearly be seen to take the ascendancy. After 600, there are no records of pagans among the Britons or Picts. On the other hand, the worship of Celtic gods, in one form or another, persisted throughout the Middle Ages. ...*
>
> *Christianity was a passive force behind the military suppression of the remaining pagan sects ...*
>
> *Conversion was made one other manner: political force. In the 480s and 490s, Clovis claimed Christianity as his religion and allied himself with the Roman church. For that, the bishop gave him the authority to conquer any non-Christian or Arian kingdom that he chose to attack. ... According to legend, only two figures commanded equal power in early Britain – Arthur and Gwrtheyrn. ... One man, (presumably Arthur) gained a period of ascendancy and used his power to demolish Celtic temples and expand his territories much as Clovis had ... If the activities were more vigilante in nature, they might have taken place at any time between the turn of the fifth century and about the year 600. After that the practitioners of the Celtic cults were forced to conduct their rituals in secret, which is why no archaeological evidence of them exists at this time.*

Much of the book deals with detail of linguistic shifts, both from the earlier British forms and how names were adapted in later tellings on the continent in French and Germanic permutations. In the Tristan material there are fascinating survivals of Pictish cultural elements (such as a particular system of royal succession, where *kings were selected from the female line of the royal family, from the maternal nephews of kings*) which explain otherwise odd plot elements, while others are connected to Celtic myth structures.

Character and place names are tracked according to various scholarly citations, pointing to assortedly plausible theories of origins. There are even suggestions of Jewish sources of the Grail rituals, brought in through Islamic troubadour influences as the stories spread. Fortunately, most of the academic detail is constrained to the end notes, as I think this is likely only interesting to hard-core language geeks.

Origins of Arthurian Romances[3] is hardly a "general interest" book, as it is a detailed look at possible sources of the tales, and not a telling of them, and unless one has an interest in either the survival of early cultural elements in the literature, the linguistic development of myths and legends, or are a hard-core Arthurian collector, this would be a bit much for most readers. On the subject of "a bit much", this is also very pricey, with a $35 cover price for a volume that's under 200 pages before notes, bibliography and index. I am, as with a previous review[4] of a McFarland title, assuming that this is intended as a *text book*, and so carrying the inflated pricing typical of that market. However, if you want to pick this up (in anything other than the e-book edition), you're going to have to pay in that ballpark, as even the used channel is at that level *or more*. Again, if this is "your thing", it's a fascinating study of the underlying literary, linguistic, historical, cultural, etc. granularity of the legends, and it might be worth it, but for most folks, it's a one that you can safely take a pass on.

Notes:

1. http://btripp-books.livejournal.com/140721.html

2-3. http://amzn.to/1gBidjt

4. http://btripp-books.livejournal.com/114983.html

Monday, December 31, 2012[1]

Old #10 ...

Sometimes I pick up books just because the price ... yeah, I know, not the best reason, and it's likely a character flaw, but I probably wouldn't have picked up a sports biography if it wasn't at a deep discount ... so when I saw Ron Santo: A Perfect 10[2] on the shelf at Walgreens at a deep clearance price this summer, I grabbed it. Now, if you don't know who Ron Santo is, you're not from Chicago. Santo was the star third baseman for the '69 Cubs, back when I was 12 years old. I can still remember the names of that team, and have ephemera from those days etched into my mind (like the plastic cap liners from Coke bottles that had their pictures, which you'd pull out and put on display cards, etc.). And, I suppose, if you're not a Cubs fan, you wouldn't be aware that Santo, who lived and breathed Cubs baseball, despite having incredible stats, had repeatedly been passed over for the Hall of Fame while he was alive (he made it in posthumously, a bittersweet honor, as he would have been so thrilled to have that happen). You also might not know about his struggles with diabetes, and how he lost both legs to the disease, yet still kept up a grueling travel schedule as a Cubs broadcaster.

Anyway, I was of the age where Santo was a Big Deal from my youth, and a familiar piece of my on-going Cubs rooting. His death was a pretty big deal in town here too, and so I was happy to get the book penned by his broadcast partner Pat Hughes, and sports author Rich Wolfe. I really didn't have any expectations about the book, and was somewhat surprised to find that it was largely a collection of reminiscences from many who knew Santo, but that makes sense as this was published a scant six months after his death, so it wasn't a long-term production or in-depth biography.

The book is split into thematic chapters, covering various aspects of his life, starting with a foreword by his namesake son, and then the longest section by Pat Hughes. Chapters cover his family, his youth in Seattle, baseball, Chicago, broadcasting, and a general "Santopalooza", with 33 people talking about him. From family members and childhood friends, to the Commissioner of baseball to a half-dozen broadcasters, the tone is something akin to a gentle "roast" ... with Santo's quirks and foibles (his toupee rates its own chapter!) being lovingly aired, along with personal stuff that, but for this format, might not ever have reached the general public.

I suspect that this is as well-rounded look at the man thanks to the groundwork laid by his son Jeff's 2004 documentary *This Old Cub*, which provided an existing biographical context for the authors to reach out to get interviews. They mention that there were almost twice as many people interviewed for this than made it in, and that extra material would likely end up in the third volume of Wolfe's *For Cub Fans Only*.

There's a 25-page section of color photos which seem to be based on (or at least includes) the memorial piece done for Santo's funeral. This section includes some classic images from he 60's, and was a great "trip down memory lane" for me.

One thing that was *interesting* in the format of the book, is that there are numerous all-caps, bolded, and underlined people and places through the text that have footnotes highlighting "interesting facts" that are, oddly, not directly related to Santo. I don't know if these are a hallmark of Wolfe's other books, or what, but they seemed a bit out of place (not that they aren't individually quite amusing) in a memorial book like this. Just sayin'.

Ron Santo: A Perfect 10[3] is still in print, and the on-line big boys have it at 60% off of cover (the copies that were at Walgreens were at a discount as well, even before being on clearance). I'm surprised, after having *been* on clearance, that this isn't going for less via the "new/used" vendors, but at least at the moment, there's not a big discount there beyond what's being offered by Amazon. If you're a Chicagoan, a Cubs fan, or even just a baseball fan, you should look into getting a copy of this ... it's a bit sad, but it's a feel-good look at one of the greats.

Notes:

1. http://btripp-books.livejournal.com/140859.html

2-3. http://amzn.to/1gBhG0P

QR code links to the on-line reviews:

Beyond Religion: Ethics for a Whole World
by
H.H. The Dalai Lama

The Dhammapada: The Path of Perfection
by
Juan Mascaro

And So It Goes: Kurt Vonnegut: A Life
by
Charles J. Shields

Tourist's Guide - Agra & Fateh Pur Sikri
by
Lal Chand & Sons

101 Funny Things About Global Warming
by
Sidney Harris & Colleagues

The Ten Golden Rules: Ancient Wisdom from
the Greek Philosophers on Living the Good Life
by
M. A. Soupios & Panos Mourdoukoutas

America the Edible:
A Hungry History, from Sea to Dining Sea
by
Adam Richman

The Long Tail: Why the Future of Business
is Selling Less of More
by
Chris Anderson

The Google Resume:
How to Prepare for a Career and Land a Job at
Apple, Microsoft, Google, or any Top Tech Company
by
Gayle Laakmann McDowell

Google+ for Business:
How Google's Social Network Changes Everything
by
Chris Brogan

Civil Disobedience and Other Essays
by
Henry David Thoreau

Manage Your Depression Through Exercise:
The Motivation You Need
to Start and Maintain an Exercise Program
by
Jane Baxter, PhD

A Modest Proposal and Other Satirical Works
by
Jonathan Swift

Enter the Past Tense: My Secret Life as a CIA Assassin
by
Roland W. Haas

The Dip: A Little Book That Teaches You When to Quit
by
Seth Godin

Digital Leader: 5 Simple Keys to Success and Influence
by
Erik Qualman

Darwin Among The Machines:
The Evolution Of Global Intelligence
by
George B. Dyson

Gurdjieff: Making a New World
by
J.G. Bennett

Aquarius Now: Radical Common Sense
And Reclaiming Our Personal Sovereignty
by
Marilyn Ferguson

The Seven Against Thebes
by
Aeschylus

Essence of the Bhagavad Gita:
A Contemporary Guide to Yoga, Meditation,
and Indian Philosophy
by
Eknath Easwaran

Winging It: A Memoir of Caring for a Vengeful Parrot
Who's Determined to Kill Me
by
Jenny Gardiner

Rubies in the Orchard:
How to Uncover the Hidden Gems in Your Business
by
Lynda Resnick

The Pluto Files:
The Rise and Fall of America's Favorite Planet
by
Neil deGrasse Tyson

Six Tires, No Plan: The Impossible Journey
of the Most Inspirational Leader
That (Almost) Nobody Knows
by
Michael Rosenbaum

Abundance: The Future Is Better Than You Think
by
Peter Diamandis

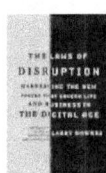

The Laws of Disruption: Harnessing the New Forces
that Govern Life and Business in the Digital Age
by
Larry Downes

Résumé 101: A Student and Recent-Grad Guide
to Crafting Resumes and Cover Letters that Land Jobs
by
Quentin J. Schultze

Lucy's Legacy: The Quest for Human Origins
by
Donald Johanson & Kate Wong

Blink: The Power of Thinking Without Thinking
by
Malcolm Gladwell

Socialnomics: How Social Media Transforms
the Way We Live and Do Business
by
Erik Qualman

A Black Hole Is Not a Hole
by
Carolyn Cinami DeCristofano

BTRIPP BOOKS - 2012   207

The Rubáyát of Omar Khayyám: First and Fifth Editions
by
Edward FitzGerald

R.U.R. (Rossum's Universal Robots)
by
Karel Capek

Groundswell: Winning in a World
Transformed by Social Technologies
by
Charlene Li & Josh Bernoff

Bliss Now!: My Journey with Sri Sri Anandamayi Ma
by
Swami Ramananda

Networking: 150 Ways to Promote Yourself
by
Bette Daoust

A Continual Feast: Words of Comfort and Celebration,
Collected by Father Tim
by
Jan Karon

The Big Moo: Stop Trying to Be Perfect
and Start Being Remarkable
by
Seth Godin & "The Group of 33"

The Damn Good Resume Guide, Fifth Edition:
A Crash Course in Resume Writing
by
Yana Parker & Beth Brown

I Know I Am, But What Are You?
by
Samantha Bee

The Next Ten Minutes:
51 Absurdly Simple Ways to Seize the Moment
by
Andrew Peterson, EdD

Masters of the Planet:
The Search for Our Human Origins
by
Ian Tattersall

Return On Influence: The Revolutionary Power of Klout,
Social Scoring, and Influence Marketing
by
Mark W. Schaefer

A Creator's Guide to Transmedia Storytelling:
How to Captivate and Engage Audiences
across Multiple Platforms
by
Andrea Phillips

The Little Book of Talent:
52 Tips for Improving Your Skills
by
Daniel Coyle

The Book of Business Awesome: How Engaging Your
Customers and Employees Can Make Your Business
Thrive / The Book of Business UnAwesome: The Cost of
Not Listening, Engaging, or Being Great at What You Do
by
Scott Stratten

The Reality of Being:
The Fourth Way of Gurdjieff
by
Jeanne de Salzmann

Mob Rule Learning: Camps, Unconferences,
and Trashing the Talking Head
by
Michelle Boule

Masterminds of Terror:
The Truth Behind the Most Devastating
Terrorist Attack the World Has Ever Seen
by
Yosri Fouda & Nick Fielding

Word of Mouth Marketing:
How Smart Companies Get People Talking
by
Andy Sernovitz

America A.D. 1000: The Land and the Legends
by
Robert Fisher

The Guinea Pig Diaries:
My Life as an Experiment
by
A.J. Jacobs

The Birth of Tragedy
by
Friedrich Nietzsche

Liars and Outliers:
Enabling the Trust that Society Needs to Thrive
by
Bruce Schneier

Man's Search for Meaning
by
Viktor E. Frankl

Death Metal Music:
The Passion and Politics of a Subculture
by
Natalie J. Purcell

Mencius
by
Mencius

The Impact Equation:
Are You Making Things Happen or Just Making Noise?
by
Chris Brogan & Julien Smith

The Tao of Twitter: Changing Your Life and Business
140 Characters at a Time
by
Mark W. Schaefer

Pinterest for Business:
How to Pin Your Company to the Top
of the Hottest Social Media Network
by
Jess Loren & Edward Swiderski

Kitchen Con: Writing on the Restaurant Racket
by
Trevor White

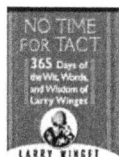

No Time for Tact: 365 Days of
the Wit, Words, and Wisdom of Larry Winget
by
Larry Winget

Great by Choice: Uncertainty, Chaos, and Luck -
- Why Some Thrive Despite Them All
by
Jim Collins & Morten T. Hansen

The Millionaire Messenger:
Make a Difference and a Fortune Sharing Your Advice
by
Brendon Burchard

Reinventing the Sacred:
A New View of Science, Reason, and Religion
by
Stuart A. Kauffman

Ho! For the Black Hills:
Captain Jack Crawford Reports
the Black Hills Gold Rush and Great Sioux War
by
Paul L Hedren

Linchpin: Are You Indispensable?
by
Seth Godin

Risky is the New Safe: The Rules Have Changed
by
Randy Gage

Robot Haiku: Poems for Humans to Read
Until Their Robots Decide It's Kill Time
by
Ray Salemi

Brand Resilience: Managing Risk and Recovery
in a High-Speed World
by
Johnathan R. Copulsky

The Rebel's Guide to Email Marketing:
Grow Your List, Break the Rules, and Win
by
DJ Waldow & Jason Falls

The Classmates:
Privilege, Chaos, and the End of an Era
by
Geoffrey Douglas

Origins of Arthurian Romances:
Early Sources for the Legends of Tristan, the Grail
and the Abduction of the Queen
by
Flint F. Johnson

Ron Santo: A Perfect 10
by
Pat Hughes & Rich Wolfe

CONTENTS - ALPHABETICAL BY AUTHOR

Aeschylus	page	45
The Seven Against Thebes		
Chris Anderson	page	17
The Long Tail		
Jane Baxter, PhD	page	26
Manage Your Depression Through Exercise		
Samantha Bee	page	98
I Know I Am, But What Are You?		
J.G. Bennett	page	39
Gurdjieff: Making a New World		
Michelle Boule	page	119
Mob Rule Learning		
Chris Brogan & Julien Smith	page	147
The Impact Equation		
Chris Brogan	page	22
Google+ for Business		
Brendon Burchard	page	165
The Millionaire Messenger		
Karel Capek	page	82
R.U.R. (Rossum's Universal Robots)		
Lal Chand & Sons	page	10
Tourist's Guide - Agra & Fateh Pur Sikri		
Jim Collins &.Morten T. Hansen	page	162
Great by Choice		
Johnathan R. Copulsky	page	186
Brand Resilience		
Daniel Coyle	page	112
The Little Book of Talent		
His Holiness the Dalai Lama	page	1
Beyond Religion		

Bette Daoust — page 89
Blueprints for Success - Networking

Carolyn Cinami DeCristofano & Michael Carroll — page 77
A Black Hole Is Not a Hole

Jeanne de Salzmann — page 117
The Reality of Being

Peter Diamandis & Steven Kotler — page 59
Abundance

Geoffrey Douglas — page 192
The Classmates

Larry Downes — page 62
The Laws of Disruption

George B. Dyson — page 37
Darwin Among The Machines

Eknath Easwaran — page 47
Essence of the Bhagavad Gita

Marilyn Ferguson — page 43
Aquarius Now

Robert Fisher — page 128
America A.D. 1000

Edward FitzGerald — page 80
The Rubáyát of Omar Khayyám

Yosri Fouda & Nick Fielding — page 122
Masterminds of Terror

Viktor E. Frankl — page 139
Man's Search for Meaning

Randy Gage — page 180
Risky is the New Safe

Jenny Gardiner — page 50
Winging It

Malcolm Gladwell — page 70
Blink

Author	Title	Page
Seth Godin	Linchpin	176
Seth Godin	The Big Moo	93
Seth Godin	The Dip	32
Roland W. Haas	Enter the Past Tense	30
Sidney Harris	101 Funny Things About Global Warming	12
Paul L. Hedren	Ho! For the Black Hills	173
Pat Hughes & Rich Wolfe	Ron Santo	197
A.J. Jacobs	The Guinea Pig Diaries	130
Donald Johanson & Kate Wong	Lucy's Legacy	68
Flint F. Johnson	Origins of Arthurian Romances	194
Jan Karon	A Continual Feast	91
Stuart A. Kauffman	Reinventing the Sacred	169
D.C. Lau & Mencius	Mencius	145
Charlene Li & Josh Bernoff	Groundswell	84
Jess Loren & Edward Swiderski	Pinterest for Business	153
Juan Mascaro	The Dhammapada	4

Gayle Laakmann McDowell *The Google Resume*	page	20
Friedrich Nietzsche *The Birth of Tragedy*	page	133
Yana Parker *The Damn Good Resume Guide, Fifth Edition*	page	95
Andrew Peterson, EdD *The Next Ten Minutes*	page	100
Andrea Phillips *A Creator's Guide to Transmedia Storytelling*	page	109
Natalie J. Purcell *Death Metal Music*	page	142
Erik Qualman *Socialnomics*	page	74
Erik Qualman *Digital Leader*	page	35
Swami Ramananda *Bliss Now!*	page	87
Lynda Resnick *Rubies in the Orchard*	page	52
Adam Richman *America the Edible*	page	15
Michael Rosenbaum & Bruce Halle *Six Tires, No Plan*	page	57
Ray Salemi *Robot Haiku*	page	184
Mark W. Schaefer *The Tao of Twitter*	page	150
Mark W. Schaefer *Return On Influence*	page	106
Bruce Schneier *Liars and Outliers*	page	136

Quentin J. Schultze — *Résumé 101* — page 65

Andy Sernovitz — *Word of Mouth Marketing* — page 125

Charles J. Shields — *And So It Goes* — page 7

M. A. Soupios & Panos Mourdoukoutas — *The Ten Golden Rules* — page 13

Scott Stratten — *The Book of Business Awesome/Unawesome* — page 114

Jonathan Swift — *A Modest Proposal and Other Satirical Works* — page 28

Ian Tattersall — *Masters of the Planet* — page 103

Henry David Thoreau — *Civil Disobedience and Other Essays* — page 24

Neil deGrasse Tyson — *The Pluto Files* — page 55

DJ Waldow & Jason Falls — *The Rebel's Guide to Email Marketing* — page 189

Trevor White — *Kitchen Con* — page 156

Larry Winget — *No Time for Tact* — page 159

CONTENTS - ALPHABETICAL BY TITLE

101 Funny Things About Global Warming
Sidney Harris — page 12

Abundance
Peter Diamandis & Steven Kotler — page 59

America A.D. 1000
Robert Fisher — page 128

America the Edible
Adam Richman — page 15

And So It Goes
Charles J. Shields — page 7

Aquarius Now
Marilyn Ferguson — page 43

Beyond Religion
His Holiness the Dalai Lama — page 1

The Big Moo
Seth Godin — page 93

The Birth of Tragedy
Friedrich Nietzsche — page 133

A Black Hole Is Not a Hole
Carolyn Cinami DeCristofano & Michael Carroll — page 77

Blink
Malcolm Gladwell — page 70

Bliss Now!
Swami Ramananda — page 87

Blueprints for Success - Networking
Bette Daoust — page 89

The Book of Business Awesome/Unawesome
Scott Stratten — page 114

Brand Resilience
Johnathan R. Copulsky — page 186

Civil Disobedience and Other Essays Henry David Thoreau	page	24
The Classmates Geoffrey Douglas	page	192
A Continual Feast Jan Karon	page	91
A Creator's Guide to Transmedia Storytelling Andrea Phillips	page	109
The Damn Good Resume Guide, Fifth Edition Yana Parker	page	95
Darwin Among The Machines George B. Dyson	page	37
Death Metal Music Natalie J. Purcell	page	142
The Dhammapada Juan Mascaro	page	4
Digital Leader Erik Qualman	page	35
The Dip Seth Godin	page	32
Enter the Past Tense Roland W. Haas	page	30
Essence of the Bhagavad Gita Eknath Easwaran	page	47
The Google Resume Gayle Laakmann McDowell	page	20
Google+ for Business Chris Brogan	page	22
Great by Choice Jim Collins &.Morten T. Hansen	page	162
Groundswell Charlene Li & Josh Bernoff	page	84

Author	Title	Page
A.J. Jacobs	The Guinea Pig Diaries	page 130
J.G. Bennett	Gurdjieff: Making a New World	page 39
Paul L. Hedren	Ho! For the Black Hills	page 173
Samantha Bee	I Know I Am, But What Are You?	page 98
Chris Brogan & Julien Smith	The Impact Equation	page 147
Trevor White	Kitchen Con	page 156
Larry Downes	The Laws of Disruption	page 62
Bruce Schneier	Liars and Outliers	page 136
Seth Godin	Linchpin	page 176
Daniel Coyle	The Little Book of Talent	page 112
Chris Anderson	The Long Tail	page 17
Donald Johanson & Kate Wong	Lucy's Legacy	page 68
Jane Baxter, PhD	Manage Your Depression Through Exercise	page 26
Viktor E. Frankl	Man's Search for Meaning	page 139
Yosri Fouda & Nick Fielding	Masterminds of Terror	page 122
Ian Tattersall	Masters of the Planet	page 103

Title	Author	Page
Mencius	D.C. Lau & Mencius	145
The Millionaire Messenger	Brendon Burchard	165
Mob Rule Learning	Michelle Boule	119
A Modest Proposal and Other Satirical Works	Jonathan Swift	28
The Next Ten Minutes	Andrew Peterson, EdD	100
No Time for Tact	Larry Winget	159
Origins of Arthurian Romances	Flint F. Johnson	194
Pinterest for Business	Jess Loren & Edward Swiderski	153
The Pluto Files	Neil deGrasse Tyson	55
R.U.R. (Rossum's Universal Robots)	Karel Capek	82
The Reality of Being	Jeanne de Salzmann	117
The Rebel's Guide to Email Marketing	DJ Waldow & Jason Falls	189
Reinventing the Sacred	Stuart A. Kauffman	169
Résumé 101	Quentin J. Schultze	65
Return On Influence	Mark W. Schaefer	106
Risky is the New Safe	Randy Gage	180

Ray Salemi	*Robot Haiku*	page	184
Pat Hughes & Rich Wolfe	*Ron Santo*	page	197
Edward FitzGerald	*The Rubáyát of Omar Khayyám*	page	80
Lynda Resnick	*Rubies in the Orchard*	page	52
Aeschylus	*The Seven Against Thebes*	page	45
Michael Rosenbaum & Bruce Halle	*Six Tires, No Plan*	page	57
Erik Qualman	*Socialnomics*	page	74
Mark W. Schaefer	*The Tao of Twitter*	page	150
M. A. Soupios & Panos Mourdoukoutas	*The Ten Golden Rules*	page	13
Lal Chand & Sons	*Tourist's Guide - Agra & Fateh Pur Sikri*	page	10
Jenny Gardiner	*Winging It*	page	50
Andy Sernovitz	*Word of Mouth Marketing*	page	125

www.ingramcontent.com/pod-product-compliance
Lightning Source LLC
Chambersburg PA
CBHW071309110426
42743CB00042B/1238